MORALITY AND THE NATURE OF LAW

Morality and the Nature of Law

KENNETH EINAR HIMMA

OXFORD
UNIVERSITY PRESS

OXFORD
UNIVERSITY PRESS

Great Clarendon Street, Oxford, OX2 6DP,
United Kingdom

Oxford University Press is a department of the University of Oxford.
It furthers the University's objective of excellence in research, scholarship,
and education by publishing worldwide. Oxford is a registered trade mark of
Oxford University Press in the UK and in certain other countries

First Edition published in 2019

Impression: 1

Published in the United States of America by Oxford University Press
198 Madison Avenue, New York, NY 10016, United States of America

British Library Cataloguing in Publication Data
Data available

Library of Congress Control Number: 2018961313

ISBN 978–0–19–872347–9

Printed and bound by
CPI Group (UK) Ltd, Croydon, CR0 4YY

This volume is dedicated to my mom, who has taught me more about courage, patience, honor, and kindness than anyone else. I have never known anyone who has faced so much adversity with so much grace and elegance. She is and will always be an inspiration to me.

Preface

This volume turned out to be quite different from what I had expected. When I first contemplated writing it, I thought that I would just take a number of previously published papers and do some minor edits to make them suitable as chapters of the volume. I figured that I would have to write no more than two new chapters, one introductory and the other purely expository, as I had previously published papers on the topics of all but two of the issues I had planned to address. Then I set about reading those papers with an eye toward revising them, and quickly realized that I had overestimated the quality of my published work. Each was riddled with errors that were so glaringly bad that I was appalled and embarrassed that I had published them.

It is important to be honest about one's mistakes, so I want to own them with the kind of public apology one hopes never to have to make: if you read these papers, I sincerely apologize for having wasted your time. From where I now sit, I think there were ideas worth developing in all of them, but I let them go much too quickly; as written, those papers were not worth reading. While there is nothing I can do to get them back, I believe that I have learned from my mistakes.

Obviously, I cannot claim that this volume is free from errors. What I can say is that I have spent much more time with each of these chapters than I spent on any of my previously published work. I have always felt uncomfortable imposing on others for detailed comments for various reasons; that has not changed and likely will not change. Even so, I am hopeful that the quality of the work here is significantly better than anything I have produced up to now.

That said, I would like to acknowledge the following people who have helped and encouraged me over the years: Matthew Adler, Larry Alexander, Brian Bix, Evgeny Borisov, David Brink, Carlos Bernal, Luka Burazin, Thomas Bustamante, André Coelho, Jules Coleman, Jennifer Corns, Jorge L. Fabra, Kenneth Ehrenberg, Imer B. Flores, John Gardner, Leslie Green, Mark Greenberg, Douglas Husak, Miodrag Jovanović, Nina Kaneda, Matthew Kramer, Massimo La Torre, C. Stephen Layman, Brian Leiter, Lucas Miotto, Adam Moore, Ronald Moore, Mark Murphy, Aleš Novak, Vitaly Ogleznev, Stephen Perry, Joseph Raz, Andrea Romeo, Corrado Roversi, Frederick Schauer, Stefan Sciaraffa, Scott Shapiro, Lawrence Solum, Bojan Spaić, Horacio Spector, Juan Pablo Sterling Casas, Noel Struchiner, Valeriy Surovtsev, William Talbott,

Jeremy Waldron, and Wilfrid Waluchow. In addition, I would like to thank the following people who have commented on some of the chapters, discussed some of the ideas with me, or helped me in other ways: Claudia Ceniceros, Andrew Jordan, Milena Jovanović, Marija Momic, Zrinka Mrkonjić, Juan Jose Otalvares, Svan Relac, and Ashley Robles. I would also like to acknowledge the following universities for having supported my work in one form or another over the years: National Autonomous University of Mexico (UNAM), Seattle Pacific University, Tomsk State University, University of Washington, University of Belgrade Faculty of Law, and University of Zagreb Faculty of Law.

Finally, I want to thank Maria Elias Sotirhos for everything that she has done for me over the nearly thirty years we have been together. She has been astoundingly supportive, as just about anyone who knows both of us can attest, putting up with more than any partner can reasonably be expected to put up with. Maria has painstakingly proofread every chapter of the book, despite utterly, unrelentingly, and, at times, loudly despising its topic. I cannot imagine how people go through life without the sort of unconditional love and kindness that she gives so naturally. I adore you, my boo.

Contents

Introduction

What Do You Mean by "Law," Anyway?

The notion of law that is typically the focus of conceptual jurisprudence applies to all and only institutional systems of norms; it is clearly part of the nature of law that it is institutional. As such, the concept-term "law" picks out paradigms of institutional systems of both municipal law and international law. These systems regulate different kinds of behavior: institutional systems of municipal law, as a conceptual matter, necessarily involve state regulation of both official and non-official behavior while institutional systems of international law necessarily involve multinational regulation of *only* official behavior on the part of nation-states. While it might be conceptually possible to have systems of international law that regulate non-official behavior, it is not conceptually necessary that they even purport to regulate non-official behavior.[1]

But this general notion of law also applies to institutional normative systems that are like and unlike these legal systems in theoretically significant ways. Like systems of municipal and international law, a system of religious law has something fairly characterized as a rule of recognition for recognizing, applying, or enforcing norms that govern the behavior of members of the relevant community, as well as a set of authorized sanctions, such as excommunication, reasonably contrived to induce compliance among subjects otherwise disposed to violate norms of the system. Unlike systems of municipal and international law, a system of religious law is necessarily concerned

[1] A federal system that brings together subnational entities into a unified national entity is somewhat more difficult to characterize. Conceived as conceptually independent of the subnational entities it unites, a federal legal system more resembles systems of international law than it does systems of municipal law in virtue of necessarily containing only norms governing the official behavior of the states. But conceived as conceptually dependent upon the subnational entities it brings together, it incorporates the law of those subnational entities and hence more resembles a municipal system than it does systems of international law.

with articulating, codifying, and enforcing a shared morality deemed to be the canon of the faith.

Although there is something to be gained in our understanding of law by explicating the content of a concept that applies to both systems of religious law and to systems of municipal and international law, there is also something to be lost. On the one hand, systems of religious law have much in common with systems of municipal and international law; that is why the term "law" can be taken to refer to both types of system. On the other hand, systems of religious law differ in theoretically significant ways from systems of municipal and international law. To pursue an explication of a general notion of law that applies equally to each will of necessity suppress theoretically significant features of one that distinguish it from the other and will hence result in a theory that under-explicates both.

Another potential drawback to focusing on a general notion that applies to both subtypes is that it can lead to confusion with respect to our understanding of each subtype. Consider H.L.A. Hart's puzzling remarks about the conceptual function of law:

> [W]hereas Dworkin's interpretive legal theory in all its forms rests on the presupposition that the point or purpose of law and legal practice is to justify coercion, it certainly is not and never has been my view that law has this as its point or purpose. Like other forms of positivism my theory makes no claim to identify the point or purpose of law and legal practices as such; so there is nothing in my theory to support Dworkin's view, which I certainly do not share that the purpose of law is to justify the use of coercion. In fact, I think it quite vain to seek any more specific purpose which law as such serves beyond providing guides to human conduct and standards of criticism of such conduct.[2]

These remarks are usually interpreted as asserting that the conceptual function of law is to guide behavior, but a more careful look indicates that Hart is skeptical about the very possibility of identifying a distinctive conceptual function of law. It is not just that he states "[l]ike other forms of positivism, my theory makes no claim to identify the point or purpose of law and legal practices as such"; it is also that he thinks it "quite vain" to say anything more about law's conceptual function than that it "provides guides to human conduct."

Notice that the claim that law's conceptual function is to guide behavior would not distinguish systems of municipal or international law from systems of religious law. Although both systems are concerned with doing something

[2] H.L.A. Hart, *The Concept of Law* 3rd Ed. (Oxford: Oxford University Press, 2012), 248–49. Hereinafter *CL*.

that involves guiding behavior through the governance of norms, legal norms and norms of religious law differ, as a conceptual matter, in content because they are concerned to achieve different things. In our world, municipal and international law seek to diminish the likelihood of violent conflicts among subjects so that they can reap the social benefits of living together in a community; the norms of religious law seek to enforce moral norms grounded in theological commitments that help to distinguish one faith tradition from another. If the concern is to explicate all of these various types of norm, all that can be said about law's conceptual function is that it is concerned to regulate behavior through norm-guidance.

But if the concern is to explicate our conceptual practices with respect to the nature of law as it applies to systems of municipal and international law, as I take it to be, the failure to distinguish municipal and international law from other systems of law is far from innocuous. The claim that the conceptual function of an automobile is to transport persons or things from one destination to another is problematic because it fails to distinguish automobiles from airplanes. Just as any conceptual theory of an automobile that fails to identify a conceptual function that distinguishes automobiles from airplanes is problematic for that reason, so is a conceptual theory of law that fails to identify a conceptual function that distinguishes systems of municipal and international law from other systems of law.

Pursuing an explication of the most general concept of law can lead to other confusions. If one refers to the rules of a chess association as "law," as the World Chess Federation (WCF) does, then it is utterly uncontentious that positivism's Separability Thesis is true; if any system of norms properly characterized as "law" is artifactual all the way down in the sense that the content of its norms is fully manufactured by its officials, the norms of a chess association are.[3] Although there are good reasons to reject the conceptual claim that there can be no unjust laws, it would be silly to argue that the system of WCF rules suffices to establish the Separability Thesis and thereby to refute a view of historic importance that has been traditionally associated with classical natural law theory.

Although it is perfectly legitimate to pursue a conceptual theory that applies as much to chess and religious law as to municipal and international law, this is not the approach I take here. This volume is concerned exclusively with *jurisprudence* as the term is used among attorneys, judges, and law students. This usage is properly applied only to matters arising within systems of municipal law and international law. The approach here focuses, like most

[3] *Handbook of the World Chess Federation*, available at https://www.fide.com/component/handbook/?id=124&view=article.

scholarly inquiries concerning the nature of law, on the practices associated with law as it pertains to political entities like states, but it assumes that these systems have a metaphysical nature that is related to but distinct from the nature of other kinds of systems of law.

None of this should be taken to deny that explicating the general concept that applies equally to municipal law, religious law, and the rules of a chess association is a worthwhile endeavor. The linguistic conventions we adopt define a conceptual framework that not only gives structure to the world of our experience but also says something important about us. An analysis of the more general concept of law hence conduces to our collective understanding of who we are and what we value. That our ordinary usages permit the application of the term "law" to systems that are as different from one another as municipal law, chess law, and religious law tells us something important about ourselves. But I have no urgent interest in the conceptual nature of chess law or religious law; what I do care a lot about is the nature of the type of law studied in law schools and practiced in systems of municipal and international law—and that is the exclusive concern of this volume.

There is one more feature of the approach adopted here that should be noted. I am of the view that the substance of a conceptual theory is deeply conditioned by the methodology that underwrites the analysis. The analysis is explicitly grounded in the linguistic and legal practices that inform our ordinary usage with respect to the term "law" and is exclusively concerned with that usage. The ultimate touchstone, then, for evaluating the claims I make about the concept of law is whether they conform to ordinary usage as fleshed out to expose not only the underlying social practices that define them but also the philosophical presuppositions that ground those practices.

1

Relationships Between Law and Morality

It is not implausible to think that the project of general jurisprudence was partly motivated by disputes about conceptual relationships between law and morality. Jeremy Bentham's and John Austin's legal positivism was articulated partly in response to William Blackstone's view that it is a conceptually necessary condition for a norm to count as law that its content not conflict with objective standards of justice. Bentham and Austin denied this claim, arguing instead that the content of the law is fully determined by the commands of a sovereign willing and able to back them with the threat of a sanction.[1]

In this chapter, I distinguish three types of inquiry about law in order to explain the conceptual project with which this volume is concerned. Then I articulate the two conceptual views about morality and the nature of law that comprise the focus of this volume. First, I explain positivist and anti-positivist views with respect to whether it is a conceptual truth that the criteria of legal validity include moral constraints on the content of law. Second, I explain the dispute between inclusive and exclusive positivists with respect to whether it is conceptually possible for a legal system to have content-based moral criteria of validity.

Finally, as the intellectual legitimacy of the project of conceptual jurisprudence has recently come under fire for not having practical consequences or being "interesting" and hence as not being worth doing, I say something brief in defense of the project. My defense, such as it is, will be somewhat modest. I will dispute neither the claim that right answers to conceptual questions lack significant practical consequences nor the claim that conceptual theorizing is uninteresting.

What I will do is argue that the claim that conceptual jurisprudence should not be done is either unclear or false. On the one hand, if the claim that

[1] See, generally, Jeremy Bentham (1782). Of Laws in General Ed. H.L.A. Hart (London: Athlone Press, 1970); and John Austin (1832). *The Province of Jurisprudence Determined* Ed. Wilfred E. Rumble (Cambridge: Cambridge University Press, 1995). For an outstanding discussion of the history of these views, see Brian H. Bix, *Jurisprudence: Theory and Context* 7th Ed. (Durham, NC: Carolina Academic Press, 2015), Chapter 5. Hereinafter *JTC*.

conceptual jurisprudence should not be done is a moral claim, it is false. From the standpoint of morality, there are many things any legal scholar can do that would make the world a much better place than writing articles for academic journals; whatever difference there is between the moral value of writing in conceptual jurisprudence and that of writing in other areas of legal scholarship amounts to little. On the other hand, if it is not a moral claim, then it is not clear exactly what it amounts to.

1. Three types of inquiry about law

A frequent area of interest to those who theorize about law concerns the various relationships between law and morality. To understand these relationships, it is helpful to distinguish three kinds of inquiry concerning morality and law. The first is *empirical* in the sense that it is concerned with identifying certain contingent relationships in our world having to do with law and morality. One can ask, for example, whether officials of some existing legal system usually consider what they believe are moral requirements in making decisions about how to create, adjudicate, and enforce the law. As this question concerns the motivations of officials, addressing it requires going into the world and observing what officials say and how they behave in discharging their functions as officials.

The second kind of inquiry is *normative* in the sense that it is concerned with determining, as a matter of morality, how officials should behave in discharging their duties or what content the law should have. It is clear both that laws should be just and that legal systems should be legitimate; and the content of the law and legal practices should satisfy the appropriate moral requirements. Normative inquiry, then, is concerned with determining whether some existing law, legal system, or legal practice satisfies the relevant demands of morality.

The third kind of inquiry is *conceptual* in the sense that it seeks to describe the content of the relevant concept and hence to explicate the nature of the thing picked out by the concept. Conceptual claims purport to identify the properties that distinguish things that are members of the reference class of the concept-term from things that are not. For example, the concept-term "bachelor" is generally thought to apply only to things that are unmarried and men. The instantiation of all these properties distinguishes things that are bachelors from things that are not bachelors; married things, for example, do not fall within the reference class of the concept-term "bachelor."

As traditionally conceived, the goal of conceptual analysis is purely descriptive. Thus conceived, the goal is simply to explicate, or describe in a philosophically rigorous way, the content of the relevant concept as it is grounded in those social practices that determine the application-conditions of the relevant concept-term. Conceptual analysis seeks to describe—rather than to prescribe—the content of the relevant concept and is hence concerned to provide an account of what the content of the concept *is*, and not of what the content of the concept *should be*.

Explicating the content of a concept requires identifying those properties that are conceptually necessary for something to fall under the concept in the following sense: if p is a conceptually necessary property for being an A, then it is conceptually impossible to be an A without instantiating p. To explicate the content of a concept is to identify those properties essential to the thing picked out by the corresponding concept-term. Being unmarried, for example, is a conceptually necessary condition for being a bachelor or, otherwise put, is essential to bachelorhood. Insofar as these conceptually necessary properties are essential properties of the thing picked out by the concept, they also define the *nature* of the thing picked out by the relevant concept.

As is evident from the talk of necessary properties, the traditional methodology for conceptual analysis trades in the language of modal logic, utilizing the modalities of necessity and possibility, along with possible-worlds talk. For example, the conceptual truth that bachelors are unmarried entails that there are no conceptually possible worlds in which there is someone who is both married and a bachelor. This latter claim is logically equivalent to the claim that in every conceptually possible world all bachelors are unmarried. Accordingly, conceptual inquiry with respect to the nature of law is concerned with determining what is true of law in some, none, or every conceptually possible world.

It is important to note that the character of the relevant modal claims about the nature of a thing depend on the logical relationship between the content of the concept and the linguistic conventions governing the use of the relevant concept-term. If, on the one hand, these modal claims presuppose a particular conceptual framework grounded in contingent linguistic practices, then the character of the resulting modal claims would aptly be described as "conditionally" necessary, and not as "absolutely" necessary, since the underlying practices can change over time. If, on the other, these modal claims are thought not to be grounded in the linguistic practices that establish the application-conditions for using the relevant concept-term, then the character of the resulting modal claims would aptly be described as "absolutely" necessary.

Both of the accounts given above harmonize with the notion of a priori justification or knowledge, properly understood. To say that a proposition can be justified or known a priori does not entail that it can be justified or known independently of *all* empirical experience. To say that a proposition can be justified or known a priori is to say that it can be justified or known independently of any empirical experience *not needed to understand the meaning of the relevant terms.* Accordingly, on the assumption that conceptual jurisprudence is a priori, its focus on identifying the contingent linguistic practices that determine the lexical meanings of words coheres with the character of a priori knowledge. Likewise, the claim that conceptual claims are conditionally necessary in the sense of being dependent on contingent linguistic practices also coheres with the idea that they are a priori in the sense that they can be known or justified independently of any empirical experience not needed to understand the meaning of the relevant terms.

It is sometimes thought that conceptual analysis, conceived as being grounded in the linguistic practices that define the lexical meaning of the relevant concept-term, involves little more than providing a dictionary definition, but this is mistaken. Thus conceived, conceptual theorizing begins from core intuitions about how to use a word that are conditioned by its lexical meaning but goes much deeper than lexicography insofar as it attempts to identify and theorize the deeper philosophical commitments these intuitions imply or presuppose. While this might or might not be a distinctively philosophical enterprise, it goes well beyond the empirical task of merely identifying shared intuitions or core features of our linguistic practices, which is the job of lexicographers.

Compare what lexicographers have to say about the word "law" with what Hart has to say by way of explication of the concept of law. Oxford American Dictionary defines "law" as follows:

law | noun 1 (often the law) the system of rules that a particular country or community recognizes as regulating the actions of its members and may enforce by the imposition of penalties: they were taken to court for breaking the law | a license is required by law | [as adj.] law enforcement.

- an individual rule as part of such a system: an initiative to tighten up the laws on pornography.
- such systems as a subject of study or as the basis of the legal profession: he was still practicing law | [as adj.] a law firm ....
- a thing regarded as having the binding force or effect of a formal system of rules: what he said was law.

Notice how much of what Hart's theory addresses is omitted by the lexical definition.[2] First, there is no mention here of many pieces central to Hart's analysis: the definition says nothing about social practices; the rule of recognition; secondary and primary rules; legal validity; and many other theoretically salient features of law. Second, the lexicographer's job is accomplished in a few lines whereas Hart took more than two hundred pages to give an analysis of the nature of law in The Concept of Law. If Hart starts from shared views about the meaning of "law," he is doing something radically different from what lexicographers do—and going much deeper into what law ultimately is.

This book is a piece of traditional conceptual analysis that conceives the project as grounded in the contingent linguistic practices that determine the lexical meanings of the relevant concept-terms, but it should not be construed as disparaging the other types of inquiry concerning law or other methodological principles that have been deployed in the service of conceptual analysis. I choose this methodology simply because it is the one that has been adopted by the theorists whose work I find most interesting and with whose work I wish to engage.

As the concern of this book is to explicate certain relationships between the concepts of law and morality, I begin by briefly describing the positions that are the focus of this volume: (1) the position that it is a conceptual truth about law that the criteria of validity include moral constraints on the content of law (i.e. natural law theory); (2) the position that it is a conceptual truth that the criteria of validity are exhausted by source-based criteria (i.e. exclusive positivism); and (3) the position that it is conceptually possible for a rule of recognition to incorporate moral criteria of validity (i.e. inclusive positivism).

2. Natural law theories

It would be helpful to partition conceptual theories of law into two mutually exclusive and jointly exhaustive categories: positivist and anti-positivist theories. Positivists hold that the content of law is an artifact that is wholly manufactured through certain social activities. Both the norms that regulate the non-official behavior of subjects and those that regulate the behavior of officials acting as legislators, judges, and executives are social artifacts. Since there are thus no conceptually necessary moral constraints on what counts

[2] See, generally, H.L.A. Hart, *The Concept of Law* 3rd. Ed. (Oxford: Oxford University Press, 2012). Hereinafter *CL*.

as valid law, the content of the validity criteria is determined entirely by the social activities of those who make, adjudicate, and enforce what they characterize as law.

In contrast, so-called anti-positivist theories are traditionally interpreted to deny that the content of the validity criteria is fully determined by our practices. Thus construed, natural law theories assert that it is a conceptual truth that the criteria of validity include moral constraints on the content of valid law. On this view, it is a conceptually necessary condition for a norm to count as a valid law that its content conforms to some set of objective moral standards. Accordingly, the social processes through which people manufacture law do not fully determine the content of the validity criteria; no matter what people do by way of recognizing, applying, or enforcing what they characterize as "law," there are moral standards that constrain what really counts as law in a legal system.

Classical natural law theory is hence traditionally interpreted as asserting that "an unjust law is no law at all" (*lex iniusta non est lex*). While natural law theory goes back at least as far as Cicero, the most influential early advocate of this view is Aquinas, who appears to endorse it in the following passage:

> As Augustine says, "that which is not just seems to be no law at all"; wherefore the force of a law depends on the extent of its justice. Now, in human affairs a thing is said to be just from being right according to the rule of reason. But the first rule of reason is the law of nature, as is clear from what has been stated above. Consequently, every human law has just so much of the nature of law is it is derived from the law of nature. But if, in any point, it deflects from the law of nature, it is no longer a law but a perversion of law.[3]

Aquinas's view is subsequently picked up by Blackstone, who expresses it in language quite similar to Aquinas's:

> This law of nature, being coeval with mankind and dictated by God himself, is of course superior in obligation to any other. It is binding over all the globe, in all countries, and at all times: no human laws are of any validity, if contrary to this; and such of them as are valid derive all their force, and all their authority, mediately or immediately, from this original.[4]

While the traditional natural law view has been largely construed to assert that it is conceptually impossible for there to be an unjust law, the passages

[3] St. Thomas Aquinas, *Summa Theologiae*, Prima Secundae Partis Q. 95, Art. 2; available at: http://www.newadvent.org/summa/2095.htm.

[4] Sir William Blackstone, "Of the Nature of Laws in General," *Commentaries on the Laws of England—Book I: Of the Rights of Persons* (Oxford: Oxford University Press, 2016), 35. Hereinafter *COM*.

above are ambiguous. Aquinas is concerned with the *force* of law, which can plausibly be interpreted as referring to the *moral* force of law. Similarly, Blackstone's references to validity and authority are plausibly construed as referring to *moral* validity and *moral* authority. These passages can be construed as asserting no more than that an unjust norm posited as law would not generate a moral obligation to obey and might be such that morality obligates us to disobey it. On this interpretation, the claim would be that an unjust posited norm is not *morally* binding, and not that an unjust posited norm is not *legally* binding.

There are plausible reasons to think that Blackstone is making only claims about moral validity and moral authority. The discussion that precedes the passage quoted above is unambiguously concerned with what we are morally obligated to do, and not with what we are legally obligated to do. Consider, for example, the following statement, which precedes the last quoted remark of Blackstone's by four paragraphs:

> Man, considered as a creature, must necessarily be subject to the laws of his creator, for he is entirely a dependent being. A being, independent of any other, has no rule to pursue, but such as he prescribes to himself; but a state of dependence will inevitably oblige the inferior to take the will of him, on whom he depends, as the rule of his conduct: not indeed in every particular, but in all those points wherein his dependence consists. This principle therefore has more or less extent and effect, in proportion as the superiority of the one and the dependence of the other is greater or less, absolute or limited. And consequently as man depends absolutely upon his maker for everything, it is necessary that he should in all points conform to his maker's will (*COM* 33–34).

The deontic locutions used in this passage (such as "must necessarily be subject," "obliged," and "should in all points conform") are unquestionably moral in character. It is clear that Blackstone is not concerned with what is prudentially or legally normative—although one certainly has prudential reasons to obey God's will if eternal torment is the consequence of disobedience.

Blackstone does not begin to discuss "human law" for several paragraphs after the last two quotes:

> Upon these two foundations, the law of nature and the law of revelation, depend all human laws; that is to say, *no human laws should be suffered to contradict these* .... To instance in the case of murder: this is expressly forbidden by the divine, and demonstrably by the natural law; and from these prohibitions arises the true unlawfulness of this crime. Those human laws, that annex a punishment to it, do not at all increase its moral guilt, or super-add any fresh obligation *in foro conscientiae* to abstain from its perpetration. Nay, *if any human law should allow or enjoin us to commit it, we are bound to transgress that human law, or else we must offend both the natural and the divine. But with regard to matters that are in themselves indifferent, and are not*

commanded or forbidden by those superior laws; such, for instance, as exporting of wool into foreign countries; here the inferior legislature has scope and opportunity to interpose, and to make that action unlawful which before was not so (*COM* 35–36; emphasis added).

The italicized portion suggest that Blackstone, like Aquinas, is concerned with what is morally binding, rather than with what is legally binding in virtue of being human-made law. The claim is that what we are obligated to do all things considered is what morality obligates us to do; if a legal and moral obligation come into conflict, we must do what the moral obligation requires us to do.

The traditional interpretation of Blackstone as claiming that an unjust norm cannot be a positive law, then, is implausible. The most reasonable interpretation of Blackstone's view, given the totality of his remarks, construes him as being concerned with what is morally (or, as the matter is sometimes put, "really") binding and authoritative—and not with the project of conceptual jurisprudence as defined by the work of Austin and Bentham. On this construction, the natural law view asserts only that it is in the nature of law that it should be just; an unjust norm might be legally valid, but it is defective *qua* law insofar as it fails to instantiate the quality of justice to which it aspires.

Brian Bix has persuasively argued for this interpretation of classical natural law theory and explicates it as follows:

A more reasonable interpretation of statements like "an unjust law is no law at all" is that unjust laws are not laws "in the fullest sense." As we might say of some professional, who had the necessary degrees and credentials, but seemed nonetheless to lack the necessary ability or judgment: "she's no lawyer" or "he's no doctor." This only indicates that we do not think that the title in this case carries with it all the laudatory implications that it usually carries. It may well be that for our purposes, knowing that this doctor is not competent is the most important fact; however, the fact that he does have the required certification is not thereby negated or made entirely irrelevant. Similarly, to say that unjust laws are "not really laws" may only be to point out that they do not carry the same moral force or offer the same reasons for action that come from laws consistent with "higher law" (*JTC* 73–74).

Bix convincingly argues that Aquinas and Blackstone hold no stronger view about the nature of positive law than this and that this view is the most "probable interpretation for nearly all proponents of the position" (*JTC* 74).

Notice that there is no inconsistency between natural law theory and positivism if Bix is correct that the natural law position should be interpreted as asserting only that an unjust law is not law in the fullest sense. Positivism does not even purport to explain what it means to be law in the fullest sense of the word "law." Positivism is concerned only to explicate the existence conditions for laws and legal systems, as those terms are used in the discourses of lawyers, officials, and other legal practitioners.

Even so, the fact that this confusion about the natural law view is so widespread and persistent—indeed, it is perpetuated in part by natural law theorists who claim they are opposed to legal positivism—is indicative of a need to consider the view that it is a conceptual truth that an unjust norm cannot be law. A more rigorous examination and evaluation of this view will be undertaken in Chapter 2.

For now, it suffices to note that one can hold that it is a conceptual truth that the criteria of validity include moral norms without taking the position that it is a conceptual truth that there are no unjust laws. To see this, it would be helpful to distinguish two theses concerning a conceptual relationship between law and morality:

NL1: It is a conceptual truth that the criteria of validity include at least some moral norms; and

NL2: It is a conceptual truth that the criteria of validity include all the norms of justice such that an unjust norm cannot be valid.

NL2 logically implies NL1. Given that the norms of justice are also norms of morality, if it is a conceptual truth that the criteria of validity include all the norms of justice, then it is also a conceptual truth that the criteria of validity include at least some moral norms.

But NL1 does not logically imply NL2. The claim that the criteria of validity include *some* moral norms does not imply that they contain all the norms of justice. Indeed, NL1 does not clearly imply that the criteria of legal validity include any norms of justice; if there are norms of political morality that are not norms of justice, then NL1 is consistent with the criteria of validity including only those norms.

Consider norms requiring democratic elections. It is not preposterous to think that norms requiring procedural democracy are not properly characterized as norms of "justice." If the notion of justice is best construed as ensuring that people get what they deserve economically and otherwise, then norms of democracy are not norms of justice insofar as it is not true that people "deserve" to elect their officials.[5] It might be true that people have a moral

[5] To say that it is not true that people deserve to elect the officials that govern them is not to say that people *do not deserve* to elect the officials that govern them. When people claim that someone does not deserve some benefit, they usually intend to say that someone is *undeserving* of the benefit and should not receive it. That is not what I mean by the claim that it is not true that people deserve to elect the officials that govern them. What I mean is that the concept of desert is irrelevant with respect to explaining why people should be allowed to elect those officials. The concept is inapt here

right to elect their leaders, but having a moral right to some *X* is not logically equivalent to morally deserving *X*. I might have a moral right to inherit someone's estate, but that does not entail that I deserve that person's estate. Accordingly, NL1 does not entail NL2.

Accordingly, holding NL2, the traditional natural law theory, is not the only way to hold NL1. Ronald Dworkin, for example, is commonly thought to hold NL1 without holding NL2:

> We need not deny that the Nazi system was an example of law ... because there is an available sense in which it plainly was law. But we have no difficulty in understanding someone who does say that Nazi law was not really law, or was law in a degenerate sense, or was less than fully law. For he is not then using "law" in that sense; he is not making that sort of preinterpretive judgment but a skeptical interpretive judgment that Nazi law lacked features crucial to flourishing legal systems whose rules and procedures do justify coercion.[6]

As Dworkin describes his view, the claim that the Nazis did not have law because their norms were too wicked to count as law is false if it makes a "preinterpretive judgment," which is the type of judgment he takes to be expressed by positivism's Separability Thesis. Accordingly, it would seem that Dworkin rejects NL2.

But it seems clear that Dworkin holds NL1, at least as his view has traditionally been interpreted. As Dworkin describes his interpretivist theory of law, it is "the theory that the law of a community consists not simply in the discrete statutes and rules that its officials enact but in the general principles of justice and fairness that these statutes and rules, taken together, presuppose by way of implicit justification."[7] Elsewhere, he states that "[t]he law of a community on this account is the scheme of rights and responsibilities that meet that complex standard: they license coercion because they flow from past decisions of the right sort ... [and] are therefore 'legal' rights and responsibilities" (*LE* 93). His view, thus, seems to be that it is a conceptual truth that the criteria of validity include those moral principles that morally justify the existing institutional history of the legal system—which would, if correct, entail that he accepts NL1.

Chapter 2 considers the plausibility of anti-positivist accounts of the relationship between law and morality, arguing that classical natural law theory

because it is not true that people deserve to elect their officials and it is not true that they do not deserve to elect those officials.

[6] Ronald Dworkin, *Law's Empire* (Cambridge, MA: Harvard University Press, 1986), 103–4. Hereinafter *LE*.

[7] Ronald Dworkin, "The Law of the Slave Catchers," *The Times Literary Supplement*, December 5, 1975, 1437.

and Dworkin's interpretivism are best construed as explicating a concept of law that has evaluative content and is hence distinct from the purely descriptive concept that positivism takes itself to explicate. Although there is reason to think that many natural law theorists have been misinterpreted as rejecting the Separability Thesis and holding NL2, I nonetheless evaluate this view. The rationale is not that any particular theorist holds that view. Rather, the rationale is that, since so many theorists and students of conceptual jurisprudence have historically interpreted the natural law view as denying the Separability Thesis, the view should be evaluated in any project that explores the conceptual relationships between morality and the criteria of validity.

3. Inclusive legal positivism

As will be discussed in more detail in Chapter 3, positivist theories are typically thought to be grounded in three core theses: the Separability Thesis, the Artifact Thesis, and the Conventionality Thesis. The Separability Thesis denies that it is a conceptual truth that the criteria of validity include moral norms of any kind and hence denies both NL1 and NL2 above. According to the Separability Thesis, then, there is a conceptually possible legal system in which the criteria of validity do not include moral constraints on the content of law.

According to the Artifact Thesis, law is, by nature, an artifact in the sense that the content of every norm that counts as law is wholly determined by certain social activities. This entails that the content of both the second-order norms empowering and constraining officials in their lawmaking and adjudicative functions (and thereby define the criteria of validity) and the first-order norms legally valid in any legal system is wholly manufactured by human beings. If this is correct, there is no legal content that is determined by something other than the social activities of officials, such as norms of objective morality. Law is an artifact all the way down.

Finally, according to the Conventionality Thesis, it is a conceptual truth that the criteria of validity are determined by the content of a conventional rule of recognition governing how officials should discharge their duties and how they may exercise their powers in the institutional normative system their activities help to create and sustain. The content of a social convention that governs members of a social group is determined by the fact that people in the group converge (1) in accepting that content as governing their behavior and (2) in complying with that content. Thus, the Conventionality Thesis expresses Hart's view that the rule of recognition is a conventional rule of the system insofar as the officials take the internal point of view toward it (thereby satisfying condition (1) above) and generally conform their lawmaking and adjudicative acts to its requirements (thereby satisfying condition (2) above).

These theses are agnostic with respect to the question of whether it is conceptually possible for a legal system to have moral criteria of validity. The Separability Thesis, for example, asserts only that it is conceptually possible for a legal system to have criteria of validity that do *not* include moral constraints on the content of law; that claim implies nothing with respect to whether it is conceptually possible for a legal system to have criteria of validity that include such moral constraints. Similarly, the claims that law is a social artifact and that the criteria of validity are conventional in character do not obviously imply anything about whether it is conceptually possible for a legal system to have moral criteria of validity.

Two positions have emerged on this issue. According to inclusive positivism, it is conceptually possible for a legal system to incorporate moral criteria of validity; that is, inclusive positivism implies that there are conceptually possible legal systems with moral criteria of validity. In contrast, exclusive positivism denies that there are conceptually possible legal systems with moral criteria of validity. According to exclusive positivism, it is a conceptual truth that the criteria of validity are exhausted by source-based criteria of validity that have to do with the manner in which a norm is promulgated as law.

As it is doubtful that any major legal theorist holds NL1, most of the book will be devoted to the dispute between inclusive and exclusive positivism. Chapter 3 begins with the articulation of a methodological assumption that is the foundation for the project of conceptual jurisprudence. The chapter goes on to provide a more detailed explication of the core theses of positivism and of how these core theses are logically related to one another.

The next chapters of the book are concerned with evaluating the most influential arguments against inclusive positivism. Chapters 4, 5, and 6 address Joseph Raz's argument that the nature of law entails a claim of legitimate authority that is incompatible with the conceptual possibility of moral criteria of validity. Chapter 4 develops Raz's challenging and nuanced analysis of the nature of authority and his argument that it is incompatible with moral criteria of validity.

Chapter 5 explains and evaluates Raz's claim that it is part of the very nature of law that it claims legitimate authority. I consider a number of different interpretations of this view and challenge each. To begin, for example, I question how an institutional abstract object like a legal system could make claims. The difficulty here is roughly analogous to the metaphysical difficulties associated with the idea that the framers of the Constitution have something that would count as a collective *intention*; as has frequently been observed, it is difficult to see how collective entities can have mental states. I go on to consider other interpretations in terms of the beliefs and acts of officials and argue that none of these other interpretations adequately support the idea that every conceptually possible legal system, in any literal sense, claims legitimate authority.

Chapter 6 endeavors to rebut Raz's claim that it is part of *our* concept of authority that the content of an authoritative directive must be identifiable without recourse to the dependent reasons it is supposed to reflect, balance, and replace—a claim that implies that moral criteria of validity cannot be authoritative. I argue that if, as Raz maintains, it is not possible for officials to be systematically mistaken about the legal concepts that are defined by their adopted practices, there are empirical reasons for thinking there is nothing in *our* concepts of law and authority that would imply that moral criteria of validity are incompatible with the nature of authority. Insofar as *our* concept of law is constructed by *our* linguistic and legal practices, the best account of our concept of law includes the thesis that there can be moral criteria of validity.

Chapter 7 is concerned with the different ways in which law might be thought to guide behavior. Scott Shapiro argues that (1) a judge cannot be motivationally guided by both an inclusive rule of recognition and a norm she applies in a dispute that is valid in virtue of moral merit; and (2) an inclusive rule of recognition is incapable of informing subjects of what their non-official obligations are under valid law.[8] I argue that both those claims falsely presuppose that a rule must be capable of either guiding or informing the behavior of persons it does not purport to govern. Finally, this chapter argues that Raz's "Arguments from Authority" likewise falsely presuppose that the rule of recognition must be capable of informing ordinary citizens of what they must do under valid legal norms; a rule need inform only those persons whose behavior it governs of what they are required to do under *that* rule.

Chapter 8, the final chapter of the book, argues for the claim that inclusive legal systems are conceptually possible. Chapter 8 constructs a model of an institutional normative system that validates all and only mandatory moral norms in a possible world that resembles ours in every causal respect and shows that the system satisfies every condition that might plausibly be thought to be conceptually necessary for the existence of a legal system, thereby vindicating the Incorporation Thesis.

[8] Scott Shapiro, "On Hart's Way Out," *Legal Theory*, vol. 4, no. 4 (December 1998), 469–507.

4. Who cares?

One might wonder why an entire book should be devoted to abstruse debates about the concept of law. Many persons in the legal academy have developed an aversion to the rarified concerns of conceptual jurisprudence. The sense is that conceptual debates about the nature of law occur at such a high level of abstraction that they have no practical relevance whatsoever and are simply not worth pursuing.

The complaint is not that there are no good reasons to think conceptual jurisprudence should be done; it is that there are good reasons to think that it *should not be done*. This is a considerably stronger claim: to say that I have no reason to do something does not obviously entail that I have a reason not to do it. Skeptics argue that pursuing conceptual jurisprudence is problematic because a conceptual theory of law tells us nothing about what our laws or legal practices should be. Conceptual jurisprudence, they proclaim, should not be done.

This critique rests on two different ideas. The first is that answers to conceptual questions do not have any practical implications with respect to what our laws and associated practices should be. The second is that a theory about law should not be pursued unless it has implications with respect to what our laws and practices should be. In the next subsection, I consider whether the first claim is true. In the sequel, I consider whether the second is true.

4.1 Does a conceptual theory of law have any practical implications?

The view that conceptual jurisprudence should not be done is not a new one. Richard Posner devotes a substantial portion of the first of his 1995 Clarendon Law Lectures at Oxford University to arguing that conceptual jurisprudence should not be done because it is "futile, distracting, and illustrative of the impoverishment of traditional legal theory."[9] He explains the problem as follows:

> I have nothing against philosophical speculation. But one would like it to have some pay-off; *something* ought to turn on the answer to the question "What is law?" if the question is to be worth asking by people who could use their time in other socially valuable ways. Nothing does turn on it (*LLT* 3).

[9] Richard Posner, *Law and Legal Theory* (Oxford: Clarendon Press, 1996). Hereinafter *LLT*.

Indeed, Posner goes so far as to argue that "the central task of analytic jurisprudence is, or at least ought to be, not to answer the question 'What is law?' but to show that it should not be asked, because it only confuses matters" (*LLT* 3).

Apart from the fact that he does not explain how conceptual theories "confuses matters," Posner's argument is problematic. On the one hand, Posner argues that conceptual jurisprudence has no practical implications about what our laws and legal practices should be. On the other, he claims that answers to conceptual questions would only confuse matters. The problem is that if the only theoretical issues about law that matter are normative issues concerning what our laws and legal practices should be, then a theory that has no practical implications whatsoever simply could not create any confusion with respect to those issues.

That said, there is something to Posner's claim that answers to conceptual questions have no practical implications whatsoever. Consider the conceptual question of whether the Pope is properly characterized as a "bachelor." At first glance, the answer seems obvious: since the Pope is an unmarried adult male, he is, by definition, a bachelor. Yet many people feel uneasy with this response because the Pope has opted out of the marriage game. The thinking is that the term "bachelor" applies only to unmarried men who are institutionally or psychologically eligible for marriage. But notice that, either way, the answer tells us nothing about how we should treat the Pope or how we should treat bachelors. Conceptual analysis might go well beyond lexicography, but it is still concerned with drawing out the implications of the social practices that define the relevant concept-words; and it is hard to see how a conceptual claim could have any practical implications other than those concerned with how to use the relevant words.

One might think the situation is different with respect to the law. The idea is that whether, say, an unjust norm, *L*, that has been properly enacted in some legal system counts as valid law depends on which theory of law is correct. If, on the one hand, it is conceptually true, as NL2 asserts, that an unjust norm cannot count as law, then *L* is not a law. If, on the other, it is conceptually true, as positivists assert, that an unjust norm can count as law, then *L* is a law in that system despite being unjust. Surely, on this line of reasoning, it makes a practical difference whether positivism or NL2 is true.

There are two problems with this reasoning. The first is that, at bottom, it makes no real practical difference with respect to morally evaluating our legal practices whether positivism or NL2 is true. What matters with respect to the moral legitimacy of *our* practices—and these are the practices we should be concerned with improving—is whether officials are treating *L* as law in the sense of backing it up with coercive enforcement mechanisms, and not whether *L* is really law according to some abstract general theory. If NL2 turns out to be true, then the rule that the courts are applying might not properly be characterized as "law," but that is no consolation to the unfortunate defendant who is being held liable under the rule. As far as considerations of political morality are concerned, the legitimacy of our practices with respect to, for example, enforcement of the Fugitive Slave Act does not turn at all on whether it counts, on some conceptual theory, as being *law*. A characterization of a norm as law simply cannot carry that kind of normative weight.

The second problem is related to the first. If officials are recognizing, applying, and enforcing an unjust norm as law, then it counts as "law," on the ordinary social practices that define the content of the concept of law with which this volume is concerned. It might be true, as a matter of political morality, that it should not be law, but that tells us nothing about whether it is properly characterized, according to ordinary usage, as law; it tells us only that the officials should not, as a matter of political morality, recognize, apply, or enforce this norm. What matters morally with respect to the practices of our courts and legislatures has everything to do with the content of the practices and nothing to do with whether those practices are properly characterized as "law." Moral problems cannot be solved by simply recasting them in different language.

Even so, it is important to note that resolving conceptual issues can sometimes help clarify notions that must be understood to address other kinds of issues. Consider the normative issue of whether legal systems should permit *medical* uses of marijuana. If one is sympathetic to the idea that criminal prohibitions of marijuana use are too restrictive and the punishments unjustifiably harsh, one might be tempted by the idea all medical uses should be permitted; after all, at first blush, if purely recreational use is problematic in a sense that requires legal prohibition, surely nothing accurately characterized as a medical use could be.

But the issue is more complicated than might initially appear because the notion of what counts as a medical use is not clear. Most people, for example, use alcohol as a "social lubricant" to reduce anxiety in certain social situations or to reduce anxiety to permit sleep after a long and stressful day. One can plausibly argue that these uses are therapeutic and hence better characterized as medical than as recreational. After all, the reasons for these uses resemble the reasons for using certain prescription medications: Ambien, for example, is prescribed to induce sleep while Valium and Xanax are prescribed for episodic anxiety of a kind that resembles the sort experienced by many people in various social settings. These uses are clearly medical and resemble the ways in which people use alcohol.

Certain purely recreational uses of alcohol would seem to be medically problematic or even pathological. One recreational use might involve consuming alcohol for aesthetic reasons having to do with the taste of the relevant beverage, such as wine. But another might involve consuming alcohol for the purpose of enjoying the inebriating effects of it—i.e. to get drunk. The problem with this use is that it suggests at least the beginning of an unhealthy relationship with alcohol that can ultimately culminate in alcoholism. If so, what appears to be a purely recreational use of a legal substance is far more problematic than other uses that appear at first glance to be recreational but turn out to be medical in character.

Alcohol, I suppose, is one thing and marijuana another, but the conceptual issues that arise in connection with uses of alcohol that seem most aptly characterized as "medical" also arise in connection with the normative issue of whether legal systems should permit medical use of marijuana. And the answer is: it all depends on what one means by "medical use" and whether one thinks that all uses that are properly characterized as "medical" are sufficiently innocuous that they should be permitted by law. Answers to conceptual questions can thus produce epistemic benefits by facilitating conceptual clarity in addressing other issues that have significant practical importance.

One might thus be tempted to argue that the pursuit of conceptual inquiry with respect to the nature of law can be justified on the ground that it enables us to think more clearly and rigorously about problems that have important normative dimensions—even if the relevant conceptual theories do not imply solutions to those problems. Proponents of conceptual analysis who feel the need (and, for what it is worth, I feel no such need) to justify their interest by reference to socially useful consequences typically do so by pointing to such epistemic benefits.

The point of conceptual jurisprudence, on this line of reasoning, is not that it entails solutions to important substantive problems of law or has immediate practical implications that conduce to the betterment of humanity by improving the moral quality of legal practice. Rather it is that conceptual analysis helps us solve those problems by enabling us to formulate them more clearly. The benefit here is not morally instrumental; rather it is epistemically instrumental.

I am unpersuaded. Perhaps this is true of some conceptual issues like the issue of what constitutes a medical use of an intoxicant, but this seems true of comparatively few issues at best. We do not seem to need a plausible account of the nature of law to successfully address normative problems of law any more than we need a plausible account of the nature of a number to successfully address mathematical problems. In both cases, a pre-theoretical understanding of the relevant concept is enough for us to fruitfully address the relevant class of problems.

Nor do we need a theoretical understanding of the nature of law to do everything we want to do with a legal system. It is true that we have to be able to do a lot of things to have a working institutional system of something that we typically characterize as "law." Officials have to agree on a set of procedures for recognizing, applying, and enforcing law; citizens have to be able to ascertain what their obligations are under the law for law to be efficacious in guiding their behavior; and so on. But if our ability to characterize these norms as "law" matters with respect to ensuring that they can efficaciously regulate behavior, we do not need a conceptual theory of law to inform our use of the term.

All we need to ensure this is that we largely agree on a pre-theoretic conception of what law is. Law is, on this shared pre-theoretic conception, what is enacted by a body that efficaciously functions as a rule-making body (which we traditionally call a "legislature") and applied by a body that efficaciously functions as an adjudicative agency (which we traditionally call a "court"). It does not matter what we call these functions or whether we are correct under the right conceptual theory in characterizing these norms as law. A social group that handles the governance of its subjects in a certain way will succeed in creating an efficacious institutional system of norm-governance—regardless of whether the relevant norms are correctly characterized as "law" under the best conceptual theory of law.

If the foregoing is correct, then a purely descriptive account of the content of a concept has neither practical implications with respect to how we should structure our legal practices nor epistemic implications with respect to how we should understand the practical problems that arise in connection with how we should structure those practices. This part of Posner's argument against doing conceptual jurisprudence seems correct. The issue considered in the next section is whether this is a good reason for thinking that conceptual jurisprudence should not be done.

4.2 Should conceptual jurisprudence not be done?

Posner's claim that conceptual jurisprudence should not be done because it squanders time that could be used in "socially valuable ways" seems to entail that it is wrong to spend time on doing conceptual jurisprudence. First, wasting a socially valuable resource is usually thought to be wrong in some sense (whether prudentially or morally); if doing conceptual jurisprudence squanders a valuable resource, it would be wrong in the same way. Second, as a general matter, to say that something should not be done according to some set of standards is to say that doing it violates those standards and is hence wrong according to those standards. Doing something that should not be done might not amount to a particularly egregious wrong but doing something that should not be done is wrong under whatever standards dictate that it should not be done. Posner's complaint, then, is that it is wrong for theorists to do conceptual jurisprudence.

This is a puzzling complaint. To begin, the sense in which conceptual jurisprudence *should* not be done is not clear. On the most natural interpretation, Posner is making a moral claim, but it seems implausible to think that it is morally wrong to work in conceptual jurisprudence. If conceptual jurisprudents were arguing for wicked conclusions (e.g., that people should torture babies), that would be a reason to think that they should not do what they are doing. But the claim that law is a social artifact grounded in a conventional rule of recognition practiced by officials seems pretty clearly to be a morally innocuous one—which, of course, is partly explained by the fact that it is purely descriptive.

If Posner is properly construed as making a moral claim, perhaps a more plausible interpretation is that it would be morally better for legal theorists to devote their energies to more practical issues. But the claim that one act is morally better than another does not entail that the latter should not be done. As a general matter, we do not say that one act is better than another unless both acts are morally permissible. Someone who says giving to charity is morally better than committing murder is most plausibly construed as making a philosophically nuanced (but not very funny) joke that calls attention to vagueness with respect to the expression "morally better." We generally use that locution only to compare options that are morally permissible in the sense that neither option is either prohibited or required. As far as ordinary usage is concerned, to say that it is morally better that I give $25 to charity than it is that I give $20 to charity neither asserts nor implies that I should not give $20 to charity.[10]

But putting aside that concern, this construction of Posner's claim remains problematic. It is surely true that conceptual jurisprudents could find morally better things to do with their time, but so can most people who write in the legal academy on other issues. Perhaps what other legal theorists do with their research interests is morally better than what conceptual jurisprudents do with theirs. But if so, the difference is not enough to make a focus on conceptual jurisprudence worth complaining about. Indeed, if it is true that we

[10] The situation changes if one adds the word "just." It seems true that I should not give *just* $20 to charity.

should all attempt to work on issues likely to maximize moral value, the vast majority of us working on the kinds of issues that fill the pages of law reviews would do better to either give up our theoretical pursuits to focus on practical pursuits involving law or to leave law entirely to study medicine or something else more likely to produce social benefits than law.

None of this should be construed to disparage the efforts of those who work in these areas. Every theorist, on my view, is entitled to pursue those issues she finds most interesting. We are all entitled to considerable moral latitude to do what we need to do to make our lives meaningful; life is, after all, nasty, brutish, and short. For this reason, in the absence of special circumstances, it is as misguided to claim that legal theorists should do something morally better with their lives as it is to claim that people in any other legitimate occupation should do so.

But if the relevant sense of "should" is not moral, it is just not clear what class of norms would support the claim that conceptual jurisprudence should not be done. It makes little sense, as far as I can tell, to argue that the relevant norms are epistemic; the idea would have to be that pursuing conceptual jurisprudence is likely to result in our having false beliefs about something—a claim that is completely lacking in plausible support. Nor does it seem to make much sense to think that the relevant norms have anything to do with what is prudentially rational. As far as I can tell, Hart and Dworkin were made famous by their contributions to conceptual jurisprudence; if so, that work certainly conduced to their interests. If the norms of practical rationality encompass some other kind of normativity, that needs to be specified in order to begin to make out Posner's claim.

Even so, it is helpful to consider how implausible remarks like Posner's would be if made about other disciplines. Though a great deal of work in pure mathematics has been used to create technologies that improve our lives, one of the most celebrated mathematical accomplishments of recent years is not thought to have such applications. In 1995, Andrew Wiles of Princeton University published a successful proof of Fermat's Last Theorem, which asserts that there are no positive integers x, y, z, and $n > 2$ such that the equation $x^n + y^n = z^n$ is true. I would be surprised if any of the mathematicians who devoted countless hours to trying to prove this theorem were motivated by an expectation it would produce a significant improvement in the human condition—or, for that matter, even believed it would have such applications.

Imagine the reaction in the mathematical community to someone whose stature in mathematics is comparable to Posner's stature in law publishing the following remarks in response to the efforts to prove Fermat's Last Theorem:

I have nothing against mathematical speculation. But one would like it to have some pay-off; *something* ought to turn on the answer to the question "Is Fermat's Last Theorem true?" if the question is to be worth asking by people who could use their time in other socially valuable ways. Nothing does turn on it.

The point here is not to deny that Wiles's proof might turn out to have beneficial practical applications; highly abstract mathematical results sometimes have such applications. For example, Kurt Gödel proved the Incompleteness Theorem long before there were computers, but some of the mathematics he invented along the way wound up having many practical applications in the field of computer science. Seemingly purely theoretical advances in abstract mathematics have sometimes had unexpected technological applications.

Rather, the point is that there is no reason to think that the pursuit of knowledge, mathematical or otherwise, is justified (or justifiably motivated) only insofar as it has direct practical benefits apart from the joy of the endeavor and the knowledge it makes possible. Mathematicians recognize, as they should, that the pursuit of knowledge need not be justified by instrumental concerns and hence that a problem need not have instrumental implications to be worth discussing. Pursuit of knowledge, mathematical and otherwise, can be justified by the value of knowing for its own sake.

It is not surprising that solutions to problems in conceptual jurisprudence lack practical applications. Concept-words are used to group acts, events, and entities into certain categories and do no more than pick out particular classes of acts, events, and entities. It seems clear that we cannot solve any interesting moral problems merely by altering our conceptual characterization of some act, event, or entity. Whether hitting someone in the face is morally wrong cannot turn on whether it is properly characterized as a gift; if it is properly characterized as a gift, then we will have to rethink our moral views about the permissibility of gift-giving from the ground up. What substantive normative qualities any particular act or event has cannot turn on how it is grouped through our linguistic practices with other acts or events. To decide those questions, we need the help of propositions that express the relevant values.

But theoretical pursuits can be justified by other reasons than those having to do with their practical applications. If we think that knowledge is both intrinsically and instrumentally valuable, a theoretical pursuit can be justified by the intrinsic value of knowing the truth about the matter. Even if it turns out that neither Fermat's Last Theorem nor its proof have practical applications, we are surely made better off as a community—in some sense relevant to human flourishing—in virtue of having a proof of the theorem because (1) we know now that the theorem is true and (2) knowing the truth about a matter, other things being equal, is valuable for its own sake. Likewise, getting a handle on the nature of law, our most important normative institution, and one that contributes significantly to our collective self-understanding, is also valuable for its own sake.

Mathematics is not the only area of intellectual activity that is justified, at least in part, by the intrinsic value of pursuing it. No sensible person thinks that art must be justified by its practical applications; both the pursuit of art and its products are valuable for their own sakes. It seems reasonable to think that the same is true of philosophy, even if some areas of philosophical speculation, such as substantive moral theory, also have instrumental benefits. The pursuit of knowledge or truth on non-trivial matters (and law is certainly a non-trivial matter) is an intrinsically valuable activity.

If one needs more to justify conceptual inquiry than this, then it might help to note that a theoretical pursuit can also be justified on the ground that it presents special intellectual difficulties. Part of the reason that Wiles's achievement has been so widely celebrated is that finding a proof for Fermat's Last Theorem was so difficult that it eluded mathematicians for hundreds of years. This, of course, is no less true of non-intellectual pursuits: one can justifiably feel proud of having scaled Mount Everest precisely because of the daunting challenges it presents. Regardless of whether there is any practical payoff to the pursuit of conceptual jurisprudence, this much cannot plausibly be denied by anyone who understands the work of Hart, Dworkin, and Raz: conceptual issues present intellectual difficulties unique among issues in law and legal theory precisely because they are so much more abstract than other issues.

This, of course, is not to suggest that the issues involved in conceptual inquiry are more difficult than the issues involved in empirical or normative inquiry any more than the claim that climbing Mount Everest presents a unique challenge suggests that climbing Mount Everest is more difficult than hitting a 95-mph fastball. Such activities present challenges that are so different that there is no obvious standard by which the difficulties can be compared and ranked.

In this connection, it is worth considering how many other topics of abiding interest in philosophy have no direct practical or technological applications. As far as I can tell, there are few topics in metaphysics, one of philosophy's core areas of inquiry, that have direct practical or technological applications. It is hard to see any practical implications or technological applications associated with solving the philosophical problems associated with the nature of time, personal identity, universals and particulars, the ontology of the universe, the nature of modality, aesthetics (or the nature of beauty), and even the nature of the mind. Similarly, there are few topics in philosophy of language, another core area of philosophical inquiry, that have obvious practical or technological applications. As was true of questions of metaphysics, it is hard to see how solutions for these philosophical puzzles could have any practical implications or applications.

The justification for pursuing these highly abstract issues has to do with the intrinsic value of both the process and the results of such pursuits. Indeed, if one pursues philosophical research unconnected with normative issues of morality, the motivation and justification must have something to do with the intrinsic value of doing so. Given that we are all entitled to significant moral latitude to decide what to devote the working hours of our lives to, it seems a little puerile to single out conceptual jurisprudents for this kind of criticism. Live and let live.

In any event, I hope that even readers who think it somewhat extravagant to expend the kind of time and effort I have squandered on these issues find something in what follows that engages their interest. I find much of interest and beauty in the work of my colleagues and believe that I have learned much from reading their work that transcends the admittedly narrow concerns of conceptual jurisprudence. I hope that what I have produced in the following chapters reflects both the value of what I have learned from them and the skill with which they have imparted that value to me.

2

Rethinking the Traditional Interpretation of Anti-Positivist Theories

Classical Natural Law Theory and Dworkinian Interpretivism

This chapter challenges the traditional interpretation of classical natural law theories and Dworkinian interpretivism. Insofar as these theories, construed as rivals to positivism, are either straightforwardly false or must be grounded in methodological assumptions that call into question the epistemological viability of the project of explicating the nature of law, they are best construed as explicating a different concept of law than the one positivism seeks to explicate. The concept that positivism seeks to explicate is a purely descriptive one that applies to any norm that has been recognized, applied, or enforced in something that counts, on ordinary linguistic practices, as a legal system. In contrast, the concept that classical natural law theories and interpretivism seek to explicate is more aptly construed as grounded in the descriptive concept that positivism seeks to explicate but also has evaluative content that applies only to valid norms that can be characterized as law "in the fullest sense." Thus construed, these theories complement rather than rival positivism and are hence misleadingly characterized as "anti-positivist."

1. Modest and immodest approaches to conceptual analysis

Fundamental to the traditional project of analyzing a concept is the task of identifying those properties jointly instantiated by all and only things that, properly understood, fall under the concept. The underlying assumption is that two things fall under a concept *C* if and only if they both instantiate properties that distinguish things that are *C* from things that are not *C*. These properties explain why something that falls under *C* is properly characterized by the corresponding concept-term in the following sense: something is properly characterized as a *C* because it instantiates the properties that constitute anything that has them as *C*.

A couple of examples should suffice to secure the point. If all and only things that instantiate the properties of being unmarried and being a man are properly characterized by the concept-term "bachelor," then the properties of being unmarried and being a man distinguish things that are bachelors from things that are not bachelors; if all and only things that are unmarried men *are*, therefore, bachelors, then instantiating the properties of being unmarried and of being a man constitutes anything that instantiates them as bachelors. Similarly, if all and only things that instantiate the compound property of being a floating mass of water vapor are properly characterized by the concept-term "cloud," then the compound property of being a floating mass of water vapor distinguishes things that are clouds from things that are not clouds; if all and only floating masses of water vapor *are*, therefore, clouds, then instantiating the compound property of being a floating mass of water vapor constitutes anything that instantiates that property as a cloud.

It is crucial to note that the relationship between having the properties that are jointly instantiated by all and only things picked out by the concept-term and being a referent of that concept-term is that of *constitution*—and not that of *causation*. Being an unmarried man might have many causal effects—for example, loneliness. But being an unmarried man does not *cause* a person to be a bachelor; whatever it is that explains why that man is unmarried also explains why he is a bachelor. Being unmarried constitutes a man as a bachelor in the sense that he falls under the concept of bachelor (i.e. *is* a bachelor) wholly in virtue of being unmarried. Likewise, being a mass of floating water vapor does not cause that mass to be a cloud; whatever it is that explains why something is a mass of floating water vapor also explains why it is a cloud Being a mass of floating water vapor constitutes something as a cloud in the sense that it falls under the concept of cloud (i.e. *is* a cloud) wholly in virtue of being a mass of floating water vapor.

Conceptual analysis, as traditionally conceived, is thus concerned with the properties that distinguish things that fall under the relevant concept *C* from things that do not fall under *C* and hence with the properties that constitute something that instantiates them as *C*. The methodology is frequently described as concerned with identifying those properties that are *essential* to something in the following sense:

A property *p* is *essential* to *C* if and only if it is not possible for a thing to be *C* without also instantiating *p*.

A complete list of all the properties essential to *C* exhausts the *nature* of the thing picked out by *C* in the following sense: something that is properly characterized as *C* falls under that concept—i.e. *is* a *C*—*only* and *wholly* in virtue of instantiating *all* of the essential properties of *C*. The nature of a thing is nothing more than the essence of a thing, and the essence of a thing is fully explained by a complete description of all its essential properties. If, for example, the essential properties of bachelorhood are exhausted by the compound property of being an unmarried man, then this compound property fully defines the nature of bachelorhood.

The language of essences and essential properties is somewhat misleading insofar as it suggests that a thing picked out by the relevant concept-term has properties that define its nature independently of any social practices determining the application-conditions of the relevant concept-term; on this view, an unmarried man would fall under the concept of bachelor regardless of whether we use the term "bachelor" to pick out unmarried men. One might take that position, but one need not do so. Given that describing the relevant properties as "essential" could be construed as suggesting a substantive commitment to that view, it is potentially misleading.

It is best to speak instead of properties that are *conceptually necessary* to being in the reference class of the relevant concept-term. While the relevant terminology should not assume that the nature of a thing is fully determined by our conceptual practices, it should not rule that out either; whether or not the relevant properties are essential in the sense described above is properly conditioned by one's choice of methodology. The term "conceptually necessary" is thus preferable to the term "essential" insofar as it connotes agnosticism with respect to the idea that the content of a concept and the nature of the relevant thing can change over time.

As discussed in Chapter 1, conceptual analysis is traditionally regarded as concerned with claims that can be justified a priori—i.e. those that can be justified with no more empirical observation than is needed to learn the meanings of the relevant terms expressing the claims. Insofar as no *further* empirical observation than that needed to understand the meaning of a sentence is needed to confirm or disconfirm it, the considerations that confirm or disconfirm the truth of that claim are the same in every possible world. Claims about the nature of a thing are therefore metaphysical and expressed in terms of claims that are either necessarily or possibly true.

Conceived as a descriptive metaphysical enterprise, conceptual analysis requires a different methodology from those deployed in normative and empirical inquiries. To this end, Frank Jackson distinguishes a *modest* from an *immodest* approach to conceptual analysis. Jackson believes that, although metaphysics is about what the world is like, the relevant questions must be framed in a language, and this gives rise to an important methodological constraint:

[T]hus we need to attend to what the users of the language mean by the words they employ to ask their question. When bounty hunters go searching, they are searching for a person and not a handbill. But they will not get very far if they fail to attend to the representational properties of the handbill on the wanted person. Those properties give them their target, or, if you like, define the subject of their search. Likewise, metaphysicians will not get very far with questions like: Are there *Ks?* Are *Ks* nothing over and above *Js?* and, Is the *K* way the world is fully determined by the *J* way the world is? in the *absence of some conception of what counts as a K, and what counts as a J.* [1]

Since the goal of the modest approach is hence "the elucidation of the possible situations covered by the *words* we use to ask our questions" (*FEM* 33), it would be appropriate to begin from "serious opinion polls on people's responses to various cases" (*FEM* 36–37)—or from something like lexicographical surveys.

Conceptual analysis, on the modest approach, purports to give us insight into what the world is like *as we structure it* through the conceptual framework we impose on it through our linguistic practices; that is, conceptual analysis gives us insight into what the world is like as we view it through a lens defined by the language we adopt to describe and make sense of our experience of the world. A modest approach to conceptual analysis thus purports to give us insight into the nature of a thing as it is determined by our linguistic practices.

The immodest approach to conceptual analysis can be defined as simply the negation of the modest approach. Jackson does not say much by way of directly explicating the immodest approach, illustrating it instead with a well-known line of criticism of the idea that time constitutes a fourth dimension on par with the three spatial dimensions represented by the *x, y,* and *z* axes of a graph:

[M]any have taken this kind of consideration to show that four-dimensionalism *qua* thesis about what our world is like is false. They, in effect, argue as follows:

Pr. 1 Different things (temporal parts or whatever) having different properties is not change. (Conceptual claim illustrated in the case of temperatures)[2]

[1] Frank Jackson, *From Metaphysics to Ethics: A Defense of Conceptual Analysis* (Oxford: Oxford University Press, 1998), 30–31. Hereinafter *FEM.*

[2] As Geach describes this case with temperatures: "[T]he variation of a poker's temperature with time would simply mean that there were different temperatures at different positions along the poker's time axis. But this, as McTaggart remarked, would no more be a *change* in temperature than a variation of temperature along the poker's length would be. Similarly for other sorts of change." P.T. Geach, "Some Problems about Time," in Geach, *Logic Matters* (Oxford: Basil Blackwell, 1972),

Pr. 2 Things change. (Moorean fact)
Conc. Four-dimensionalism is false. (Claim about the nature of our world)

We now have an example of conceptual analysis in what I call its immodest role. For it is being given a major role in an argument concerning what the world is like (*FEM* 42–43).

The idea is that four-dimensionalism does not accurately describe our world as it is independent of our conceptual practices because it is inconsistent with the mind-independent fact that things change. This criticism presupposes an immodest approach to metaphysical analysis insofar as it purports to identify features of the world as it really is independent of the conceptual framework we impose on the world to understand it.

The two approaches, then, differ with respect to the proper object of study. The modest approach (MCA) seeks to understand the nature of a thing as it is defined by the conceptual framework we impose on the world through shared linguistic practices. The immodest approach (ICA), in contrast, seeks to understand the nature of a thing as it really is independent of any such conceptual framework that *we* impose on the world.[3]

The methodologies of MCA and ICA are both partly empirical in character insofar as each adopts "ordinary" intuitions as the starting point of conceptual analysis. Which intuitions are *ordinary* is a matter of which intuitions are *commonly shared* among people in the relevant population; and that is an empirically observable feature of the world.

302–18, 304. The idea is that a difference in temperature between one point on the poker and another is not properly characterized as a change in temperature; it is just a difference between the temperature at one point and the temperature at another point, such as would be the case if one end of the poker had been placed in fire and the other end in a freezer. If, however, reality is four-dimensional in the sense that time is a fourth dimension on par with the three dimensions of space, then there cannot be any changes in temperature from one moment in time to the next. What appears to us in a three-dimensional world as a change in the temperature of the poker would simply be a variation of the temperature at "different positions along the poker's time axis."

[3] Here is another way to understand the distinction. Kant distinguished between things as they appear to us mediated through the categories of space and time through which we process all sense perceptions and things as they are in themselves. Immanuel Kant, *Critique of Pure Reason* (Cambridge: Cambridge University Press, 1998) in Paul Guyer and Allen Wood (eds.), *The Cambridge Edition of the Works of Immanuel Kant* (Cambridge: Cambridge University Press, 1992–98). The categories with which Kant is concerned, of course, are not concepts picked out by some concept-term; rather, they involve the innate ability of the mind to structure experiences so that the world appears to us as having spatial dimensions and temporal qualities. Even so, it would be helpful throughout this chapter to express some of the ideas in the Kantian distinction between the world as it is and the world as it appears to us. To put it in Kantian terms, the immodest approach to conceptual analysis purports to give us knowledge of things as they are in themselves independent of the conceptual frameworks we use to make sense of the world.

If the two approaches agree on starting from ordinary intuitions, they disagree on *why* we should start there. Insofar as MCA seeks to reconcile conceptual theories with ordinary talk, it requires that we consider ordinary talk as a touchstone for evaluating theories about the nature of the relevant thing, and ordinary talk reflects ordinary intuitions conditioned by the shared social conventions for using the corresponding term. Accordingly, MCA begins from an understanding of the lexical meanings of words; these meanings form the starting point for an investigation into what deeper philosophical commitments these ordinary practices imply. In contrast, there is nothing in ICA that would logically require that we take ordinary talk as a starting point and hence nothing that grounds ICA in the shared practices defining the lexical meanings of the relevant concept-terms; insofar as we seek to understand what the world is like independent of the concepts picked out by our linguistic practices, there is no reason to think that recourse to ordinary intuitions is even helpful, much less necessary. Indeed, there is nothing in the idea that conceptual analysis seeks to articulate the nature of things as they are independent of our thoughts and practices that even gestures in the direction of starting from the lexical meanings of the relevant concept-terms or the intuitions that the corresponding social practices condition in us.

Not surprisingly, the two approaches differ according to how much epistemic weight should be assigned to the corresponding intuitions. MCA takes these intuitions as providing the ultimate standard for evaluating a conceptual theory because MCA assumes that the object of conceptual analysis is to uncover the nature of the world *as we define it* through the conceptual frameworks that *our* linguistic practices impose on it. ICA, in contrast, takes ordinary intuitions to be nothing more than a guide to understanding the nature of a thing; our intuitions or ordinary talk are not conceived as defining the nature of the thing.

Accordingly, there are certain kinds of errors that would warrant the rejection of a conceptual theory deploying MCA that would not obviously warrant the rejection of a conceptual theory deploying ICA. Insofar as our ordinary talk defines the nature of a thing, our conceptual theory of the thing must harmonize with ordinary talk; failure to do so is a fatal error for a conceptual theory under MCA. Insofar as ICA presupposes that ordinary talk does not define the nature of some thing *T*, any or all of our ordinary intuitions about *T* can be false.

To describe this difference using a term coined by J.L. Mackie, MCA cannot, while ICA can, result in an *error theory*—i.e. a theory that purports to show that everyday thought, or what has the status of being the "folk theory" in some area, is so deeply and widely in error as to warrant its rejection.[4] An

[4] J.L. Mackie, *Ethics: Inventing Right and Wrong* (London: Penguin Books, 1977), 35.

error theory about a thing, then, is a theory that implies that our folk theory about that thing is systematically in error and should be rejected. Insofar as our folk theory comprises our ordinary intuitions, an error theory implies that the relevant ordinary intuitions should also be rejected. Since, in effect, MCA makes the folk theory the *touchstone* for evaluating conceptual theories, MCA cannot result in an error theory. Since ICA assumes that ordinary intuitions are merely a guide and not a touchstone, ICA can result in an error theory.

2. Two concepts of law

There are two different concepts of law that might be the focus of a conceptual theory—a purely descriptive concept and an evaluative concept. The former is purely descriptive in the sense that whether or not something counts as law does not depend on whether it satisfies any moral standards that are *not* incorporated into the criteria of validity. The evaluative concept is grounded in the descriptive concept but also has evaluative content. Whether something that counts as law on the purely descriptive concept also counts as law on the evaluative concept depends on whether it is a good example of its kind according to certain moral standards that express values that *should* be satisfied by anything that *antecedently* counts as law on the descriptive concept. The evaluative concept thus expresses the idea of what counts as law in its fullest or ideal sense—i.e. what the law *should be* given some understanding of law's point or aspirations.

It might be thought that this account of the descriptive concept of law begs the question against the traditional interpretation of classical natural law theory, but this is incorrect. Whether a norm counts as law on the descriptive concept in some system might depend on whether it satisfies certain moral norms. If so, then those moral norms are part of the system's criteria of validity and are hence, so to speak, *internal* to the system in this sense: they determine what counts as law *in that particular system* but not what counts as good law or law in its fullest sense. If it is true that every conceptually possible legal system incorporates these moral norms as criteria of validity, then those norms are also internal to the existence conditions for law as defined by the descriptive concept.

Notice that the claim that a legal norm is consistent with certain moral requirements does not imply that it is a morally good law or that it is hence law in its fullest sense. For example, there might be laws imposing taxes on citizens that are consistent with some set of moral standards of fairness incorporated into the system's criteria of validity but are not morally ideal according to other standards. The claim that something satisfies a set of moral standards does not imply that it is morally good; my not having ever committed murder satisfies the moral prohibition against murder, but it would be odd to characterize my having refrained from murder as morally good. If the traditional interpretation of natural law theory is the correct account of the descriptive concept, then there are standards of morality *internal* to law because incorporated into the criteria of validity of every conceptually possible legal system. But there can still be additional moral standards that are *external* to a system's criteria of validity and to the existence conditions of law in the sense that they distinguish law that is morally ideal from law that is morally acceptable but not morally ideal.

Both concepts are grounded in convergent patterns of ordinary lexical usage. The purely descriptive concept might be the more familiar one, as it is the one more commonly deployed in questions about what the law requires or permits. For example, if I seek a lawyer's advice on whether I may take a certain deduction in calculating my tax liability, my question deploys a descriptive concept grounded in convergent patterns of ordinary lexical usage. What I care about on this usage is what is required by the tax statutes that are enforced by the IRS because I want to avoid having to serve a prison sentence for tax fraud. Knowing which tax statutes count as law "in the fullest sense" will not help me ascertain how much I need to pay to avoid such liability. Indeed, paying too much attention to which tax statutes count as law in the fullest sense might tempt me to pay less than is required by all the tax statutes taken together and hence to do something that would subject me to exactly the liability I wish to avoid. When I am attempting to plan my behavior to avoid criminal or civil liability, the relevant usage of "law" is the one that picks out the purely descriptive concept grounded in convergent patterns of ordinary usage.

The evaluative concept is also grounded in convergent patterns of ordinary lexical usage. Opponents of abortion rights argue that the U.S. Constitution does not define a right to reproductive privacy that requires states to legalize abortion during the first trimester. As the claim is sometimes put, "there is no constitutional right to abortion"—which, properly fleshed out, expresses the claim that there is nothing in the *law* defined by the Constitution that entails a legal right to abortion. If understood as employing a purely descriptive usage of the concept-term "law" that is conventionally defined, as all words are, by certain social practices, the claim is simply confused. If understood as employing an evaluative usage of "law" that seeks to distinguish what is just or legitimate from what is unjust or illegitimate, the claim might be false but at least it expresses a plausible position: thus construed, the claim is that, while technically (or descriptively) "law," the holding that established such a right is illegitimate because inconsistent with how the relevant provisions of the Constitution should, as a matter of political morality, be interpreted.

The concept of law resembles the concept of art in this respect. As is true of law, there are two concepts of art, one descriptive and the other evaluative. According to the institutional conception of the purely descriptive concept of art, the term "art" is properly applied to any artifact that is presented to a certain community for the purpose of creating an aesthetic experience. On this usage, any painting displayed in a museum counts as a piece of art regardless of quality. According to the evaluative usage, the term "art" is properly applied to those objects that count as art in the purely descriptive sense but also satisfy certain standards of aesthetic quality.

It is not uncommon for people to alternate between the two concepts of art depending on what the circumstances dictate as appropriate. If I am moved by a Caravaggio and exclaim "Wow, that's art," it should be clear that, absent unusual circumstances, I am not using the term to apply the purely descriptive concept. It is unnecessary to say of a Caravaggio in a museum that it is art in this sense; a Caravaggio is so paradigmatically art in the descriptive sense that an exclamation of its status as such says nothing anyone would have any reason to say. What I am claiming is that it is an exemplary piece of art or is art in the fullest sense—what art is at its aesthetic best.

In contrast, if I come across a pair of eyeglasses on the floor in an empty corner of a museum exhibit of conceptual art and ask an employee whether it is art, I am deploying the descriptive concept. In particular, I might be wondering whether it is part of the exhibit, or I might be wondering whether someone has deliberately left it there to make an ironic comment on the quality of the exhibited art. Either way, I am asking whether the eyeglasses are part of the exhibit and hence constitute a piece of art in the purely descriptive sense of the term.

It can sometimes be difficult to determine whether a concept-term is being used in a purely descriptive sense or whether it is being used in an evaluative sense. If, for example, I ask someone who does not know what motivates the question whether the pair of eyeglasses is a piece of art, she might take the question to be about the applicability of the evaluative concept. Thus construed, my question would not be whether the eyeglasses piece falls within the reference class of the descriptive concept-term; it would be whether the piece is art in the fullest sense and hence falls within the reference class of the evaluative concept-term. Alternatively, she might construe the question to be about the applicability of the descriptive concept. Thus construed, the question would be whether the pair of eyeglasses is art in the descriptive sense.

Complicating the interpretive issue is that the content of the evaluative concept is not always clear. Suppose that I notice a card posted over the eyeglasses with the name of an artist and the title "Eyeglasses" on it and ask someone, "Is this art or bullshit?" Construed as a question employing an evaluative concept, I am using the term to deploy a different evaluative concept from the one that I deployed when exclaiming "Wow, that's art" of a Caravaggio painting. In that example, I was expressing the judgment that the painting was art in the fullest sense of the term—a model for what art is at its best. In the case where I ask of the eyeglasses whether the piece is art or bullshit, I am asking whether it meets some minimum standard for counting as art on any reasonable conception of an evaluative sense of the term. In both cases, I am deploying an evaluative concept, but one picks out what is art in a normatively fullest sense while the other picks out what is art in the normatively minimal sense.

One lesson that emerges from this discussion is that it is important to be clear about which concept is being explicated by a theory of any concept-term that is ambiguous between a descriptive use and an evaluative use. It matters a great deal whether the relevant usage picks out a purely descriptive concept or whether it picks out a concept that is grounded in the descriptive concept but also has evaluative content. A failure to be clear about which concept is the relevant one can lead to systematic confusion about the character of the phenomenon under study.

Another lesson that emerges here is that there is no necessary inconsistency between a theory of a descriptive concept of a thing and a theory of an evaluative concept of the same thing that give different answers to the question of whether some particular item falls under the relevant concept. There is no necessary inconsistency between a conceptual theory that implies that some street mural is art in a descriptive sense and a conceptual theory that implies the mural is not art in an evaluative sense. They might be inconsistent, but they need not be. If the two theories agree on the content of the descriptive content of art that is presupposed by the account of the evaluative concept, there is no inconsistency between the two judgments. If the two theories disagree on the content of the relevant descriptive content and the evaluative theory denies the status of art to the mural on the ground that it is not art on the underlying descriptive concept, then the two judgments are inconsistent.

One could, I suppose, ask whether the evaluative concept better captures the *real* nature of the thing under study, but it is not clear how one could answer this question. If we consider this question in connection with the concepts of art, there are two ways to construe this question, and both are problematic. First, one might construe the question as concerned with which concept better picks out what *art* really is, as defined independently of anything we might think about it or independently of the conceptual framework we impose on the world through our linguistic practices regarding such objects. But it is not clear either what this question is really asking or what kind of evidence to which we have access that would help to answer it. Perhaps, the question is concerned with what an omniscient being would regard as "art." If this is what is intended by the question, it is simply not clear how *we* could go about answering it. Apart from having it directly answered by such a being, which I am guessing is not likely to happen soon, it is just not clear what we could do to determine which concept better captures the nature of a thing that is determined in a way that is completely independent of our thoughts, preferences, and linguistic practices. If asking such a question is coherent, there is no real point to doing so.

Second, one might construe the question as concerned with which concept better picks out what we intend to pick out with our conceptual practices concerning the use of the term "art." The problem, however, is that we have two sets of conceptual practices that are contrived to pick out different, albeit closely related, phenomena. The evaluative concept is generally deployed to pick out a proper subset of objects to which the descriptive concept-term applies. No competent speaker of English can dispute that a Caravaggio is a piece of art regardless of whether we are using the descriptive or evaluative concept. In contrast, competent speakers of English could disagree on whether a ready-made by Duchamp is "really" art under either the descriptive or evaluative concepts; I do not think that there are any real issues there, but the question can coherently be asked. Either way, there is no one set of phenomena that would tell us that one concept better picks out what we intend to pick out by "art" than the other because we use the term differently to pick out two different sets of phenomena.

The question of which use of "art" better captures the real nature of art makes no more sense than the question of which use of "bank"—the one referring to financial institutions or the one referring to the natural barriers defining the boundaries of a river—better captures what a bank *really* is. There is no single right answer to that question because, for all practical purposes, there are two logically independent concepts of bank that are picked out by two different usage patterns of the concept-term "bank." The same is true of the question of which use of "art" better captures the real nature of art. There is no single right answer to that question because the two concepts of art are likewise logically independent of one another. To say that something is descriptively art does not imply that it is a good piece of art. Conversely, and somewhat surprisingly, to say that something is art on the evaluative usage does not imply that it is art on the descriptive usage; one might characterize an exceptionally clever criminal act as "art" despite the fact that it is not presented to an audience for the purpose of producing an enjoyable aesthetic experience.

The fact that we use the same word to refer to phenomena that might be related in some way does not imply that one concept better captures the nature of the thing picked out than the other. We could just as well use a different term to express the evaluative sense of the term "art" from the one that we use to express the descriptive sense of the term. Although doing so might result in a loss of some non-cognitive expressive force (which would not be true if we used different words to express the two senses of the word "bank"), such a change would result in no significant difference in the cognitive content of the term.

For this reason, conceptual theories that purport to explain a purely descriptive use of a term do not engage conceptual theories that purport to explain an evaluative use of the same term—except in unusual cases that likely involve some confusion about the relevant notions. Insofar as a theory of an evaluative concept of a thing is properly grounded in assumptions that pick out the correct descriptive concept of a thing, there could be no logical conflict between them. Any criticism of a theory of an evaluative concept would have to be directed at the normative standards that express the evaluative content of the concept. Conversely, it makes even less sense to criticize a theory of the relevant descriptive concept on the ground that it does not jibe with the normative content of the evaluative concept because a purely descriptive concept has no normative content.

In articulating a conceptual theory of law, one must therefore be clear about which concept the theory is intended to explicate. On the one hand, an explication of the purely descriptive concept of law will not directly engage an explication of the evaluative concept of law. On the other, an explication of the evaluative concept of law will not directly engage an explication of the descriptive concept of law. If this is correct, then it is a mistake to think that a conceptual theory of the evaluative concept is an object-level rival to a conceptual theory of the descriptive concept.

3. Four possible interpretations of a conceptual theory of law

The discussions in the last two sections call attention to a couple of interpretive difficulties in assessing conceptual theories of law. The first difficulty has to do with which usage or concept the relevant conceptual theory purports to explain. Since there are two concepts of law that a theory might purport to explicate, there are two possible ways to interpret a conceptual theory of law: one interprets the theory as concerned to explicate the descriptive concept of law while the other interprets it as concerned to explicate the evaluative concept of law.

The second difficulty has to do with the character of what determines the content of the relevant concept of law. A conceptual theory of law can be interpreted as presupposing MCA and hence as purporting to explicate the relevant concept as it is determined by our shared linguistic and legal practices; thus construed, the theory purports to explicate a concept of law that is *ours* in the sense that *our* linguistic and legal practices determine its content. Alternatively, the theory can be interpreted as presupposing ICA and hence as purporting to explicate the nature of law as it is independent of any of our linguistic and legal practices; thus construed, the theory purports to tell us something about the extra-linguistic world as it pertains to the nature of law as it really is.

Accordingly, there are four possible interpretations of a conceptual theory of law: a conceptual theory can be construed (1) as an explication of the content of the *descriptive* concept of law as it is determined by our shared linguistic and legal practices and hence as presupposing *MCA*; (2) as an explication of the content of the *descriptive* concept of law as it is determined by objective features of the world independently of our shared linguistic and legal practices and hence as presupposing *ICA*; (3) as an explication of the content of the *evaluative* concept of law as it is determined by our shared linguistic and legal practices and hence as presupposing *MCA*; and (4) as an explication of the content of the *evaluative* concept of law as it is determined by objective features of the world independently of our shared linguistic and legal practices and hence as presupposing *ICA*. I argue below that positivism is best construed according to option (1) and that classical natural law theory and Dworkin's interpretivism are best construed according to option (3).

4. Legal positivism as assuming MCA to explain the descriptive concept of law

Positivism purports to explain the nature of law *as such*—and this requires an account of the existence conditions for legal systems, as well as for the valid legal norms that furnish a legal system and help bring it into existence. Since positivism is a conceptual theory of law, it is a metaphysical theory insofar as it purports to explain the nature of law by (1) identifying conceptually necessary properties that (2) constitute any norm or system as one of law. Insofar as positivism does not purport to tell us anything about which properties a norm must have to be a law that is good, it purports to explain the purely descriptive concept of law.

H.L.A. Hart provides such an account of the existence conditions for legal norms and legal systems.[5] First, on Hart's view, there is a *legal system* in *L* if and only if (1) there is a rule of recognition defining the criteria of validity that is accepted and practiced by those who serve as officials in *L*; and (2) the behavior of people in *L* generally conforms to the norms valid under the rule of recognition. Second, a norm *n* is a *law* in a legal system *L* if and only if there exists a legal system *L* in which either (1) *n* is one of the recognition norms practiced in *L* or (2) *n* is valid under the criteria of validity defined by the recognition norms practiced in *L*.

Hart understands himself to be explicating descriptive concepts picked out by ordinary linguistic and legal practices. As Hart describes his project, it is to identify those features of law that define its nature *as we ordinarily understand it*. As he puts it, "The starting-point for this clarificatory task is the widespread common knowledge of the salient features of a modern municipal legal system which … I attribute to any educated man" (*CL* 239). Insofar as the common knowledge that comprises the starting point for conceptual theorizing about law is grounded in an ordinary understanding of how the concept-term "law" is used, the descriptive concept of law that Hart purports to explicate is the one grounded in social practices that are both linguistic and legal in character.

Joseph Raz is more explicit in affirming that the descriptive concept his theory is concerned to explicate is grounded in our linguistic and legal practices. On his view, officials cannot be systematically confused about the nature of authority because it is their claims, conceptions, and practices that construct *our* concept of authority as it functions in legal practice:

> [W]hile [legal officials and institutions] can be occasionally [confused,] they cannot be systematically confused. For given the centrality of legal institutions in our structures of authority, their claims and conceptions are formed by and contribute to *our* concept of authority. It is what it is in part as a result of the claims and conceptions of legal institutions. (*ALM* 217; emphasis added)

The concept of authority that is therefore the focus of his theoretical inquiries—i.e. the one that matters—is a concept of authority that is *ours* because it is the one presupposed, and hence constructed, by *our* linguistic and legal practices.

[5] H.L.A. Hart, *The Concept of Law* 3rd Ed. (Oxford: Oxford University Press, 2012). Hereinafter *CL*.

Contemporary positivism is thus properly understood as presupposing MCA to explicate the purely descriptive concept of law. MCA attempts to explicate the nature of a thing as it is determined by ordinary patterns of linguistic usage with respect to characterizing things of that kind and hence takes the relevant social practices that pick out those things and condition our ordinary intuitions about them as the standard for understanding it. While ICA is also grounded in intuitions that are ordinary in some sense, positivism begins from those intuitions because they express the ordinary conventions we have adopted for using the terms that construct *our* concepts of law and authority. On a modest approach, those conventions, which inform our common intuitions, provide the touchstone for evaluating a theory of the concept of law.

What this means, given the arguments of the last section, is that legal positivism cannot result in an error theory since it presupposes MCA. Insofar as our core linguistic and legal practices determine or construct the content of the relevant concepts, we cannot—absent extraordinary confusion about what our core linguistic and legal practices are—be systematically mistaken in understanding law. Thus, the adoption of MCA by positivists presupposes that the intuitions informed by these core practices are largely correct and hence that an explication of the relevant concepts cannot result in an error theory of law.

5. The traditional interpretation of natural law theory construed as a rival to positivism

Classical natural law theory is traditionally construed as inconsistent with legal positivism and hence as purporting to explicate the same concept of law that positivism purports to explicate. The content of the descriptive concept of law that positivism purports to explicate is determined by convergent patterns of linguistic usage that are informed by practices understood to be paradigmatically legal; positivism thus purports to explicate the nature of law as it is determined by the core legal and linguistic practices that define the application-conditions for using *our* descriptive concept-term "law." The traditional interpretation of natural law theory construes it as a rival to positivism and hence as explicating the same concept of law as positivism. The traditional interpretation of classical natural law theory, then, presupposes that it purports to explicate a descriptive concept of law that is picked out by our core legal and linguistic practices and is hence *our* concept of law.

The problem with the traditional interpretation is that it implies that unjust norms can never be properly characterized as "law," as *we* use the term in its descriptive sense—a claim that is straightforwardly inconsistent with the ordinary practices that construct the content of the descriptive concept that positivism purports to explicate. It is clear, to begin, that there can be unjust laws and legal systems as far as our ordinary linguistic practices are concerned. Consider, again, a representative lexical definition of the concept-term "law":

law (noun): the system of rules that a particular country or community recognizes as regulating the actions of its members and may enforce by the imposition of penalties.[6]

There is nothing in this definition that even remotely suggests that unjust laws are impossible. If the relevant community recognizes and enforces rules that are unjust as part of "the system of rules recognized and enforced [as law] by [that] particular community," then the law can include rules that are unjust. Indeed, if this were not true, then the claim that there can be unjust laws or legal systems would be, from the standpoint of the lexical definition, as much a contradiction in terms as the claim that there can be married bachelors. Whatever else might be true of the claim that there can be unjust laws, it is quite clearly not a contradiction in terms.

The definition of "law" on this point should be contrasted with the definition of "bachelor," which is as follows:

bachelor (noun): a man who is not and has never been married.[7]

It should be clear that the definition of the concept-term "bachelor" explicitly precludes the conceptual possibility of a bachelor who is married. Unlike the claim that there can be just laws, the claim that there can be married bachelors is quite clearly a contradiction in terms.

Further, it is clear, as far as ordinary linguistic usage is concerned, that laws and legal systems can be illegitimate for a variety of reasons that include the unjustness of the norms. The legal system of apartheid in South Africa is universally condemned among right-minded people as illegitimate because of the wicked quality of its valid norms, which mandated pervasive racial segregation in that country; those unjust norms, as a matter of ordinary linguistic usage, were laws. If the linguistic conventions defining the lexical definition of "law" are the touchstone for ordinary usage, there can clearly be unjust laws.

[6] "Law," *Oxford Online Dictionary*; available at: https://en.oxforddictionaries.com/definition/law.

[7] "Bachelor," *Oxford Online Dictionary*; available at: https://en.oxforddictionaries.com/definition/bachelor.

Ordinary *legal* practice in many legal systems also straightforwardly presupposes that there can be unjust laws. What is properly promulgated as law in these legal systems is recognized and enforced by courts as laws that *legally* justify imposition of sanctions on subjects who violate them. A court has the legal authority (i.e. authority conferred by the convergent recognition practices of officials) to hold a subject liable under a properly promulgated norm regardless of whether the norm is unjust or is simply considered unjust. This of course does not mean that the court must do so or will do so; a court might also have legal authority to decline to enforce—or even to change—an unjust norm. The point, however, that it is clearly false as an empirically verifiable matter of ordinary legal practice that unjust norms never count as law for purposes of the practices that determine the content of the concept of law that positivists take themselves to be explicating.

Courts in Anglo-American legal systems explicitly concede that there can be unjust or morally problematic laws. U.S. courts acknowledge that they lack authority to revise properly promulgated laws on the ground that they are morally problematic; in cases where unjust norms have been properly enacted by the legislature and violate no constitutional protections, courts are—as a matter of what is recognized by the courts as settled law—required to defer to the judgment of the legislators. Consider the following remarks from the U.S. Supreme Court:

> Whether embodied in the Fourteenth Amendment or inferred from the Fifth, equal protection is not a license for courts to judge the wisdom, fairness, or logic of legislative choices .... [A] legislative choice is not subject to courtroom factfinding and may be based on rational speculation unsupported by evidence or empirical data .... Only by faithful adherence to this guiding principle of judicial review of legislation is it possible to preserve to the legislative branch its rightful independence and its ability to function.[8]

Insofar as this principle requires federal courts, other things being equal, to defer to the judgment of the legislature in cases regardless of whether the court believes it is "fair" or "wise" to do so, it acknowledges that there can be unjust federal laws.[9]

[8] *FCC v. Beach Communications*, Inc., 508 U.S. 307 (1993). Similarly, in *Williamson v. Lee Optical*, 348 U.S. 483 (1955), the Court stated that "the day is gone when this Court uses the Due Process Clause to strike down state laws, regulatory of business and industrial conditions, because they may be unwise, improvident, or out of harmony with a particular school of thought." The Court indicated that in cases where a challenged statute implicates no fundamental constitutional rights it must uphold the law unless there is no conceivable reason for enacting the bill. In such cases, the only ground for striking down the law is that it is utterly irrational. Even if the challenged law is morally problematic, it must be upheld if a coherent rationale can be given for its enactment. I am grateful to Todd Shaw, Ashley Robles, and David Brink for these and other examples.

[9] Similar comments can be found in judicial opinions in cases from the U.K. In *Madzimbamuto v. Lardner-Burke* [1969] 1 AC 645, 723, the court argued: "It is often said that it would be

The same is true of state law. State courts not uncommonly indicate that they lack authority to modify statutory enactments on the ground that they are unjust or otherwise ill-advised. As the Washington Supreme Court unambiguously explains:

> [H]owever much members of this court may think that a statute should be rewritten, it is imperative that we not rewrite statutes to express what we think the law should be. We simply have no such authority.[10]

The claim by the court that it lacks authority to modify problematic statutes implicitly acknowledges the possibility that a statute with the status of *law* might be unjust. Whether unjust or unwise, courts in Washington state are legally bound to defer to the judgment of the legislature.

Indeed, the rules of civil procedure governing both the federal system and many state systems preclude bringing lawsuits on purely moral grounds. Federal Rule of Civil Procedure 11(b)(2) provides as follows:

> By presenting to the court a pleading, written motion, or other paper—whether by signing, filing, submitting, or later advocating it—an attorney or unrepresented party certifies that to the best of the person's knowledge, information, and belief, formed after an inquiry reasonable under the circumstances ... the claims, defenses, and other legal contentions are warranted by existing law or by a nonfrivolous argument for extending, modifying, or reversing existing law or for establishing new law.

Washington Court Rule 11(a)(2) similarly provides that an attorney's signature on a pleading constitutes an affirmation that the action "is warranted by existing law or a good faith argument for the extension, modification, or reversal of existing law or the establishment of new law." While these rules permit grounding an action to *change* an existing law in moral considerations,[11] this

unconstitutional for the UK Parliament to do certain things, meaning that the moral, political and other reasons against doing them are so strong that most people would regard it as highly improper if Parliament did these things. But that does not mean that it is beyond the power of Parliament to do such things. If Parliament chose to do any of them the courts could not hold the Act of Parliament invalid." See also *R (Countryside Alliance) v. Attorney General* [2008] 1 AC 719, para. 45. ("The democratic process is liable to be subverted if, on a question of moral and political judgment, opponents of the Act achieve through the courts what they could not achieve in Parliament.") I am grateful to Kenneth Ehrenberg for these examples.

[10] *State v. Groom*, 133 Wash.2d 679, 689, 947 P.2d 240 (1997).

[11] There is no distinction that matters here between changing existing law and creating new law. It is true that the rules permit grounding an action to "establish[] new law" in moral argument, the act of creating a new law is simply a certain kind of change in existing law. A new law that imputes a duty to subjects that they did not have because there was no legal norm imputing such a duty has the effect of changing existing law to make impermissible behaviors that were formerly permissible under the law.

presupposes that the relevant rule both has the status of law and is arguably and hence possibly unjust. If what is regarded by ordinary citizens and legal practitioners as paradigmatic *legal* practice in legal systems like that of the U.S. is taken as defining the relevant concept of law, it is clear that there can be unjust laws.

Note that the problem with interpreting classical natural theory as a rival theory to positivism is worse than that it is just false; the problem is that it implies an error theory of law. Thus construed, the traditional interpretation of classical natural law theory is inconsistent with the claims that (1) a legal system exists wherever the appropriate institutions, practices, and normative outputs can be found without regard to the moral quality of these institutions, practices, or normative outputs; (2) a norm is a law whenever it is properly promulgated (which might or might not include moral constraints on the content of law); and (3) every mandatory legal norm gives rise to a legal obligation. It seems clear that (1), (2), and (3) express obvious truths about the content of a descriptive concept of law that is defined by practices that are pre-theoretically characterized as *legal* and form the touchstone against which a conceptual theory of law must be evaluated. Insofar as positivism is grounded in these assumptions, then, this interpretation of traditional natural law theory implies an error theory of law.

Given that a conceptual theory of law employing MCA cannot result in an error theory, the traditional interpretation of classical natural law theory as a rival to positivism should be rejected. Whatever else classical natural law theory might be, it cannot charitably be construed as a rival to positivism that directly conflicts with it. Given the ambiguities in Aquinas's and Blackstone's description of their natural law position, it is most charitably and plausibly construed as doing something other than as adopting MCA to explicate the descriptive concept of law that positivism purports to explicate.

There remain three options for interpreting classical natural law theory: classical natural law theory can be construed as either (1) adopting *ICA* to explicate the real nature of law in a *descriptive* sense determined independently of the linguistic practices that construct the content of *our* descriptive concept of law; (2) adopting *ICA* to explicate the real nature of law in an evaluative sense (i.e. law in its fullest sense) that is determined independently of the linguistic practices that determine the content of *our* evaluative concept of law; or (3) adopting *MCA* to explicate an *evaluative* concept of law that is grounded in the descriptive concept positivism seeks to explain but has normative content as well. Which option is the best one depends on whether it is plausible to think that officials, legal theorists, and ordinary citizens could be systematically mistaken about what counts as law in legal systems like that of the U.S.—i.e. whether there are any reasons to adopt an error theory, either as a theory of the descriptive concept of law or as a theory of the evaluative concept of law.

6. Dworkin's interpretivism construed as a rival to positivism

The core thesis of Dworkin's interpretivism is expressed in the claim that "the law of a community consists not simply in the discrete statutes and rules that its officials enact but in the general principles of justice and fairness that these statutes and rules, taken together, presuppose by way of implicit justification."[12] Whether he is explicating the content of a descriptive concept of law or is explicating the content of an evaluative concept, then, Dworkin's view can be expressed as follows:

Dworkinian Interpretivism: A norm *n* is a law in *L* if and only if either *n* is duly promulgated by a court or legislature or *n* can be rationally derived from the general moral principles of justice and fairness that show the totality of the law in *L* in its best moral light.

Construed as a rival to positivism that adopts MCA to explicate a purely descriptive theory of law defined by ordinary linguistic and legal practices, Dworkin's interpretivism is straightforwardly inconsistent with two elements of institutional practices that are paradigmatically *legal* in character according to both ordinary linguistic usage and the unambiguous practices of courts and other officials in Anglo-American legal systems.

The first element of judicial practice with which Dworkin's theory, construed as a rival to positivism, is inconsistent has to do with the putatively legal authority of courts to create new norms that legally bind other officials of the legal system. Thus construed, Dworkin's theory denies that judges have anything plausibly characterized as a quasi-lawmaking authority—a denial that is inconsistent with the convergent practices of judges and officials with respect to court holdings and orders. As far as the ordinary legal practices of common law adjudication in the U.S. are concerned, legislatures have implicitly delegated authority to common law courts to develop and construct certain areas of law, such as contract law and the law of torts.

It is true that legislatures in legal systems like that of the U.S. have authority to take control over any area of the law that they have delegated to judges to develop—and they have sometimes done exactly that. Sales of

[12] Ronald Dworkin, "The Law of the Slave Catchers," *The Times Literary Supplement*, December 5, 1975, 1437.

certain goods, which were formerly governed by the common law of contracts in the U.S., are now governed by statutory law in most states.[13] Liability for defective design or manufacture of products, which was formerly governed by the common law of torts in the U.S., is now also governed by statutory law in most states.[14] The legal authority of courts in the U.S. to make and change the common law is impliedly delegated by the legislature,[15] but it is clear that officials in the U.S. converge on recognizing that courts have a quasi-legislative discretion to change the content of the common law until such time as the legislature enacts statutes that bring the relevant area of law under legislative control. If what counts as law is determined by the convergent practices of officials, then it is clear that judges in the U.S. have some legal authority to make and change the content of the law.

There is another way to see this. Insofar as a common law court overrules or otherwise departs in a holding from a line of precedents, the court's holding has the effect of changing, to some extent, the norms of the common law that were recognized as binding. Insofar as a common law court has *legal* authority to do this (i.e. can bind lower courts with such a holding), it has the authority to change norms of the common law. There is simply no way to explain the fact that a common law court can bind itself and lower courts with either of two conflicting holdings other than to acknowledge that courts have a limited legal authority to modify the common law. If Dworkin's theory is intended to explicate the content of a descriptive concept of law that is grounded in ordinary linguistic and legal practices, it is simply false; officials in the U.S. clearly converge on recognizing judicial holdings that either depart from existing precedent or decide novel issues of law as establishing the content of what counts as law in the purely descriptive sense of the term that positivists seek to explicate.

But this quasi-legislative authority of the courts to make law in this descriptive sense is not limited to changing the content of the common law. In many cases, courts also have legal authority to modify statutes by exercising a quasi-legislative discretion to make new law to fill gaps in the coverage of statutes. As one Washington appellate court put it:

[13] See, e.g., Revised Code of Washington (RCW) 62A.2-100 et seq.; available at: http://app.leg.wa.gov/rcw/default.aspx?cite=62A.2-106.

[14] See, e.g., RCW 7.72 et seq.; available at: http://app.leg.wa.gov/rcw/default.aspx?cite=7.72.

[15] I say "impliedly delegated" here because, as far as I know, there is no statutory enactment that explicitly delegates responsibility for various areas of law to the courts. The authority of common law courts over such areas derives from practices of common law courts in the U.K. that were adopted by officials in the U.S. without an explicit statutory delegation of authority.

Washington courts have also construed this statute to permit the adaptation of the common law to address gaps in existing statutory enactments, providing that the common law may serve to "fill interstices that legislative enactments do not cover."[16]

Judicial authority to modify statutory law is clearly conferred upon courts in the relevant jurisdictions by conventional recognition norms having the status of law under the descriptive concept constructed by ordinary linguistic and legal practices. It might be true that, depending on what one means by "really," that courts do not *really* have such authority to change law. What is indisputable, however, is that, according to the empirically observable practices of officials that reflect their understanding of what counts as law in the U.S., common law courts have a limited quasi-legislative authority to modify the content of both statutory and common law.

The second element of judicial practice with which Dworkin's theory, construed as a rival to positivism, is inconsistent has to do with the status of certain norms that are paradigmatically law under the descriptive concept that positivism purports to explicate. Here is the problem. If Dworkin is correctly construed as a rival to positivism, then either *Plessy v. Ferguson*, which held that public school race-based discrimination does not violate the Equal Protection Clause of the Fourteenth Amendment, or *Brown v. Board of Education*, which held that such discrimination violates the Equal Protection Clause, is mistaken in the sense that it is inconsistent with the principles showing the existing legal history in its best moral light. Accordingly, one of those holdings—presumably *Plessy*, decided nearly sixty years before *Brown*—is mistaken in this sense: only one of them could be derived from the general moral principles showing the legal history in the best light; the other is logically inconsistent with those principles. If consistency with moral principles showing the legal history in the best light is a conceptually necessary condition for being law, then one of those two holdings *cannot count as law*.

Construed as purporting to explicate the content of the descriptive concept of law grounded in ordinary linguistic and legal practices, Dworkin's view that one of these holdings does not count as establishing the content of the law in the U.S. is clearly false. Even dissenting officials converged on recognizing and treating *Plessy* as establishing the content of the law for nearly one hundred years. Statutes permitting or mandating public school segregation were enacted with the expectation that they would be applied and enforced by the courts. The courts met those expectations, applying and enforcing those statutes in ways that significantly changed the lives of millions of people. If, by "law," Dworkin intends the purely descriptive concept that is determined by

[16] *Dep't of Soc. & Health Servs. v. State Pers. Bd.*, 61 Wn.App. 778, 783–84, 812 P.2d 500 (1991).

what is pre-theoretically treated as law by the officials of the legal system, then it is clearly false that the *Plessy* holding was *not* law.

Accordingly, if Dworkin's claims about what counts as law are construed as explicating the content of the same purely descriptive concept that positivism purports to explicate, then they are inconsistent with legal practices in the U.S. that are characterized, according to the legal practices that construct the content of that concept, as paradigmatically *legal* in character. To begin, officials, as a matter of standard practice, regard judicial holdings that result in new common law rules as being legally binding. Additionally, judges, lawyers, and officials, also as a matter of standard practice, regard statutes upheld by the courts as law and treat them as such regardless of whether they are consistent with the moral norms showing the existing legal history in its best moral light.

As was true of the traditional interpretation of natural law theory, the problem with construing Dworkin's interpretivism as a rival to positivism is not just that it is false; the problem is that it entails an error theory of law. Otherwise put, the problem is not just that Dworkin's view that judges lack quasi-lawmaking authority is inconsistent with official practices regarding morally problematic holdings like *Plessy*; it is rather that, thus construed, Dworkin's view potentially calls into question whether too many of what are treated by officials as legal norms are really "law." For all we know, we all might be mistaken about whether many legal norms are consistent with the objective moral norms that Dworkin believes constrain the content of the law. It is certainly reasonable to hypothesize that many people at the time *Plessy* was decided believed that the separate-but-equal doctrine was consistent with the relevant standards of objective morality. For all we know, then, officials, legal theorists, and ordinary citizens could all be systematically mistaken about what counts as law in any legal system. Thus construed, Dworkin's theory entails an error theory insofar as it entails that, for all we know, we *could* all be mistaken about what constitutes even the settled law in any paradigmatic instance of a legal system.[17]

Given that a conceptual theory that presupposes MCA cannot result in an error theory, Dworkin's theory, like classical natural law theory, must be

[17] Dworkin's theory does not, strictly speaking, entail that we *are* systematically mistaken about the law; since we do not have infallible access to what an objective morality requires, I am not justified in claiming that his theory entails that we *are* mistaken about whether the relevant legal norms conform to the relevant standards of an objective political morality. But it is enough that we might, for all we know, be mistaken about the status of those norms. It is thus more accurate to say that Dworkin's theory might, for all we know, entail an error theory than it is to say that Dworkin's theory does entail an error theory of law. Either way, the result is problematic, and for the same reasons.

construed either as employing ICA to explicate what is *really* the content of the descriptive concept of law positivism purports to explicate or as explicating a concept of law that is grounded in the descriptive concept but also has evaluative content. Which option is the better one depends in part on whether it is plausible to think that officials, legal theorists, and ordinary citizens could be systematically mistaken about what counts as law in legal systems like that of the U.S. In other words, which interpretive option is preferable depends on whether we have plausible reason to believe that the presuppositions of ordinary legal practice entail an error theory of law.

7. Construing classical natural law and interpretivism as deploying MCA to explain an evaluative concept of law

The fact that ICA can, while MCA cannot, result in an error theory has important implications with respect to evaluating a conceptual theory. Error theories attribute a special kind of mistake to commonly held views about the nature of something that are quite stubborn because they seem self-evident. From an ordinary point of view, the law consists of those rules that the state promulgates in some official way and enforces with its police power. An error theory of law entails that these seemingly obvious views are systematically in error and should be rejected.

Insofar as the "folk" views challenged by an error theory enjoy a strong presumption of being correct, an error theory requires a strong showing to justify its acceptance. Consider, for example, the eliminative materialist's view that the furniture of the world contains no substances, properties, functions, or states that have the properties thought to distinguish the mental from the physical. As Paul Churchland describes the problem with our folk psychology: "[O]ur common-sense psychological framework is a false and radically misleading conception of the causes of human behavior and the nature of cognitive activity." Thus, the eliminative materialist holds that our folk psychology, which is grounded in the idea that people have beliefs, thoughts, desires, and other mental states, is systematically in error and should be rejected. Like the term "phlogiston," the terms "belief," "thoughts," "desires," and "perceptions" refer, on the eliminative materialist's view, to nothing that *really* exists; there are no such things as beliefs, thoughts, desires, or perceptions.

The intuitive implausibility of eliminative materialism calls attention to the issue of what must be shown to justify the acceptance of an error theory. Although it is not clear what would be needed to justify accepting such a theory, what is clear is that the burden that must be met to justify accepting an error theory is quite demanding. What is needed is a line of reasoning that is sufficiently compelling to outweigh the very stubborn intuitive confidence we have in the folk views challenged by the theory in question. For example, a justification for eliminative materialism can succeed only insofar as the evidence for accepting an error theory of mind strikes us as more compelling than the evidence provided by our own experiences of having beliefs, desires, and perceptions, which we take to exist in some real sense.

This is where eliminative materialism falls short. Eliminative materialists point, for example, to what they take to be failures on the part of our folk psychology to explain phenomena it must explain to be justifiably accepted. For example, eliminative materialists argue that the hypothesis that we have mental states contributes nothing to an explanation of why we need sleep, how we catch fly balls, or why some people have mental illnesses. Insofar as the hypothesis that we have mental states is not needed to explain such phenomena, the principle of Ockham's Razor dictates that the hypothesis should be rejected.

These considerations strike most theorists and laypersons as inadequate to justify accepting an error theory of mind. It might be true that the hypothesis that we have mental states does not figure into a *causal* explanation of why we need sleep or how we catch fly balls. But there is no way to make sense of our conscious experiences without assuming that we have mental states and that these states have some kind of existence in the world—even if their existence is causally dependent on the brain states that produce them, and even if these states are epiphenomenal in the sense that they do not cause any acts or behaviors. At bottom, this argument lacks the resources to convince people to accept an error theory of mind because most people have far more intuitive confidence in the claim that they *really* have beliefs, desires, and perceptions than in any claim that the eliminative materialist could marshal in support of the idea that there are no such things.

It is important to be clear on what is being claimed here with respect to the viability of eliminative materialism. The claim is not that we have any *conclusive* reason to accept the idea that mental states "really" exist. Rather, the claim is that the arguments adduced by the eliminative materialist do not give us adequate reason, given that it implies an error theory, to reject the folk theoretic view that mental states exist in some sense. While a folk theory might enjoy some special presumption of correctness, the claim that the proponent of an error theory fails to meet the argumentative burden for justifying an error theory neither implies that the error theory is false nor that the folk theory is true. It merely implies that the proponent has not given adequate reason for rejecting the folk theory in favor of the error theory.

The difficulties in giving persuasive reasons to accept an error theory militate decisively against construing classical natural law theory and Dworkin's interpretivism as conceptual theories of law that directly engage positivism. It is simply not clear what kind of reasons one could give that would justify accepting the view that what we regard as paradigmatic instances of law might not *really* be law in the descriptive sense of the term. I have far more intuitive confidence, given ordinary linguistic and legal practices, in the claim that the normative outputs of courts and legislatures characteristically result in something properly characterized as "law" in the descriptive sense than in anything a proponent of an error theory of law could adduce in support of it.

Accordingly, there is little to be gained in construing classical natural law theory and Dworkin's interpretivism as deploying ICA to explicate the *real* nature of law as it is defined independently of our conceptual practices. Although ICA can, while MCA cannot, result in an error theory of law, it does nothing to make those theories more plausible to understand them as deploying ICA, rather than MCA because it does nothing to meet the burden that must be met to justify accepting an error theory of law. Positivism purports to explicate the content of a purely descriptive concept of law that is grounded entirely in ordinary linguistic and legal practices. To justify rejecting positivism on the ground that these ordinary practices tell us nothing about what law *really* is, the proponent of an error theory needs to articulate a compelling reason that we should think that the practices that construct *our* shared concept of law are systematically misleading with respect to what law really is, properly understood. In the absence of a sufficiently compelling reason to accept such an interpretation of these putatively "anti-positivist" theories, the better option is to construe them as deploying MCA to explicate a different, but related, concept of law—a concept that is grounded in the descriptive concept that positivism purports to explicate but has evaluative content.

Thus construed, positivism, classical natural law theory, and interpretivism converge on adopting MCA in attempting to give an analysis of the nature of law but diverge with respect to which concept of law they are attempting to explicate. Whereas the positivist adopts a methodology that assumes MCA in order to explicate the content of a purely descriptive concept of law grounded in ordinary usage patterns, classical natural law and interpretivism adopt, like the positivist, a methodology that assumes MCA but, unlike the positivist, deploy it to explicate the content of an evaluative concept that is also grounded in ordinary usage patterns. On this interpretation, then, all three theories converge in rejecting ICA as a meta-methodological principle but diverge with respect to which usage of the term "law" they are attempting to explicate. The positivist attempts to flesh out the deeper philosophical commitments of the descriptive usage of "law" as it picks out those norms that are treated and characterized as law in practices that are pre-theoretically regarded as legal. Classical natural law theories and Dworkin's interpretivism attempt to flesh out the deeper philosophical commitments of the evaluative usage of "law" as it picks out those norms that are law not only in a purely descriptive sense but also in a morally normative *fullest* sense of the term.

8. What do Finnis and Dworkin say?

Blackstone's classical natural theory has traditionally been interpreted as a rival theory to positivism that claims that an unjust norm cannot be a positive law. On this interpretation, Blackstone's theory purports to deploy MCA to explicate the descriptive concept of law defined by our linguistic and legal practices. This interpretation can be challenged, as discussed in Chapter 1, on the ground that a more careful study of the relevant texts suggests that he is concerned with what is morally (or "really") binding and authoritative—and not with the project of conceptual jurisprudence as defined by the work of Austin and Bentham.

There are similarly persuasive textual reasons to think that contemporary natural law theorists and Dworkin are concerned to deploy MCA to explicate the evaluative concept of law. John Finnis, the most influential contemporary natural law theorist, endorses the Separability Thesis and hence denies the view that it is conceptually impossible for there to be an unjust legal norm and rejects the attribution of that view to Aquinas.:

> "There is no necessary or conceptual connection between positive law and morality." True, for there are immoral positive laws; "there are two broad categories (with many sub-classes) of unjust laws …". And a conceptual distinction or disconnection is effortlessly established by the move made in the *Summa*, of taking human positive law as a subject for consideration in its own right (and its own name), a topic readily identifiable and identified *prior* to any question about its relation to morality …. "The identification of the existence and content of law does not require resort to any moral argument." True, for how else could one identify wicked laws such as Israel's prophet denounced in words so often quoted by Aquinas: "Woe to those who make unfair laws [*leges iniquas*] who draw up instruments imposing injustice [*iniustitiam*], and who give judgments oppressing the poor"?[18]

[18] John Finnis, "The Truth in Legal Positivism," in Robert P. George (ed.), *The Autonomy of Law* (Oxford: Clarendon Press, 1996), 203, 204.

Similarly, while it is true that Dworkin took himself in his early work to be articulating a view inconsistent with positivism, Dworkin is clear in Law's Empire that he is explicating an evaluative concept of law—and indeed acknowledges that his theory is consistent with positivism:

> We need not deny that the Nazi system was an example of law ... because *there is an available sense in which it plainly was law*. But we have no difficulty in understanding someone who does say that *Nazi law was not really law, or was law in a degenerate sense, or was less than fully law.* For he is not then using "law" in that sense; he is not making that sort of preinterpretive judgment but a skeptical interpretive judgment that Nazi law lacked features crucial to flourishing legal systems whose rules and procedures do justify coercion.[19]

Dworkin concedes, as he must, that in a purely descriptive sense (the "preinterpretive" sense) the Nazis "plainly" had a system of law, but this is the sense of the term that is expressed by the purely descriptive concept that positivism purports to explicate. What the Nazis did not have, on his view, was something that was "really" or "fully" law in the interpretive—or evaluative—sense of the term.

It turns out, then, that the traditional interpretation of classical natural law theory and Dworkin's interpretivism as inconsistent with positivism does not cohere with what these theorists have had to say about the matter. Properly construed, those theories are not inconsistent with positivism because they are not rival accounts of the same concept. While positivism is concerned to explicate the content of a purely descriptive concept of law, classical natural law theory and Dworkin's interpretivism are concerned to explicate the content of an evaluative concept that does not engage a positivist theory of law.

9. Can ICA ground a viable conceptual methodology?

One might nonetheless still be tempted at this point to reject the arguments given above and to attempt to rescue an interpretation of Dworkin and classical natural law theories as anti-positivist. On this line of argument, classical natural law theorists and Dworkin are best construed, despite any ostensible evidence to the contrary, as deploying ICA to explicate a descriptive concept of law the content of which is determined independently of our shared linguistic and legal practices.

[19] Ronald Dworkin, *Law's Empire* (Cambridge, MA: Harvard University Press, 1986), 103–04. Hereinafter *LE*.

The problem with this line of interpretation is that ICA is just not a methodological approach that beings like us could adopt with respect to explicating the nature of law. If ICA requires being able to understand the nature of law independent of the lexical meanings that fix our concept of it, it seems clear we are not equipped to do this; the only epistemic access that we could have to the nature of law is through the conventions that define the application-conditions for using the term "law." To put the point in Kantian terms, we can apprehend the nature of things only as they appear to us mediated through the concepts we deploy to organize and make sense of our experience; we simply have no way to apprehend things as they are utterly independent of the concepts through which we organize the materials of our experience. We do not have reliable epistemic access to what the nature of law is if determined by considerations utterly independent of the practices that define the lexical meaning of the term.

It is true that ICA starts from the lexical meaning of the term "law" in attempting to identify the unconstructed real nature of law but it is utterly mysterious as to how such an approach could produce a theory that we have any reason to accept. As Jackson describes it, ICA purports, like MCA, to begin from ordinary intuitions, but there is no reason to think that ordinary intuitions would be reliable in explicating a concept or the nature of a thing that is not even partly determined by our linguistic practices. Ordinary intuitions are reliable in identifying the content of concepts defined by our linguistic practices because those intuitions are conditioned by those practices. I have the strong intuition that only unmarried people can be bachelors only because our linguistic practices converge on defining the term "bachelor" as "unmarried adult male." In contrast, if I have any intuitions about what a bachelor is that are independent of our linguistic conventions for using the term, I have no clue how to go about identifying them. ICA simply cannot ground an epistemically accessible conceptual methodology.

There are hence two reasons for thinking that anti-positivist theories are most charitably construed as explicating a different concept of law than the purely descriptive concept that positivism purports to explicate. First, as discussed in the last section, construing anti-positivist theories as explicating the purely descriptive concept of law that positivism purports to explicate implies an error theory of law that we have no reason to accept. In the absence of an argument that meets the difficult standard for justifying an error theory, any theory of law that implies an error theory should summarily be rejected. Construing anti-positivist theories as deploying ICA to explain the descriptive concept does nothing to meet the requisite standard for justifying an error theory. But, second, given that it is clear that we have no way of knowing how we could identify the nature of law as defined utterly independently of our conceptual practices, it is more plausible to construe anti-positivist theories as deploying MCA to explain an evaluative concept of law that is grounded in the descriptive concept with which positivism is concerned, but also has evaluative content—namely that which expresses what counts as law in its morally fullest sense or what counts as law in its morally best light.

10. Conclusions

The idea that one theory X entails that another theory Y is an error theory presupposes that the two theories are attempting to explain exactly the same phenomenon. It is reasonable to think that only a theory of the descriptive concept of law can entail that another theory of the same concept is an error theory. Construed as rival accounts that purport to explicate the content of a descriptive concept of law fixed by ordinary legal and linguistic practices, positivist theories and putatively anti-positivist theories, like interpretivism and the traditional interpretation of natural law theory, would both be candidates for error theories.

But, as discussed above, there is another way to construe the disagreement between positivism and so-called anti-positivist views—namely, as explicating different concepts of law that are both grounded in ordinary linguistic and legal practices. On this view, positivists are explicating a purely descriptive concept of law while natural law theory and interpretivism are explicating a concept that is grounded in the descriptive concept positivism purports to explicate but also has evaluative content. On this construction of natural law theory and interpretivism, a morally problematic norm that is properly promulgated is properly characterized as a "law" in a purely descriptive sense but not in the fullest evaluative sense of the term. Just as the evaluative concept of art incorporates aesthetic standards that are external to the existence conditions for art in its descriptive sense, the evaluative concept of law incorporates moral standards that are external to the existence conditions for law in its descriptive sense. Positivists and theorists traditionally characterized as anti-positivist are, thus construed, answering different questions about the nature of law.

This should not be thought to disparage either conceptual project relative to the other. As discussed in Chapter 1, we need to approach the institution of law from empirical, normative, and conceptual points of view to fully understand it. But, even as far as conceptual jurisprudence is concerned, it is not enough to explicate one purely descriptive concept of law to fully understand the nature of the institution of law. In addition, there are the concepts of obligation, normativity, norm-guidance, and a host of other related concepts—including the evaluative concept that is frequently used, for example, to express disapproval of court holdings interpreting the U.S. Constitution. If understanding the purely descriptive concept of law is the foundation for a comprehensive conceptual understanding of law, understanding the evaluative concept is equally crucial. Thus construed, positivism, classical natural law theory, and Dworkinian interpretivism all have something crucial to contribute to a fully comprehensive understanding of the institution of law.

3

Legal Positivism and the Possibility of Moral Criteria of Validity

This chapter provides an overview of the theses associated with the various forms of legal positivism. It begins with a discussion of the assumption, which grounds the project of conceptual jurisprudence, that legal norms and systems have certain properties that distinguish them from other norms and systems that purport to govern or regulate the behavior of subjects. It continues with a description of the core theses of legal positivism that are intended to identify the conceptually necessary properties that constitute something as law and distinguish things that count as law from things that do not count as law. The chapter closes with an explication of inclusive and exclusive positivism, which comprise the focus for the remaining chapters of the volume.

1. The Differentiation Thesis

The project of conceptual jurisprudence is concerned with explicating the content of those concepts that figure most prominently in practices pre-theoretically regarded as legal in character; these concepts include the concepts of law, validity, authority, and a legal system. As traditionally described, the point of a conceptual theory of law is to explicate the content of each of these concepts, locating them among a general conceptual framework determined by the linguistic and legal practices that define the application-conditions for using the corresponding concept-terms.

There are a couple of methodological approaches to the project of conceptual jurisprudence but the most common, and only epistemically viable, approach grounds the content of our concepts in the ordinary linguistic practices that define the lexical meanings of the corresponding concept-terms. Given that the lexical meaning of a term fixes the content of the corresponding concept, any viable approach to explicating the content of a concept must begin with the lexical meaning of the corresponding concept-term.

This does not imply, as discussed in Chapter 1, that there is no significant difference between the methodologies of conceptual analysis and empirical lexicography. The lexical meaning of a word contributes to fixing the content of a concept but need not exhaust it. Insofar as the social practices that fix the lexical meaning of a word are indeterminate with respect to the application of the word in some theoretically interesting case, the lexical meaning fails to exhaust the content of the corresponding concept. In this case, conceptual analysis is needed to eliminate the indeterminacy by identifying the deeper philosophical commitments grounding the relevant practices. The methodology of conceptual analysis, unlike the purely sociological methodology of lexicography, is concerned to identify these philosophical commitments presupposed by the relevant social practices and is hence philosophical in character.

Consider, again, the term "bachelor." While the lexical meaning of the term "bachelor" is reported in dictionaries as "unmarried man," the meaning seems to be indeterminate with respect to whether the Pope is properly characterized as a bachelor. Many people have the intuition that the term "bachelor" connotes a formal eligibility for marriage or a psychological openness that is lacking in the case of the Pope and take the view that the Pope is not properly characterized as a bachelor. Others have the intuition that being an unmarried man exhausts the notion of a bachelor and hence take the view that the Pope is as paradigmatically a bachelor as any other unmarried man.

The existence of conflicting intuitions on the applicability of the term to the Pope gestures in the direction of thinking that the lexical meaning of "bachelor" is indeterminate with respect to the Pope but is not enough to *establish* that it is indeterminate with respect to this application. The problem is that we do not know what percentage of speakers would affirm that the Pope is a bachelor and what percentage of speakers would deny that the Pope is a bachelor. If, on the one hand, there were an even split on the matter, then the lexical meaning of the term would be indeterminate with respect to whether the Pope is a bachelor because there is no linguistic convention with respect to whether the Pope is properly characterized as a bachelor. If, on the other hand, 99 percent of speakers hold that the Pope is a bachelor while 1 percent deny this, then there is a convention that equates being a bachelor with being an unmarried man; the dissenting 1 percent are confused about the lexical meaning of the term. Since we do not know the extent of the split among speakers on this case, we do not know whether the lexical meaning of "bachelor" is indeterminate with respect to the Pope.

This tells us something about how a conceptual issue requiring philosophical explication arises. When there is a significant split among speakers about the application of a term to a case that has some theoretical importance, the issue cannot be resolved by purely empirical means because an empirical analysis can disclose only what people believe about the meaning of a term and cannot provide reasons for resolving an issue of indeterminacy one way or another. In the case of a 99–1 split on the application of "bachelor" to the Pope, the term clearly applies to the Pope. In the case of the 50–50 split above, there is an indeterminacy with respect to the lexical meaning that requires resolution. While any indeterminacy in meaning can be resolved by brute stipulation, this will not usually be regarded as satisfactory insofar as competent speakers believe that there is an objectively correct answer; this objectively correct answer would be determined by the deeper shared commitments grounding the convergent patterns of usage.

It is important to note that these deeper commitments are philosophical in character—even if people in the relevant community of speakers would not think to characterize them as such. To begin, if one thinks that the Pope is not a bachelor, it is not because the lexical definition rules it out; the Pope is clearly a bachelor, on this definition. In this case, one is expressing skepticism that the lexical definition fully expresses what a bachelor ultimately is, and what a bachelor ultimately is defines the nature of bachelorhood.

Further, someone who accepts the claim that the Pope is a bachelor also does so on the strength of a philosophical intuition concerning the nature of bachelorhood. Insofar as skepticism about whether the Pope is a bachelor is grounded in philosophical intuitions about the nature of a bachelor, so is the intuition that the Pope is as much a bachelor as any other. In this case, the view is that the lexical definition of a bachelor as an unmarried man fully expresses the nature of a bachelor.

Ordinary speakers might not be likely to describe their intuitions about whether the Pope is properly characterized as a bachelor as philosophical, but the underlying intuition in each case is metaphysical insofar as it concerns the nature of the thing picked out by the relevant concept-term. Claims about the nature of a thing are claims about what properties constitute something as belonging to the reference class of the concept-term picking out the thing and are hence claims about the essential properties of the thing. As such, they are properly understood as metaphysical and hence philosophical in character.

Conceptual analysis, then, purports to identify these deeper philosophical commitments shared by a community of speakers that would resolve theoretically significant issues of lexical indeterminacy. These deeper commitments are implicitly grounded in the conventions for using the term but do not usually rise to the surface except in the form of puzzles, such as is posed by the question of whether the Pope is a bachelor or, more to the point, by the question of whether there can be objective moral constraints on the content of law if it is a social artifact. Because these puzzles are ultimately metaphysical in character, none can be resolved wholly on the strength of empirical observations having to do with convergent patterns of usage; these puzzles arise only insofar as there is no convergence with respect to the usage in question. What is needed to resolve the indeterminacy is an analysis that is explicitly philosophical in character but one that is also grounded in the empirical patterns of usage that fix the lexical meaning of the term.

The methodology of conceptual analysis attempts to resolve lexical indeterminacy by deploying various logical tools and the methodology of possible cases to identify deeper intuitions about the nature of the thing picked out by the concept-term in order to explicate these intuitions in the form of a conceptual theory of the thing. Just as ethical theorizing proceeds by eliciting intuitions on possible cases in order to extract deeper commitments in the form of general ethical norms, conceptual analysis proceeds in a similar way by eliciting intuitions on possible cases to extract deeper commitments with respect to the nature of the thing picked out by the relevant concept-term.

Insofar as an analysis of a concept is concerned to disclose the nature of the thing referred to by the corresponding concept-word, it is expressed in claims that purport to be necessarily true. The nature of a thing is constituted by a list of those properties that a thing *must* have in order to be properly characterized as falling within the reference class of the relevant concept-term. It is hence a necessary truth that a thing properly picked out by some concept-term has every property defining the nature of the thing picked out by the concept-term; it is, for example, a necessary truth that every bachelor has the compound property of being an unmarried man.

A conceptual analysis of law, then, is intended to explicate the nature of law by displaying all of the properties that make something that has them an instance of *law*, rather than an instance of something else. As discussed in Chapter 2, these properties do not merely distinguish things that are law from things that are not law; they also explain why something that counts as an instance of law has that status. In other words, the relevant properties constitute something that is law as law in this sense: something that is law has that status wholly in virtue of instantiating each of the relevant properties. Just as, for example, instantiating the property of being an unmarried man constitutes something as a bachelor, instantiation of all the conceptually necessary properties of law constitutes something as law.

The idea that conceptual jurisprudence is concerned to identify properties that distinguish things that are law from things that are not law presupposes the claim that in every conceptually possible legal system there exist necessary and sufficient conditions for a norm to count as law. Since the law of a system includes both the norms that are legally valid and recognition norms that define the criteria of validity, the relevant membership criteria include not only the conditions something must satisfy to be a valid legal norm but also include the conditions something must satisfy to be a legal recognition norm. Accordingly, the project of conceptual jurisprudence presupposes the following:

The Differentiation Thesis: In every conceptually possible legal system *S*, there is a set of criteria of *legality* (as opposed to legal validity) such that, for every norm *n*, *n* is a law in *S* at time *t* if and only if *n* satisfies the criteria of legality at *t*.

The Differentiation Thesis is a metaphysical thesis and not an epistemological thesis. The Differentiation Thesis neither presupposes nor implies any claims about the extent to which the criteria of *legality* can be identified in any possible legal system. Although the Differentiation Thesis implies that there is a set of common properties that distinguishes things that count as law from things that do not, the claim that there exists such a set of properties implies nothing with respect to our ability to reliably determine whether a particular thing instantiates these properties or not. The former claim is a purely ontological one while claims concerning the latter issue are epistemological in character. Whatever views a theorist takes on the epistemological qualities of the criteria of legality—or, for that matter, the criteria of validity—must be grounded in other commitments that rest, in part, on considerations of normative epistemology and, in part, on observable facts about legal practice in the legal system of interest.

Further, the Differentiation Thesis implies nothing about the nature or moral character of the law in any or every conceptually possible legal system. As far as the Differentiation Thesis is concerned, legally valid content might—or might not—be necessarily constrained by moral principles or by the inherently interpretive character of law. Since the Differentiation Thesis is agnostic on its face with respect to such claims, it is consistent with any non-skeptical theory of the nature of law.

The Differentiation Thesis simply expresses the truism that, in every conceptually possible society with a legal system, legal norms have certain properties that distinguish them, as a conceptual matter, from moral norms and from other social norms that might be used to appraise the behavior of subjects in that society. Every conceptual theory of law has assumed the Differentiation Thesis as a starting point because it implies that there exists a set of properties that distinguish norms of law from norms of other kinds and that constitute a norm with those properties as being a legal norm. As such, the Differentiation Thesis entails that there is a unique set of existence conditions that constitute something as law—and hence implies that our practices define a concept of law that can be explicated in the form of necessary and sufficient membership conditions.

2. Conceptual foundations of legal positivism

2.1 The Artifact Thesis

The most fundamental of positivism's core commitments is the Artifact Thesis, which asserts that law is, in essence, a social creation and artifact. What distinguishes law from non-law, according to this thesis, is the occurrence of some contingent social fact (or facts) that constitutes a norm or system as one of law. It is the occurrence of the relevant social fact (or facts) that constitutes any norm or system that has the status of law as having this status.

The relevant facts constituting something as a norm or system of law can be expressed in terms of some social property instantiated by the relevant thing. For example, if the relevant social fact that must occur for a norm to count as law is that it be officially promulgated, then a norm counts as law in virtue of instantiating the social property of having been officially promulgated. According to the Artifact Thesis, then, anything that counts as law in any possible legal system has that status wholly in virtue of instantiating the relevant social properties. It is the occurrence of the relevant social facts or, otherwise put, the instantiation of the relevant social properties that brings a legal norm into existence as one of law and sustains it as having that status. The occurrence of the relevant social facts manufactures the norm as one of law.

The Artifact Thesis implies that both valid legal norms and the rule of recognition have the status of law in virtue of instantiating some contingent social property. The Artifact Thesis holds that law is wholly a social creation, and this means that *every* norm that has the status of law is an artifact. Since both the rule of recognition and the norms it validates all have the status of law, the content of the rule of recognition, the legal system to which it gives rise, and every norm it validates can be explained in terms of the relevant social facts or properties. Law is an artifact all the way down

The type of social fact or social property that explains, or manufactures, the content of the rule of recognition and hence the criteria of validity will be different from the type of social fact that explains, or manufactures, the content of the norms that are validated by the rule of recognition. The type of social fact that explains the content of the valid norms of the system can differ from one legal system to another because the content of the rule of recognition can differ from one legal system to another; since the content a rule of recognition defining the properties a norm must have to be valid can differ from one legal system to the next, so can the properties a norm must have to be valid.

In contrast, the general type of social fact that explains the existence and content of the rule of recognition is the same in every conceptually possible legal system; and the relevant social fact must have something to do with what certain people—i.e. those who serve as officials of the system—believe, say, and do. What these people believe, say, and do manufactures the law and determines its content. If there are no people doing things like promulgating, applying, and enforcing norms that tell people what to do, then there is nothing that could count as law. Law requires the existence of someone in a community who is doing something that purports to make certain behaviors non-optional on the part of other persons in the community.

The issue, then, with respect to applying the Artifact Thesis to the rule of recognition is to determine the type of social fact having to do with the beliefs and behavior of officials that would manufacture in every conceptually possible legal system the content of the rule of recognition. While all positivists, of course, are committed to the Artifact Thesis, they differ with respect to which type of social fact manufactures the rule of recognition—and hence with respect to which social fact manufactures the criteria that determine what counts as valid law.

John Austin fleshes out the Artifact Thesis in terms of a community of people who habitually obey the commands of a sovereign that are backed with the threat of a sanction. On Austin's view, the distinguishing feature of a legal system is the presence of a sovereign who is habitually obeyed by most people in the society but who is not in the habit of obeying anyone else. On Austin's view, a norm *n* is legally valid in a society *S* if and only if (1) *n* is the command of the sovereign in *S*; and (2) *n* is backed up by the threat of a sanction. The social fact that explains the content of the rule of recognition that validates all and only commands of a sovereign is the existence of a community of people who habitually obey those commands, while the social fact that explains the content of a valid legal norm is that it is commanded by the sovereign. In both cases, the content of law is artifactual in virtue of being manufactured by social facts.

Hart rejects Austin's view that it is a conceptually necessary condition for law that the norms be backed by coercive sanctions for noncompliance. Since Hart denies that being enforced by a sovereign is a conceptually necessary feature of either a legal system or a legal norm, he must also deny that being enforced by a sovereign is one of the properties that distinguishes legal systems or norms from other systems or norms. Insofar as he thereby denies that the property of being enforced by a sovereign constitutes something as law, Hart rejects Austin's view of the social property that manufactures law.

On Hart's view, the social fact that manufactures the legally authoritative rule of recognition is a convergent practice of officials with respect to what is recognized, applied, and enforced as law in a community in which citizens generally satisfy the standards that officials recognize, apply, and enforce as law. It is the behavior of officials with respect to what they recognize, apply, and enforce as law—and not the disposition of citizens to obey certain norms—that constitutes a norm that has the status of law as having this status. Thus, on Hart's well-known view, the social fact that establishes the rule of recognition as legally authoritative is that officials converge in practicing a norm that governs official behavior in recognizing, applying, and enforcing law and thereby defines the content of the criteria of validity in that system. The social fact that constitutes a norm as a valid law of the system is that it is recognized, applied, or enforced in a manner that conforms to the content of the rule of recognition practiced by the officials in the system. Hart, like Austin, conceives of law as wholly artifactual in character.

Either way, the Artifact Thesis explains the content of the rule defining the system's criteria of validity and hence the authority of valid legal norms in terms of some set of social facts and thereby conceptualizes law as an artifact all the way down. On Hart's version of the thesis, the relevant social fact is the convergence of officials in practicing a rule of recognition that defines the criteria of validity in the system; on Austin's version, the relevant social fact is the sovereign's ability to coerce compliance. But, in either case, since the content of every legal norm is authoritative wholly in virtue of instantiating some social property, the legal system and valid legal norms to which they give rise are social creations. According to the Artifact Thesis, then, it is a conceptual truth that law is a social artifact all the way down in the sense that the legal system, rule of recognition, and valid legal norms are legally authoritative in virtue of the occurrence of some contingent social fact or the instantiation by the relevant entity of some contingent social property. The content of any law, then, is wholly manufactured by the occurrence of the relevant social fact.

The Artifact Thesis should be distinguished from the so-called Sources Thesis, according to which it is a conceptual truth that the existence and content of law are fully determined by social sources. To understand the substantive difference between the two theses, it is helpful to note the logical relationship between the Sources Thesis and Artifact Thesis. To begin, the Sources Thesis logically implies the Artifact Thesis. If it is a conceptual truth that the content of every law is fully determined by its sources, then it follows that it is a conceptual truth that the content of every law is fully determined by social facts that manufacture that content. If the Sources Thesis is true, then law is an artifact all the way down.

In contrast, the Artifact Thesis does not imply the Sources Thesis. The claim that the content of every law is manufactured by certain social facts does not imply anything about what the content of the criteria of validity must be; it implies only that what content the criteria of validity have they have wholly in virtue of the occurrence of the relevant social facts. Since the Artifact Thesis makes a claim only about what makes the rule that defines the criteria of validity legally authoritative as a general matter, it does not imply that the artifactual criteria of validity cannot incorporate constraints on the content of law. The Artifact Thesis implies only that if the rule of recognition incorporates constraints on the content of valid law, those constraints are legally authoritative in virtue of the same general social facts that confer such authority upon source-based criteria of validity.

The Artifact Thesis is hence related to the Sources Thesis but distinct from it. Whereas the Sources Thesis states a conceptual constraint on the *content* of the rule of recognition that determines what counts as valid law in the system, the Artifact Thesis states only that the rule of recognition is authoritative in virtue of instantiating some general social property that manufactures its content and hence its existence as law. The Artifact Thesis, in essence, states a claim about what accounts for the existence and authority of the rule of recognition as a legal norm; in contrast, the Sources Thesis limits the content of the criteria of validity defined by an authoritative rule of recognition to source-based considerations.

The Artifact Thesis states a defining thesis of legal positivism, while the Sources Thesis does not. One can, as inclusive positivists do, reject the Sources Thesis and still be a positivist, but one cannot reject the Artifact Thesis and still be a positivist. Unlike the Sources Thesis, the Artifact Thesis is part of the shared foundation that distinguishes legal positivism from other conceptual theories of law and is thus accepted by all positivists.

2.2 The Separability Thesis

The Separability Thesis can be understood at the most general level as simply the negation of the distinguishing thesis of classical natural law theory as traditionally interpreted. Classical natural law theory asserts, on this construction, that it is a conceptual truth that the criteria of validity incorporate moral constraints on the content of law. The Separability Thesis denies this claim as it applies to the concept of law constructed by our ordinary linguistic and legal practices and thereby acknowledges the conceptual possibility of wicked laws and legal systems.

Thus construed, the Separability Thesis asserts no more than that it is conceptually possible for a legal system to have criteria of validity that consist entirely of considerations having to do with the source and manner in which a norm is promulgated or recognized by officials. In such a legal system, whether or not a norm counts as law is wholly determined by whether it has been properly promulgated, which would include its having its source in the appropriate official agency.

There is little logical distance between the Separability Thesis and the Artifact Thesis. To begin, the Separability Thesis seems to be a straightforward logical consequence of the Artifact Thesis. If it is a conceptual truth that the content of every legal norm is *fully* manufactured by certain contingent social processes, it seems to follow that there are no conceptually necessary content-based restrictions on what can count as a *valid* legal norm; since these social processes can change with respect to any element, so can the content that is determined by that particular element. But insofar as a moral constraint on the content of law would be a content-based restriction on what can count as a valid law, it follows that it is not a conceptually necessary feature of law that its content conforms to moral standards and hence that there are no conceptually necessary moral criteria of validity.

Conversely, the Artifact Thesis can be derived from the Separability Thesis. If there are no conceptually necessary moral constraints on the content of valid law, then it would seem to follow that the content of every valid legal norm, as a conceptual matter, is fully determined by the occurrence of some contingent social fact. The only determinant of legal content that could obtain independently of any contingent fact would have to be content-based in character. But if, as the Separability Thesis asserts, there are no necessary moral constraints on the content of law, assuming moral constraints are the only plausible candidates for necessary content-based constraints on the content of valid law, then the only other possible contingent determinants of legal content would have to be social in character—and the only plausible candidate for the contingent fact that determines the content of a valid legal norm is some social fact involving the acts and dispositions of certain persons in the community. Since the content of *every* legal norm is manufactured, it follows that the legal system is manufactured and hence that law is an artifact all the way down.

The important point, for our purposes, is this: while it is typically thought that the core of positivism can be fully expressed only by reference to both the Artifact and Separability Theses, the Artifact Thesis is sufficient to express the distinguishing core of positivism since it implies the Separability Thesis. At its foundation, then, positivism is nothing more than the Artifact Thesis.

Lending further support to the idea that the Artifact Thesis fully expresses the core of legal positivism is the fact that the logical relationship between the Separability Thesis and the Sources Thesis parallels that between the Artifact Thesis and Sources Thesis. To begin, if there are no conceptually possible legal systems with moral criteria of validity, then every conceptually possible legal system lacks moral criteria of validity. But if there is at least one conceptually possible legal system and there are no conceptually possible legal systems with moral criteria of validity, then there is at least one conceptually possible legal system without moral criteria of validity. The Sources Thesis, then, implies the Separability Thesis—as it does the Artifact Thesis.

In contrast, as was also true of the logical relationship between the Artifact and Sources Theses, the Separability Thesis does not imply the Sources Thesis. The claim that there can be legal systems *without* moral criteria of validity does not imply that there cannot be legal systems *with* moral criteria of validity; the claim that there can be families without children, for example, does not imply that there cannot be families with children. Otherwise put, the claim that there can be legal systems without moral criteria of validity is consistent with the claim that there can be a legal system with moral criteria of validity. Since it is therefore possible for the Separability Thesis to be true and the Sources Thesis false, the Separability Thesis does not imply the Sources Thesis.

Inclusive and exclusive positivism are hence both *prima facie* options for a positivist theory of law. Although the Sources Thesis logically implies both the Artifact Thesis and Separability Thesis logically implies the Sources Thesis, it is logically implied by neither the Artifact Thesis nor the Separability Thesis. This entails that a positivist can, at least at first glance, consistently hold that it is conceptually possible for a legal system to incorporate moral criteria of validity and hence that there is nothing in the core commitments of legal positivism as expressed by the Artifact Thesis or the Separability Thesis that is facially inconsistent with the conceptual possibility of moral criteria of validity.

2.3 The Conventionality Thesis

If the Artifact Thesis is true, as seems plausible, of the purely descriptive concept of law defined by ordinary usage, then there are no other determinants of the content of the validity criteria than what those persons who serve as officials of the system believe, say, and do with respect to what counts as law. What we characterize as "law," according to ordinary usage, in any conceptually possible legal system is fully defined by what officials converge in characterizing as law in the course of performing their functions as officials. The only determinants of the content of the criteria of validity have to do, then, with what officials recognize, apply, and enforce as valid law in the system.

Subjects of valid law, which include every person within the relevant jurisdiction, must generally acquiesce to official actions in the following minimal respect: their behavior must conform sufficiently to the norms that officials recognize, apply, and enforce as valid law in the community. This implies that subjects of valid law acquiesce with respect to what officials treat and characterize as "law." But apart from this minimal efficacy condition, what counts as law in any stable community that is plausibly characterized as governed by law is fully determined by what officials recognize, apply, and enforce as law.

This implies that officials must largely agree with respect to what they recognize, apply, and enforce as law. The existence of a stable legal system depends on there being some minimal degree of consistency and clarity with respect to what norms will be applied and enforced against citizens as law, and this could not be achieved without officials converging in their behavior with respect to what counts as law in the system. Further, this convergence of behavior must be mutually conditioned in the following sense: part of what explains why one official treats a norm as law with respect to her behavior as an official of the system must have something to do with the fact that she is aware that the other officials converge in treating that norm as law.[1]

What this means, then, is that the content of the criteria of validity is wholly determined by the mutually responsive practices of officials with respect to what they recognize, apply, and enforce as law in the following respect: insofar as the content of the criteria of validity is determinate with respect to whether some norm counts as law, its content is determined by and only by the convergent practices of officials.

The relevant official practices might be indeterminate with respect to whether some norm counts as valid law, but that is not a problem for the Artifact Thesis. The Artifact Thesis asserts only that what content the law has it has wholly in virtue of the occurrence of certain social facts that manufacture it as law. By itself, the claim that all legal content is an artifact implies nothing whatsoever about the substantive coverage of that content. It asserts no more than that whatever content the criteria of validity have in any instance is wholly manufactured by the convergent practices of officials with respect to what they recognize, apply, and enforce as law.

This raises an issue with respect to how to characterize the relationship between the relevant official practice and the rule of recognition. There are two possibilities. The relationship between the rule of recognition and the relevant official practice could be characterized as one of identity; thus conceived, the rule of recognition would be identical with the practice in the

[1] It might be that, as a purely conceptual matter, one cannot rule out the possibility of a system in which officials always converge accidentally on what they recognize, apply, and enforce as law. But if that is a conceptual or nomological possibility, it picks out a fringe state of affairs that tells us little of significance about the nature of law as it is defined by our practices.

sense that the term picking out the rule of recognition and the term picking out the relevant practices refer to exactly the same object. Alternatively, the relationship between the two could be characterized as one of determination; thus conceived, the rule of recognition would be determined by the practice but would not be the same object as the practice.

Hart is not clear on this issue but seems to think that the relationship between the rule of recognition and the social practice that determines its content is one of identity:

> The account I have given of [social rules] has become known as "the practice theory" of rules because it treats the social rules of a group as *constituted by a form of social practice comprising both patterns of conduct regularly followed by most members of the group and a distinctive normative attitude to such patterns of conduct which I have called "acceptance"*.[2]

To say that these patterns of conduct "constitute" the social rules of a group seems to say something stronger than just that the patterns of conduct fix or determine the content of the rule; it seems to say that they comprise the rule. Insofar as these patterns of conduct constitute the rule in the sense of comprising it, the *aggregate* of these practices is ontologically identical with the rule; that is, the term referring to the rule of recognition and the term referring to the practice pick out the same object.

This is a much stronger claim than the claim that the practices fix or determine the content of the rule. Since, on the former view, everything that can correctly be said of the rule can correctly be said of the aggregate of these practices and conversely, it follows that the rule and the aggregate of these practices have *every* property in common and hence do not differ from one another in *any* respect. Since, on the latter, the rule is fixed or determined by the aggregate of the practices but is not the same as those practices, the content of the rule merely supervenes on the content of the practices in the sense that there can be no changes in the content of the rule without there being corresponding changes in the content of the practices.

In any event, whether he believes that the rule of recognition is identical with, or merely determined by, the aggregate of the practices, Hart accepts the following claim:

The Conventionality Thesis: In every conceptually possible legal system, the content of the criteria of validity is fully determined by a rule of recognition that is conventional in character.

[2] H.L.A. Hart, *The Concept of Law* 3rd Ed. (Oxford: Oxford University Press, 2012), 255. Emphasis added. Hereinafter *CL*.

The Conventionality Thesis, as is evident, asserts two conceptual claims about the rule of recognition and the criteria of validity. It asserts, first, that the rule of recognition is a conventional rule and, second, that there are no other determinants of the content of the criteria of validity than the content of the conventional rule of recognition.

The distinguishing feature of a conventional rule is that it is adopted and followed by members of the group as a standard that governs their behavior. It is a rule for the group because and only because they have converged on accepting and following it. While the group might converge on accepting and following it because they take a favorable attitude toward its content, it is not a rule for members of the group in virtue of its having this favored content; it is a rule for members of the group in virtue of their converging on accepting the rule and conforming their behavior to its content.

This distinguishes conventional norms from other norms that govern a group in virtue of their content. If, for example, moral norms are objective in character, then it is true that what morality requires of people in any given instance does not depend on what people believe about what morality requires of them. But it is also true that these requirements govern their behavior regardless of whether they accept those moral norms; objective moral norms apply to rational subjects and govern their behavior because of the content of those norms. In contrast, conventional norms do not apply to subjects in virtue of what content they have; they apply to a group only insofar as members of the group converge in accepting and following them.

To situate the Conventionality Thesis relative to positivism, it is worth noting that it logically implies each of the distinguishing theses of positivism. First, the Conventionality Thesis logically implies the Artifact Thesis. To begin, the content of the rule of recognition is artifactual if fully determined by a conventional rule. If the rule of recognition is a conventional rule, then its content is wholly determined by the practices of officials, who converge on accepting it and satisfying its requirements. These practices bring the rule into existence as a legal norm and hence manufacture its content; accordingly, if the rule of recognition is a conventional rule, its content is artifactual in character.

The content of valid law is also artifactual in character if the Conventionality Thesis is true. If the content of the rule of recognition is fully determined by a contingent conventional rule, the content of the criteria of validity is also fully determined by a contingent conventional rule. Since there are thus no necessary constraints on the content of valid law, the content of valid law is fully determined by the contingent occurrence of the social facts that, according to the criteria of validity, constitute a norm as legally valid. Insofar as the occurrence of the relevant social facts constitutes a piece of content as legally valid, those social facts manufacture the content of valid law. If the Conventionality Thesis is true, law is an artifact all the way down.

Second, the Conventionality Thesis logically implies the Separability Thesis. If the rule of recognition is a conventional rule, then its content is wholly determined by the contingent practices of officials. But this latter claim implies that there are no conceptually necessary moral criteria of validity. Since (1) the content of the criteria of validity in any conceptually possible legal system is fully determined by the content of the conventional rule of recognition in that system and (2) the content of the rule of recognition is fully determined by the contingent practices of officials in that system, the content of the rule of recognition and the content of the validity criteria it determines are both contingent and hence can vary with respect to all particulars from one possible legal system to the next. Thus, there are no conceptually necessary criteria of validity—moral or otherwise.

The Conventionality Thesis thus bears the following relationship to positivism. Insofar as the Conventionality Thesis implies both the Separability Thesis and the Artifact Thesis, any theory that logically presupposes or implies the Conventionality Thesis is also a positivist theory. Assuming the Artifact Thesis does not imply the Separability Thesis, those two theses would, taken together, define the core distinguishing content of positivism; since the Conventionality Thesis logically implies both, one cannot hold the Conventionality Thesis and reject positivism as a theory of law. The adoption of the Conventionality Thesis constitutes any coherent theory as positivist in character.

The converse is not true: a theory can reject the Conventionality Thesis and still be a positivist. Scott Shapiro, for example, rejects the idea that the rule of recognition is a conventional rule, holding instead that the rule of recognition is a plan:

> The existence conditions for law are the same as those for plans because the fundamental rules of legal systems *are* plans. Their function is to structure legal activity so that participants can work together and thereby achieve goods and realize values that would otherwise be unattainable.[3]

Despite rejecting the Conventionality Thesis, Shapiro's theory is clearly positivist in character. Note, to begin, that he accepts the Separability Thesis:

> My strategy is to show that there is another realm whose norms can only be discovered through social, not moral, observation, namely, the realm of *planning*. The proper way to establish the existence of plans, as I argue below, is simply to point to

[3] Scott Shapiro, *Legality* (Cambridge, MA: Harvard University Press, 2011), 119. Hereinafter *LEG*.

the fact of their adoption and acceptance. Whether I have a plan to go to the store today, or we have a plan to cook dinner together tonight, depends not on the desirability of those plans but simply on whether we have in fact adopted (and not yet rejected) them. In other words, positivism is trivially and uncontroversially true in the case of plans: the existence of a plan is one thing, its merits or demerits quite another (*LEG* 199).[4]

Further, he also accepts the Artifact Thesis: "[p]ositivists disagree with one another about the nature of [the relevant] social facts, [but] ... all legal facts are ultimately determined by social facts alone" (*LEG* 27). Shapiro's planning theory of law is thus a positivist theory in virtue of accepting the Separability Thesis and Artifact Thesis.

The Conventionality Thesis should not be thought of as a defining thesis of positivism. The Conventionality Thesis is just one way to flesh out the Artifact Thesis as it applies to the content of the rule of recognition and criteria of validity; that is, the Conventionality Thesis expresses just one way in which the rule of recognition and criteria of validity can be explained as social artifacts. It is true, as we have seen, that anyone who accepts the Conventionality Thesis is a positivist, but that is because the rule of recognition and valid legal norms would be social artifacts if the rule of recognition is a conventional rule. But it is not true that anyone who accepts the Artifact Thesis and Separability Thesis—and who is hence a positivist—thereby accepts the Conventionality Thesis; accepting the Conventionality Thesis is sufficient to constitute a view as positivist, but it is not necessary.

2.4 The relationship between the criteria of validity and the rule of recognition

The terms "rule of recognition" and "criteria of validity" differ in both meaning and reference. The rule of recognition purports, by nature, to be normative insofar as it has the form of a rule. It is a conceptual truth that anything with the form of a rule, which incorporates deontic operators such as "should" or "must," purports to be normative; that is, in part, the work that deontic operators necessarily do.

Something with the form of a rule might not, in fact, be normative but it is *purportedly* normative. For example, the deontic proposition expressed by the sentence "people should kill their first-born child" purports to be normative

[4] This would also be true of conventions. The existence of a convention is one thing; its merit is another. If so, then there is nothing in Shapiro's plan positivism that makes positivism more plausible than it would be if the rule of recognition is, as the Conventionality Thesis asserts, a conventional rule.

given that it incorporates deontic operators that purport to *prescribe* an act and hence to tell people what they should do. The proposition merely claims, so to speak, to have some kind of normative force in virtue of its form; that claim might be true, or it might not be. The rule of recognition, then, is purportedly normative by its very nature insofar as it takes the form of a norm and purports to tell officials how they should behave with respect to what they recognize, apply, and enforce as law.

The rule of recognition is also *subjectively* and *intersubjectively* normative. It is subjectively normative for a particular official insofar as she takes the internal point of view toward it and accepts it as governing *her* behavior. It is intersubjectively normative for the group of officials insofar as officials converge in adopting the rule of recognition as a norm that governs their behavior as officials and hence converge in accepting it as a norm governing *their* official behavior. The rule of recognition, then, is purportedly normative in virtue of having the form of a norm but is subjectively and intersubjectively normative in virtue of the social practice that, as a conceptual matter, brings it into existence.

A rule of recognition might not *actually* be normative from the standpoint of objective right reason. A rule of recognition that, by nature, is purportedly, subjectively, and intersubjectively normative might not be *objectively* normative because its authority over officials is not morally legitimate; in that case, the rule of recognition has legal, but not legitimate, authority over them. A rule of recognition that lacks objective normativity might justifiably govern the behavior of officials from the standpoint of what the law requires or permits but would not justifiably do so from the standpoint of what morality requires. In such a case, its requirements might create obligations that are legal in character, but they would not necessarily create obligations that are moral in character.

A morally illegitimate rule of recognition could thus *legally* bind officials without *morally* binding them. Insofar as apartheid South Africa had a system of law in the purely descriptive sense of the term defined by ordinary linguistic practices, it had a rule of recognition that was purportedly, subjectively, and intersubjectively normative and hence that legally bound officials. But insofar as a rule of recognition that requires judges to apply and enforce racially discriminatory rules could not be morally legitimate, the rule of recognition in apartheid South Africa was not objectively normative and did not morally bind officials. By nature, then, a rule of recognition, *qua* rule, is purportedly normative and, *qua* rule that is authoritative in virtue of being accepted by officials, is subjectively and intersubjectively normative; however, a rule of recognition is not, by nature, objectively normative.

To say that a rule of recognition is objectively normative is not necessarily to say that the legal system to which it gives rise is morally legitimate. Whether a legal system is morally legitimate surely depends on more than just whether the rule of recognition that defines how law is recognized, applied, and enforced in the system satisfies the relevant standards of political morality; whether a legal system is morally legitimate would also depend, in part, on whether citizens largely consent to its authority and, in part, on whether the content of its valid laws conforms to that of other moral standards. Even so, it is not unreasonable to think that it is a necessary condition for a legal system to be legitimate that its rule of recognition is objectively normative.

In contrast, the criteria of validity cannot be purportedly, subjectively, intersubjectively, or objectively normative because the content of the criteria of validity simply reports the properties that distinguish legally valid norms from all other norms. Consider a legal system *S* in which all and only commands of a sovereign are legally valid. The content of the criteria of validity in *S* does no more than assert that what distinguishes legally valid norms in *S* from all other norms is that each of the former and none of the latter instantiates the property of having been commanded by the sovereign in *S*. Since the criteria of validity for any legal system merely describe the properties that distinguish valid laws from other norms in the system—rather than *prescribe* what properties *ought* to distinguish valid laws from other norms in the system—the content of the criteria of validity is purely descriptive in character.

This is true even if the criteria of validity include moral constraints on the content of law. If, for example, it is conceptually possible for there to be a legal system *S* in which the rule of recognition validates all and only commands of a sovereign that are morally just, then the properties that distinguish content that is legally valid in *S* from content that is not legally valid in *S* include not only procedural properties but also the substantive property of being morally just. Either way, a statement of the criteria of validity in *S* merely describes—rather than prescribes—the properties that all and only legally valid norms have and that explain why norms in *S* that are legally valid have that status.

The criteria of validity are as purely descriptive in character as the semantic criteria for applying the term "bachelor." Something counts as a bachelor, according to the lexical definition, if and only if it instantiates the compound social property of being an unmarried man. Similarly, something counts as a valid law in a system if and only if it has all of the social properties that officials converge in accepting as constituting something as valid law. The criteria of validity, like semantic criteria governing the application of terms, are purely descriptive in content.

The content of the criteria of validity resembles the content of semantic criteria governing the application of a term in two additional respects. First, both the criteria for applying the term "bachelor" and the criteria of validity state existence conditions: the former state the existence conditions for bachelorhood while the latter state the existence conditions for valid law. In the former case, a person's being an unmarried man wholly explains his existence *as a bachelor*; in the latter case, a norm's satisfying the criteria of validity wholly explains its existence *as a valid legal norm* of the system.

Second, both the content of the criteria for applying the term "bachelor" and the content of the criteria of validity are determined by a convergence among people in the relevant social group on accepting and conforming their behavior to the relevant *norm*. The content of the semantic criteria for applying the term "bachelor" is determined by the content of a *semantic norm* practiced by speakers that defines a standard of correctness for using the term; according to this norm, "bachelor" should be used to refer only to unmarried men. The content of the criteria of validity is determined by the content of a *rule of recognition* practiced by officials that defines standards for how officials may recognize, apply, and enforce valid legal norms; according to this norm, "valid law" should be used to refer to only norms properly recognized, applied, or enforced under the rule of recognition.

While the content of both the semantic criteria and the criteria of validity are determined by standards that purport to be normative and are intersubjectively accepted as subjectively normative, the content of each kind of criteria is purely descriptive; such purely descriptive content does not even purport to be normative because it lacks the form of a norm and hence *cannot be* subjectively, intersubjectively, or objectively normative. Only something that can be subjectively, intersubjectively, or objectively normative can purport to be normative; and only something that has the form of a norm in virtue of deploying deontic operators can be subjectively, intersubjectively, or objectively normative.

Descriptive content can be incorporated into a norm that can be purportedly, subjectively, intersubjectively, and objectively normative but that does not entail that such content is itself normative. Insofar as one treats, for example, the lexical meaning of a term as defining a standard for using the term to which one ought to conform, one has adopted a norm that requires one to conform one's use of a term to the lexical meaning and hence that incorporates in the relevant way the descriptive lexical meaning of the term. Similarly, insofar as officials converge in treating properties defined by certain descriptive content as criteria of validity, they have adopted a rule of recognition that incorporates that descriptive content and thereby makes it normative. But because the content of semantic criteria or the content of the criteria of validity can be fully expressed without the use of deontic operators or other normative language, such content is purely descriptive in character and hence, by itself, lacks the resources to be normative in any respect. That is, such criteria are neither purportedly, subjectively, intersubjectively, nor objectively normative because they can be fully expressed without deontic operators and hence, properly expressed, do not have the form of a rule.

The existence conditions defined by the relevant criteria can nonetheless be deduced from the corresponding norm. It is true that people regard the relevant relationship between being a bachelor and being an unmarried man as defining the lexical standard for using the term that is normative in every relevant respect. While this relationship defines or presupposes a lexical standard for applying the term, the relationship itself is not the standard. The standard is a norm that warrants applying the term "bachelor" to all and only unmarried men. The existence conditions can be deduced from the norm, but they do not fully comprise or constitute a norm—and could not because, as discussed above, they can be completely expressed without the use of deontic language.

The same, of course, is true for the criteria of validity, which define the existence conditions for valid law: the existence conditions can be deduced from the rule of recognition that is, by nature, purportedly, subjectively, and intersubjectively normative, but the existence conditions do not comprise or constitute a norm—and are hence not themselves normative in any sense. The purely descriptive criteria of validity, which distinguish norms that count as legally valid from those that do not count as legally valid and which state the properties that constitute something as legally valid, can hence be expressed without using any deontic operators according to the following schema:

Criteria of Validity Schema: A norm *x* is a valid law in S if and only if *x* satisfies the conditions described in the proposition *P*, where *P* expresses a set of properties necessary and sufficient for a norm to count as valid law in the system.

The foundations for law and language resemble one another in another theoretically significant respect. Consider, for example, a recognition norm that requires officials to recognize, apply, and enforce as valid law any norm enacted by the majority of legislators in the legislature. Such a norm empowers the legislature to make law but does not impose any duties on the legislature to enact any laws and is hence not categorically normative. But it is normative in the sense that it defines a procedural requirement for something to be recognized, applied, and enforced as valid law—namely, the norm must be promulgated by the vote of a majority of legislators. Although the norm does not provide a reason to enact any laws, it provides a reason for any legislator with some antecedent reason to enact a law to do certain things to introduce the bill to the legislature and to secure a majority vote. Such a norm is thus fairly characterized as conditionally or hypothetically normative.

In this respect, such a recognition norm resembles those defining standards for the correct use of words. A norm that requires that "bachelor" be used only to refer to unmarried men provides no reason whatsoever to use the term; there are many words I will never use despite my knowing the semantic norms that define the correct application conditions. But insofar as I have an antecedent reason to use some word *correctly*, the norms that accurately state the application-conditions for the word give rise to a reason to use the word in a manner that conforms to those conditions. The semantic norm that prescribes using the term "bachelor" only to refer to unmarried men gives me no reason ever to use the word "bachelor," but it does give me a conditional reason to conform my use of the term to that norm—at least when I want to use the term correctly in order to communicate some thought. Both semantic norms and recognition norms defining powers are conditionally normative in precisely the same way because both explicitly make normative certain existence conditions.

A rule of recognition is likely to be comprised of a number of recognition norms that specifically define either how officials of the system must be selected (e.g., by election or lineage) or how official functions of various types (e.g., legislative, judicial, and executive) must be performed with respect to recognizing, applying, and enforcing valid legal norms. We can call the former Selection Norms and the latter Substantive Norms. The general form of each can be expressed as follows:

Selection Norm Schema: To count as an official of some type (legislative, judicial, or executive), selection of that person *must* be preceded by the occurrence of social facts, *F1, F2, . . . , Fn.*

Substantive Norm Schema: To be legally authoritative, officials (i.e. those persons who satisfy the relevant Selection Norm) *must* conform their legislative, judicial, and executive acts to conditions *C1, C2, . . . , Cm.*

Both the Selection Norm and Substantive Norm Schemas define powers and duties that are associated with recognizing, applying, and enforcing law and can be expressed in the form of a norm that is, by nature, purportedly normative and that can be subjectively, intersubjectively, and objectively normative. To properly select an official, the selecting agency must behave such as to ensure the occurrence of the social facts *F1, F2, . . . , Fn.* To ensure that an official act with respect to recognizing, applying, and enforcing valid law is authoritative, she must ensure that her behavior conforms to the social conditions expressed by *C1, C2, . . . , Cm.* Accordingly, the rule of recognition, which is comprised of all the various selection and substantive norms practiced by officials of the system, derives its purported, intersubjective, and subjective normativity from the purported, subjective, and intersubjective normativity of all the selection and substantive norms that fully comprise its content. Unlike the criteria of validity, then, the rule of recognition has the logical resources in the form of incorporated deontic notions—such as is picked out by the term "must" in the above schemas—to define and express duties.

Insofar as the purely descriptive criteria of validity for a society must be extrapolated from the rule of recognition that is accepted and practiced by officials, the recognition norm is metaphysically basic while the criteria of validity are derived from the recognition norm. In this respect, the relationship between the two parallels the relationship between a semantic norm that defines the application-conditions for using a word and the lexical definition of a word; it is the convergence of a community of speakers on satisfying a semantic norm that defines the descriptive criteria for applying the word and, so to speak, brings into existence the thing to which the relevant word applies. Likewise, it is the convergence of officials on satisfying a rule of recognition that defines the descriptive criteria of validity and brings valid law into existence in a system where citizens generally conform their behavior to norms validated by the rule of recognition.

3. Inclusive legal positivism

The Separability Thesis asserts that it is conceptually possible for a legal system to have criteria of validity that do not include any moral norms constraining the content of what counts as valid law in that system; that is, it asserts that there is a conceptually possible legal system in which the criteria of validity are exhausted by considerations having to do with the source and manner in which a norm is recognized or promulgated as law. In such a legal system, it is neither a necessary nor a sufficient condition for a norm to be legally valid that its content satisfies some set of moral norms.

In contrast, the Incorporation Thesis asserts that it is conceptually possible for a legal system to have criteria of validity that include moral constraints on the content of valid law in the system. The Incorporation Thesis implies, then, that there is a conceptually possible legal system in which the criteria of validity are *not* exhausted by considerations having to do with the source of a norm or the manner in which it is recognized, applied, or enforced as law. In such a legal system, whether a norm counts as valid depends, at least in part, on its moral merit.[5]

There are a number of different claims that one might associate with the Incorporation Thesis:

(1) it is conceptually possible for there to be a legal system in which officials converge in *believing* they are practicing a norm that requires them to recognize, apply, and enforce as valid law only properly promulgated norms that satisfy certain moral standards;

(2) it is conceptually possible for there to be a legal system in which officials converge in *actually* practicing a norm that requires them to recognize, apply, and enforce as valid law only properly promulgated norms that satisfy certain moral standards; and

(3) it is conceptually possible for there to be a legal system in which officials converge in practicing a recognition norm that succeeds in incorporating moral criteria of validity.

The first is a claim about what is possible for officials to *believe* about the recognition norm they are practicing; that is, the first is a claim about whether officials can believe they are practicing a recognition norm that defines moral

[5] There are two ways in which the validity of a norm *could* depend on the moral merit of its content. First, it might be a sufficient condition in a legal system for a norm to be legally valid that it reproduces the content of some moral norm. In this case, a norm would be valid wholly in virtue of the moral merit of its content—and not even partly in virtue of having its source in some authoritative act of promulgation. Second, it might be a necessary condition in a legal system for a norm to be legally valid that its content be consistent with some set of moral norms. In this case, morality would function as a constraint on legislative or judicial authority to promulgate law by enactment or declaration in the course of adjudication.

The relevant logical relation will generally differ depending on whether moral merit is a necessary or sufficient condition for validity. While the relevant relation with respect to necessary conditions will usually be the consistency relation, the relevant notion with respect to sufficient conditions will usually be the conformity relation. One could not plausibly use the consistency relation in expressing sufficient conditions because it would validate inconsistent norms; there are many propositions *P* such that *P* and *~P* are each consistent with morality. A law that requires drivers to drive on the right side of the road is no less consistent with morality than a law that requires drivers to drive on the left side. Likewise, as a practical matter, one could not plausibly use the conformity relation in expressing necessary conditions because it would result in too few norms—at least in modern legal systems like ours. Many laws are intended as solutions to coordination problems and hence do not reproduce the content of some moral norm.

This should not be construed to imply that it is conceptually impossible for a system to make it a necessary condition for a properly promulgated norm to count as valid law that it reproduces the content of a moral standard. If officials properly promulgate the minimum content of the natural law and the peace is largely kept in the resulting system, then it arguably constitutes a legal system. The point here is not that such a system is conceptually impossible; it is that it is not likely to be practicable in worlds like ours given the features of our psychology and the features of the world of scarcity in which we live.

constraints on the content of valid law. The second is a claim about what is possible for officials to *do* with respect to the moral quality of the recognition norm they are practicing; that is, the second is a claim about whether officials can converge on *correctly* applying some standard that purports to define moral constraints on the content of valid law. The third is a claim about whether it is conceptually possible for there to be a legal system in which officials practice a recognition norm that succeeds in defining moral criteria of validity; that is, the third claim is just another way of expressing the Incorporation Thesis.

Claims (1) and (2) are logically independent. Claim (1) does not imply claim (2). Officials might believe they are practicing a recognition norm that requires them to recognize, apply, and enforce as valid law only properly promulgated norms that satisfy certain moral standards but be mistaken because their practices are so patently immoral that they could not plausibly be described as conforming to standards that are moral in character; in this case, officials know which recognition norm they are practicing but are mistaken about its moral quality.

Conversely, claim (2) does not imply claim (1). Officials might in fact be practicing a recognition norm that requires them to recognize, apply, and enforce as valid law only properly promulgated norms that satisfy certain moral standards without believing that the relevant standards are moral in character; in this case, they are practicing a norm that incorporates moral standards as criteria of validity without realizing that the relevant standards are moral in character. Since the relevant beliefs and actions of officials can come apart in both directions, claims (1) and (2) are logically independent.

Claims (1) and (3)—i.e. the Incorporation Thesis—are also logically independent. Claim (1) does not imply claim (3). The claim that officials *believe* they are practicing a recognition norm that requires them to recognize, apply, and enforce as valid law only properly promulgated norms that conform to certain moral standards does not logically imply the claim that the recognition norms succeed in incorporating moral criteria of validity. Officials could believe they are practicing a recognition norm that implicates certain moral standards when the recognition norm they are practicing fails to incorporate moral criteria because they are mistaken in believing the relevant standards are standards of morality.

Conversely, claim (3) does not imply claim (1). The claim that the recognition norms officials are practicing incorporate moral criteria of validity does not logically imply the claim that officials *believe* that the recognition norm they are practicing requires them to recognize, apply, and enforce only properly promulgated laws that satisfy standards that are moral in character. Officials could mistakenly believe that the recognition norm they are practicing does not implicate standards that are moral in character when that norm does implicate such standards and succeeds in incorporating them into the criteria of validity of the system. What officials believe about whether they are practicing a norm that implicates moral standards in the relevant way is logically independent of whether the norm they are practicing succeeds in incorporating moral criteria of validity into the system.

In contrast, claims (2) and (3) are not logically independent. It is helpful to note that claim (3) logically implies claim (2), on a positivist theory of law, because it is not possible for there to be a legal system with moral criteria of validity unless officials succeed in practicing a recognition norm that defines moral constraints on the content of law; the criteria of validity in every conceptually possible legal system are fully determined, on a positivist theory, by the convergent practices of officials with respect to what they recognize, apply, and enforce as law.

But claim (2) does not obviously logically imply claim (3). And the problem here is not just the one mentioned above, namely that officials might have objectively mistaken beliefs about the moral quality of their official actions. The problem, rather, is that the existence of moral criteria of validity might be inconsistent with some feature thought to be a conceptually necessary property of a legal system, such as a claim to legitimate authority. If so, then the claim that officials in an institutional normative system converge in practicing a recognition norm that requires them to treat as valid legal norms only norms satisfying some moral principle does not imply the claim that the criteria of validity in that system incorporate moral constraints on the content of law. Officials could succeed in *practicing* a recognition norm that defines moral constraints on the content of valid norms but that nonetheless fails to actually incorporate moral criteria of *legal* validity because such a system would lack some conceptually necessary feature of a legal system.

Assuming that the possibility of moral criteria of validity is incompatible with some conceptually necessary feature of a legal system, there are two ways to characterize an institutional normative system in which officials practice a recognition norm that putatively defines moral constraints on the content of valid law. It might be that the system is not properly characterized as a legal system because it fails to instantiate some conceptually necessary feature of a legal system. Alternatively, it might be that the system is a legal system but that the criteria of validity are best characterized, despite the beliefs of officials, as exclusively source-based in character because the system instantiates all the conceptually necessary features of a legal system thought to be inconsistent with the existence of moral criteria of validity.

In essence, the Incorporation Thesis asserts that there are conceptually possible legal systems in which the legal validity of a norm depends on the moral merits of its content. To say that there is a conceptually possible legal system with moral criteria of validity is simply to say that there is a conceptually possible legal system in which the properties that distinguish valid legal norms from other norms and that constitute a norm as legally valid include whether a norm satisfies some specified moral standard. In such systems, the validity of a norm depends on the moral merit of its content.

Exclusive positivists deny the Incorporation Thesis and instead hold the Sources Thesis, according to which it is a conceptual truth that the existence and content of law are fully determined by social sources. If the Sources Thesis is true, then the criteria of validity are fully defined in terms of criteria having to do with a norm's being properly promulgated by an authorized official act. It follows, then, that it is not conceptually possible to have content-based criteria of validity of any kind. Since the only possible criteria of validity, on the Sources Thesis, are those that define certain procedures for manufacturing law, the Sources Thesis implies that the Incorporation Thesis is false.

Even so, it is important to note that the Sources Thesis is *not* logically equivalent to the negation of the Incorporation Thesis. While, as just shown above, it is true that the Sources Thesis implies the negation of the Incorporation Thesis, it is not true that the negation of the Incorporation Thesis implies the Sources Thesis. The negation of the Incorporation Thesis implies that there are no conceptually possible legal systems with content-based constraints on what counts as valid law that are *moral* in character, but the Sources Thesis implies that there can be no content-based constraints *of any kind* on what counts as valid law. Thus, the Sources Thesis and the Incorporation Thesis are mutually exclusive but not jointly exhaustive with respect to what kinds of criteria of validity are conceptually possible for a legal system.

Although the Sources Thesis is typically expressed in terms of a norm's having the appropriate sources, it is more perspicuously expressed in terms of certain procedural constraints. To say that a norm is valid in virtue of its source is to say something about the procedures by which the *appropriate* officials recognize or promulgate it as law. To say that all and only commands of a sovereign are law is to indicate a required source (i.e. that the norm must originate with the sovereign) and a procedural constraint (i.e. the norm must be commanded by the sovereign). Insofar as the notion of an appropriate source can be understood in terms of authority conferred by something that can roughly be characterized as procedural, the Sources Thesis is better understood as claiming that the only possible criteria of validity are those having to do with the procedures by which a norm is recognized, applied, and enforced, which would include procedures for selecting the appropriate officials. The only possible criteria of validity, on the Sources Thesis, are those that define certain procedures for manufacturing law *and* for selecting persons authorized to do so.

Either way, exclusive positivists do not—and need not—deny either claim (1) or (2) above. It should be clear, to begin, that exclusive positivism has nothing to say whatsoever about the issue, addressed by claim (1), of whether it is conceptually possible for officials to *believe* that they are practicing a recognition norm that requires them to recognize, apply, or enforce as valid law only norms that are consistent with some set of moral requirements—or whether it is possible, for that matter, for officials to have the more explicitly theoretical but related belief that they are practicing a rule of recognition that incorporates moral criteria of validity. Although there is no plausible reason to doubt that it is possible for officials to have either belief, there is nothing in any conceptual theory of law that would have anything to say about what kinds of beliefs an official could have about such matters.

Nor does exclusive positivism entail a position with respect to the issue addressed by claim (2) of whether it is conceptually possible for officials to converge on practicing a recognition norm that requires them to recognize, apply, and enforce as valid laws only norms that satisfy certain moral standards. For example, the officials of a legal system might converge in recognizing, applying, and treating as valid law only those properly promulgated norms that satisfy certain moral standards of justice. What an exclusive positivist must deny is that these recognition practices succeed in establishing conformity to some moral standard as a necessary or sufficient condition for a norm to count as a valid law of the system. It might be true that exclusive positivists typically deny claim (2) but, strictly speaking, the Sources Thesis, like the Incorporation Thesis, is agnostic with respect to the issues addressed by claim (1) and claim (2).

What the exclusive positivist denies is claim (3) that it is conceptually possible for a legal system to have moral criteria of validity, which is the distinguishing thesis of inclusive positivism. On this view, the only conceptually possible criteria of legal validity consist exclusively of source-based considerations having to do with the procedures by which officials are selected and the procedural norms to which they must conform in executing their powers and duties in making, changing, and adjudicating valid law. Although the exclusive positivist view precludes all types of content-based criteria of validity, it directly engages the Incorporation Thesis insofar as a moral constraint on the content of valid law is also a content-based constraint on the content of valid law. The Sources Thesis is fairly, if not fully, characterized in terms of denying the Incorporation Thesis.

The claim that it is conceptually impossible for a *legal* system to have moral criteria of (legal) validity, again, does not imply that it is conceptually impossible for an institutional normative system of *some other kind* to have moral criteria of (institutional) validity. Since, by its own terms, the Incorporation Thesis is limited to stating a thesis concerning what is conceptually possible for an institutional normative system that counts as a system of *law*, its negation is limited to stating a thesis about the existence conditions only for legal systems. The Sources Thesis is a thesis that is limited by its own terms to the existence conditions for systems *of law*.

Exclusive positivism, as will be discussed below, denies the conceptual possibility of a legal system with moral criteria of validity on the ground that any institutional normative system with content-based criteria of validity lacks some conceptually necessary feature of a legal system. Chapters 4, 5, and 6 consider the argument that the existence of content-based criteria of (legal) validity is inconsistent with the nature and justification of authority. Chapter 7 considers the argument that an institutional normative system with moral criteria of (institutional) validity is incapable of guiding subject behavior in a way that it must be able to do in order to count as a legal system. Chapter 8, the final chapter of this volume, provides a positive argument for the Incorporation Thesis by defining a model of an institutional normative system validating all and only mandatory moral norms that satisfies every condition that is plausibly thought conceptually necessary for the existence of a legal system.

4

Inclusive Positivism and the Arguments from Authority

All positivists accept the Separability Thesis, according to which there can be legal systems *without* moral criteria of validity, but positivists disagree on whether there can be legal systems *with* moral criteria of validity. Exclusive positivists hold that it is not conceptually possible for there to be a legal system with moral criteria of validity; on this view, the criteria of validity in every conceptually possible legal system are exhausted by considerations having to do with how and by whom norms are promulgated. Inclusive positivists accept the Incorporation Thesis, according to which there is a conceptually possible legal system with moral criteria of validity; in such a legal system, the properties that constitute a norm as legally valid include properties having to do with whether its content satisfies certain moral standards.

Critics of inclusive positivism argue that the conceptual possibility of moral criteria of validity is inconsistent with the nature and justification of practical authority. On this line of reasoning, the possibility of moral criteria of validity is inconsistent with law's conceptual claim to authority because an institutional normative system with moral criteria of validity is incapable of instantiating all the conceptually necessary features of authority. Joseph Raz argues that an institutional normative system with moral criteria of validity cannot be legitimately authoritative because the norms of such a system cannot replace the judgments of its subjects in their practical deliberations about what they should do and hence cannot be legitimate.

This chapter explores the various tensions that might be thought to arise between the Incorporation Thesis and practical authority. It begins with a general discussion of the differences between practical and epistemic authority. It then articulates the various theses associated with the so-called service conception of authority and concludes with a summary of the arguments for the claim that this conception of authority is inconsistent with the Incorporation Thesis (henceforth the "Arguments from Authority").

1. Epistemic and practical authority

There are two kinds of authority: epistemic and practical authority. *P* has *epistemic authority* over *Q* with respect to a proposition *x* if and only if *P* sincerely asserting that *x* is true is a reason for *Q* to believe that *x* is true. An example of an epistemic authority with respect to cancer would be an oncologist; an oncologist sincerely informing a patient that she has cancer provides the patient with a new reason to believe she has cancer. In contrast, *P* has *practical authority* over *Q* with respect to the performance of an act *x* if and only if *P* sincerely directing *Q* to perform *x* provides *Q* with a reason to do *x*. An example of a practical authority would be a police officer; a police officer's directive to drive slower provides the driver with a new reason to drive slower.

These two forms of authority are logically independent of each other. The claim that *P* has practical authority over *Q* does not imply that *P* has epistemic authority with respect to *Q* over the domain of relevant propositions; a police officer might still have practical authority over someone who knows better what the relevant traffic laws and considerations of public safety require drivers to do. Conversely, the claim that *P* has epistemic authority with respect to *Q* does not imply that *P* has practical authority over *Q* over the domain of relevant propositions; a moral theorist might have epistemic authority with respect to what someone is obligated to do, but this does not make her a practical authority with respect to what she is obligated to do.

It is true, of course, that if *P* is an epistemic authority with respect to what *Q* is *obligated to do, P*'s expressed judgments about what *Q* is obligated to do will give *Q* a reason to *believe* what *P* has *claimed Q* should do, but those judgments do not, simply in virtue of being expressed by *P*, provide *Q* with a new reason to *do* what *P* has claimed *Q* is obligated to do. An attorney correctly informing me that I am legally obligated to pay a $100 fine does not give me a new reason to pay the fine; whatever reason I have to pay the fine is fully determined by the content of the applicable legal norms. The two forms of authority, as well as the reasons to which they give rise, are sufficiently different in character that there are no obvious logical connections between them; reasons to believe and reasons for action do not bear any obvious relationships of logical entailment to one another.

The foregoing gestures in the direction of an important similarity with respect to the character of the reasons that each form of authority provides. Although different with respect to the type of reasons they provide, both kinds of authority provide reasons that are content-independent in the following sense: it is the source—and *not* the content—of the directive that provides the subject with a new reason. The reason to believe that the oncologist's opinion provides is content-independent; had the oncologist sincerely asserted that the patient does not have cancer, that would be a reason for the patient to believe she does not have cancer, as it is the oncologist's expertise that makes her opinion trustworthy, and not the content of her opinion. Likewise, the new reason for action that the police officer's directive provides is content-independent; had the police officer directed the driver to drive faster, that would be a new reason to drive faster, as it is the police officer's status as a practical authority that makes her directive binding, and not the content of the directive.

Contrast this with the reasons that moral norms would provide if morality is objective. It is the content of the norm that it is wrong to intentionally harm innocent persons that provides a reason not to intentionally harm innocent persons—and not the source. Even if objectively true moral norms have a source in divine promulgation, the content of those norms would still provide reasons to comply with them. If the norm that it is wrong to intentionally harm innocent persons has an authoritative source that gives rise to a source-based reason to comply, the content of the norm would also give rise to a reason not to intentionally harm innocent persons—namely, that it is wrong to do so. Objective moral norms are the kind of thing, if anything is, that provide content-based reasons to conform one's behavior to those norms.

There is a conceptual issue as to whether, on the ordinary usages with which this volume is concerned, a proposition can be authoritative in virtue of its content. On the one hand, the notion of having authority—and hence the notion of being authoritative—seems conceptually connected to the notion of having an author in virtue of the two terms being etymologically related: only norms that have an *author* can have *author*ity or be *author*itative. If so, the norms of an objective morality, assuming they lack an author, would be binding and would provide content-independent reasons for action *without* being authoritative.

On the other hand, ordinary usage seems to permit characterizing binding norms as authoritative even if they are not grounded in the directives of some personal practical authority. It is not utterly counterintuitive to distinguish, as some philosophers of religion have, between the authority of reason and the authority of faith; if it is true that the authority of faith is source-based, the authority of reason is not. Whether a norm has authority in virtue of being derivable from reason—and not in virtue of having an appropriate source in an author—would seem to depend on whether its content is authoritative. Similarly, it does not seem implausible, as far as ordinary usage goes, to characterize the norms of an objective morality as authoritative, regardless of whether they have an author since mandatory moral norms function the same way that any other authoritative norm does.

The reported lexical meanings seem indeterminate with respect to the issue of whether a proposition can be authoritative only if it has a source in the directives of something with practical authority. Merriam-Webster, for example, defines the notion as follows:

Authoritative—1: having, marked by, or proceeding from authority; 2: possessing recognized or evident authority: clearly accurate or knowledgeable.[1]

Whereas the first definition seems to suggest that a norm or proposition can be authoritative only in virtue of having a source, the second seems to allow for the possibility that a norm can be authoritative if its content is clearly accurate. The lexical meanings thus appear consistent with the possibility of norms that are authoritative in virtue of source and with the possibility of norms that are authoritative in virtue of content.

Either way, the notions of epistemic authority and practical authority seem to function differently with respect to propositions. If propositions can be either epistemically or practically authoritative, the considerations that determine whether a proposition is epistemically authoritative will be different from those that determine whether a proposition is practically authoritative for the following reason: a proposition can give rise to a reason for action solely in virtue of its content but cannot give rise to a reason for belief solely in virtue of its content. The content of the proposition expressed by "it is morally wrong to set living human infants on fire" would appear to provide a reason to refrain from setting living human infants on fire; the fact that it is wrong to set living human infants on fire, by itself, provides a reason not to do so. In contrast, the content of the proposition expressed by "2 + 2 = 4" does not appear to provide a reason to believe it; the fact that the sum of 2 and 2 is 4 does not, by itself, appear to provide a reason to believe that 2 + 2 = 4; otherwise, we would have a reason to believe every proposition that is true simply in virtue of its being true.

One might think that the self-evident quality of the proposition expressed by "2 + 2 = 4" is what gives rise to its epistemic authority but that has more to do with the abilities of rational knowers than with any inherent quality of the content. The claim that a proposition is self-evidently true merely asserts that its truth can reliably be discerned from a cursory inspection of its content

[1] "Authoritative," *Merriam-Webster Online Dictionary*; available at: https://www.merriam-webster.com/dictionary/authoritative. The notion of authority being defined should be construed, given that it is a general definition of "authoritative," as the general one of which epistemic authority and practical authority are subspecies.

by a rational agent with certain abilities; however, the fact that its truth can be discerned in such a manner is not enough by itself to make the proposition epistemically authoritative for any *particular agent.* That some particular agent has, in fact, reliably discerned from a cursory inspection of its content that the truth of the proposition is self-evident might make that proposition epistemically authoritative *for her*, but it would not make the proposition authoritative for any person who has not discerned its self-evidence.

There is another important way in which the notion of authority seems to apply differently in epistemic contexts than it does in practical contexts. The directives of practical authority bind subjects in the sense that they create an obligation on the part of subjects to conform their behavior to the requirements of the authority as expressed in its directives. This obligation might be moral in character, but it need not be. The authoritative rules of a chess club, for example, bind in virtue of defining an obligation to comply that is institutional, rather than moral, in character. It might also be true, of course, that the directives of a chess club are morally obligatory but the obligation to which its directives give rise in virtue of having an authoritative source in the chess club is institutional. The precise character of the relevant type of institutional obligation and the mechanism by which it binds are not clear but there is no obvious *prima facie* reason to think that it is a conceptual truth that authoritative directives of every kind create or purport to create moral obligations.

The capacity to create obligations distinguishes the directives of a practical authority from the opinions of an epistemic authority. It is commonly thought that legitimate (or morally justified) practical authorities have the capacity to bind subjects by providing reasons in the form of a moral obligation to comply. If one can freely choose one's acts, then one can freely choose to act, other things being equal, in a manner that conforms to the relevant moral obligation. Of course, it might not be true that we freely choose our acts; however, the idea that our behavior is conditioned by choices that are responsive to reasons is presumptively plausible insofar as it conforms to our experience of ourselves.

In contrast, the idea that epistemic authority gives rise to reasons that *obligate* the subject cannot be reconciled with our experience with respect to belief formation. Consider, for example, the proposition expressed by "2 + 2 = 5." There is nothing I could do to make myself genuinely *believe* that proposition. There are many acts I could *perform* with respect to that proposition: I could balance my checkbook adding 2 to 2 as if the sum were 5; I could tell people that this proposition is true; perhaps I could even make an effort to bring it about somehow that I come to believe it is true. But one thing I cannot do is bring it about that I believe that 2 + 2 = 5 merely by choosing to believe it. My belief that the sum of 2 and 2 is 4, and not 5, is not a matter of choice.

The same is true of propositions that are not necessarily true. There is nothing I could do to bring it about that, despite the sun shining brightly through my window as I write this sentence, I believe it is now raining outside. What I believe is conditioned by how the evidence strikes me; while I can freely choose to seek out evidence that confirms what I want to believe and to avoid evidence that disconfirms what I want to believe, how the evidence strikes me is not within my direct volitional control. Insofar as it is clear that we do not choose what to believe, we cannot be obligated to believe any particular proposition. The idea that epistemic authority can give rise to an obligation of any kind simply does not cohere with certain obvious facts of our experience.

Nevertheless, if it makes sense to think that we have obligations to believe that are epistemic in character, there is an important respect in which these obligations would differ from other paradigmatic forms of obligation: practical obligations are almost always owed to other people, but it is implausible to think that one owes an obligation to believe what an epistemic authority says. Suppose, for example, that a patient, for whatever reason, does not believe her oncologist's opinion that she has cancer. It might make sense to characterize her as irrational, although even that seems too strong. But it seems implausible to characterize her as having wronged the oncologist by violating some sort of obligation she has to believe the oncologist's opinions.

This is not to say that the notion of obligation has no application with respect to issues of what or whom we should believe; it is rather to say that the notion of obligation, assuming that the same notion applies in both contexts, has different properties when applied in the context of theoretical rationality (i.e. epistemically) than when applied in the context of practical rationality. Insofar as the concepts of authority and obligation are conceptually linked across all contexts, this is enough to show that an opinion from an epistemic authority would function quite differently in a subject's reasoning than a directive by a practical authority.

While it is nevertheless true that the notion of epistemic authority is relevant in addressing many issues that arise in connection with law, the concept of authority that figures most prominently in law is that of practical authority. Law is not primarily contrived, by nature, to create epistemic obligations or reasons to believe something. Law is primarily contrived, by nature, to regulate behavior by issuing directives that create practical obligations that provide new reasons to do what the directives require. It might be true that the law must ensure that people know what the law requires to be efficacious, but that function is subordinate to, and derives from, its primary function of creating new reasons to do certain things. Insofar as law has an epistemic function by its nature, the epistemic function is secondary to its practical function of regulating the outward expression of certain mental states in the form of acts or behaviors.

2. Practical authority as grounded in a claim of right

Practical authority is typically, if not as a matter of conceptual necessity, asserted or exercised under a claim of *right* of some kind; that is, practical authority is characteristically grounded in, or justified by, some sort of right on the part of the authority to tell the subject what to do. The right that grounds a claim to, or exercise of, authority might be moral in character, as in the case of parental authority, or it might be legal in character, as in the case of the authority of the police to order me to park my car elsewhere.

The fact that practical authority is asserted under a claim of right explains why authoritative directives obligate the subject. Insofar as practical authority regulates the behavior of subjects by means of directives issued under some claim of right, authoritative directives obligate subjects in some sense that depends on the character of the right claimed by the authority. If a person's authority over another is grounded in a legal right, then directives that fall within the scope of that authority will create a legal obligation on the part of the latter to comply. If, in contrast, a person's authority over another is grounded in a moral right, then directives that fall within the scope of that authority will create a moral obligation on the part of the latter to comply. It would be hard to make sense of the idea that I have a legal/moral right to tell you what you *must* do with respect to doing p if my directive that you do p did not bind you by creating a legal/moral obligation to do p.

The directives of practical authority hence purport, at least, to provide the kind of reasons generally associated with obligations, but the strength of the reasons will depend on what grounds the relevant claim of authority. Insofar as one person's practical authority over another is grounded in a claim of legal right, the novel reasons to which her directives give rise will be of the sort to which legal obligations give rise; insofar as one person's practical authority over another is grounded in a claim of moral right, the novel reasons to which her directives give rise will be of the sort to which moral obligations give rise. If moral obligations trump conflicting legal obligations, the directives of a moral authority will win over the directives of a merely legal authority in cases where they conflict.

The claim of right that entitles a practical authority *P* to tell *Q* what she must do allows *P* to direct *Q*'s behavior only within certain largely determinable limits. *P*'s authority over *Q* might be general in the sense that *P*'s claim of right embodies a wide range of behaviors and contexts within which *Q*'s behavior is subject to being regulated by the former; the political authority of a legislature might be an example of such general authority. In contrast, *P*'s authority over *Q* might be limited with respect to both behaviors and contexts; a teacher's practical authority over a student is limited to what goes on in the classroom during school hours and is limited with respect to what she can require of students during those hours.

3. Power, *de facto* authority, legitimate authority, and law

Raz distinguishes between *de facto* authority and legitimate authority (or authority per se). A *de facto* authority "either claims to be legitimate or is believed to be so, and is effective in imposing its will on many over whom it claims authority."[2] Not every *de facto* authority is legitimate; some practical authorities might claim legitimacy without being legitimate, as is the case with corrupt totalitarian regimes that systematically violate the moral rights of citizens. A *de facto* authority, on Raz's view, is *legitimate*—or is an authority per se—when either its claim that it has legitimate authority is true or, what comes to the same thing, its subjects' beliefs that it has legitimate authority is true.

The notion of legitimacy is concerned with the moral justification of practical authority. To say that a practical authority is legitimate is to say that the authority is morally justified in issuing directives that tell subjects what to do. As Raz puts the point:

> [Authorities] claim ... a right [to rule], i.e. they are *de facto* authorities because they claim a right to rule as well as because they succeed in establishing and maintaining their rule. *They have legitimate authority only if and to the extent that their claim is justified.*[3]

The relevant form of justification is *moral* justification: "If [a legal system] lacks the moral attributes required to endow it with legitimate authority then

[2] Joseph Raz, *Ethics in the Public Domain* (Oxford: Oxford University Press, 1994), 211. Hereinafter *EPD*.

[3] Joseph Raz, *The Morality of Freedom* (Oxford: Oxford University Press, 1988), 26; emphasis added. Hereinafter *MF*.

it has none .... To claim authority it must be ... a system of a kind which is capable in principle of possessing the requisite moral properties of authority" (*EPD* 215). A legitimate practical authority is, then, one that is morally justified in "imposing its will" on subjects by issuing directives that tell them what they must do.

Both *de facto* authority and legitimate authority should be distinguished from *power*. A person can have power over another person without having either *de facto* or legitimate authority. *P* can be a *de facto* authority over *Q* only insofar as *P* either claims legitimate authority over *Q* or is generally accepted as a legitimate authority in the relevant community. All that is needed for *P* to have power over *Q* is that *P* has some reliable means for coercively inducing *Q* to comply with *P*'s commands. Someone who points a loaded gun at me and demands my money has power over me but does not have *de facto* authority over me.

The notions of having *de facto* authority and having power are logically independent. To begin, if someone has the kind of compromising information on me that could, if disclosed, result in my being incarcerated for an extended period of time, then, in the absence of some sort of claim of right to direct my behavior, that person has power over me without having *de facto* authority. Conversely, assuming that the one can be effective in "imposing one's will" over another person without having a reliable means to coercively induce her to do what one directs, a person can have *de facto* authority over another person without having power over that person. If, for example, I accept as an authority someone with no reliable coercive means of inducing me to comply with her directives because I believe she has legitimate authority over me, she has *de facto* authority over me without having power.

Similar things can be said about the relationship between power and legitimate authority. Assuming, again, that one can be effective in imposing one's will over another person without having a reliable means to coercively induce her to do what one directs, one can have legitimate authority over someone without having power over her, as might be true of someone without any means to coercively induce my compliance whom I accept as an authority and whose commands always accurately express the requirements of right reason. Alternatively, one can have morally legitimate authority with respect to someone over whom one has coercive power. Depending on (1) whether the authority of the U.S. government is legitimate with respect to citizens and (2) whether the enforcement mechanisms authorized for violations of civil and criminal laws rise to the level of being reliably coercive, the U.S. government might be an example of a morally legitimate authority with coercive power over its subjects.

The above shows that it is possible for a legal system to have power, *de facto* authority, and legitimate authority over its subjects. If it is possible for there to be a legitimate legal system with coercive power over its subjects, then it is surely possible for there to be a legitimate legal system with coercive power over its citizens that is believed by subjects to be legitimate.

Although it is clear that there can be a legal system that has *de facto* authority without having morally legitimate authority, there is a question as to whether there can be a morally legitimate authority without *de facto* authority. As Raz defines the notion, a *de facto* authority "either claims to be legitimate or is believed to be so" (*EPD* 211). The question is thus whether there could be a morally justified authority who neither claims to be legitimate nor is believed by subjects to be so.

The answer depends on both moral and conceptual considerations. Consider the role that consent might play in legitimizing practical authority. To begin, if we assume that it is possible, as a matter of political morality, for *P* to have legitimate practical authority over *Q* without *Q* giving meaningful consent, then it would seem that something could be a legitimate authority without also being a *de facto* authority. Suppose that some putative authority, *P*, who succeeds in imposing her will on subjects and does nothing that would imply a *claim* of morally justified authority, satisfies all the moral conditions for being a morally justified authority. Suppose, further, that subjects do not consent to *P*'s authority and do not believe *P*'s authority is morally justified. Then *P* would be an example of someone who has morally legitimate authority without having *de facto* authority.

But if we assume that it is not possible, as a matter of political morality, for *P* to have legitimate practical authority over *Q* unless *Q* gives meaningful consent, then it would appear that it is not possible for something to be a legitimate authority without also being a *de facto* authority. If one cannot give *meaningful* consent to being subject to an authority without believing that the authority is morally legitimate, then there could not be a morally legitimate authority that is not also a *de facto* authority.

The assumption that one cannot give meaningful consent to an authority without believing the authority is legitimate seems reasonable both as a normative matter of morality and as a descriptive matter of human psychology. As a normative moral matter, consent must be meaningful to be effective, and it is reasonable to think that consent is not meaningful in the absence of a minimally informed belief that the authority is legitimate. As a descriptive psychological matter, it seems reasonable to think that, in the absence of duress or other factors that would problematize consent from a moral standpoint, people would not give consent to be subject to an authority unless they believe the authority is legitimate. If so, then there could not be a morally legitimate authority that is not a *de facto* authority—on the assumption that one can have legitimate authority only over subjects who give meaningful consent to authority.

The notion of legitimate authority is both descriptive and evaluative while the notions of power and *de facto* authority are purely descriptive. To determine whether *P* has legitimate authority over *Q*, one must determine whether *P* satisfies the *morally* normative conditions for having *morally* justified authority over *Q*; and this requires an analysis that has both normative and empirically descriptive elements. First, one must identify the appropriate moral norms for evaluating whether a putative authority is legitimate and determine what observable properties a putative authority must have to be legitimate; and both of these tasks require morally normative analysis. Second, one must determine whether the putative authority instantiates the relevant observable properties; and this involves empirically descriptive analysis. If, for example, a morally normative analysis correctly concludes that it is both necessary and sufficient for a putative authority to be legitimate that the subject expresses meaningful consent to the authority, then one will have to determine whether the subject has, as an empirically observable matter, expressed consent and whether that consent is, as a morally normative matter, meaningful.

In contrast, one can determine whether *P* has *de facto* authority over *Q* by purely empirical means. To determine whether *P* has *de facto* authority over *Q*, one must determine whether (1) *P* is generally successful in imposing her will on *Q*; (2) *P* claims legitimate authority over *Q*; and (3) *Q* believes that *P* has legitimate authority over *Q*. If (1) is true and either (2) or (3) is true, then *P* has *de facto* authority over *Q*.

But notice that one can determine whether each of these conditions is true by purely empirical means. Whether, first, *P* is generally successful in imposing her will on *Q* can be determined by empirical means that require determining whether *Q*'s behavior generally conforms to *P*'s commands. Whether, second, *P* claims legitimate authority over *Q* can be addressed by empirical means that require determining whether any of *P*'s behaviors imply a claim of legitimate authority. Whether, third, *Q* believes that *P* has legitimate authority over *Q* can be determined by asking *Q*, assuming *Q* answers sincerely. Since the satisfaction of each of these three conditions can be determined by purely empirical means, the issue of whether one person has *de facto* authority over another person is purely descriptive.

Similarly, the issue of whether *P* has power over *Q* is purely descriptive. To determine whether *P* has power over *Q*, one must determine whether a number of empirically observable conditions are satisfied. One must determine whether (1) *P* issues directives to *Q*; (2) whether *Q* generally complies with these directives; (3) whether *P* has a means of coercing *Q* to comply with

P's directives and is willing to use these means, if necessary, to secure *Q*'s compliance; and (4) whether *Q* is inclined to comply with *P*'s directives, when otherwise disinclined to do so, solely to avoid the application of such coercive means by *P*. Since whether each of these conditions have been satisfied can be determined by purely empirical means, the issue of whether one person has power over another person is a purely descriptive issue.

4. Conceptual relations between law and authority

As a conceptual matter, legal systems are authoritative in the minimal sense that they issue directives in the form of mandatory legal norms that tell people what they must do and that are treated by officials of the system as binding against subjects. These mandatory legal norms might be categorical as with the norms of the criminal law, which tell people what they must not do regardless of any desires they might have; these norms are categorical in the sense that they purport to provide reasons for action that are not conditional on other reasons the subject might have. Alternatively, they might be hypothetical as with the norms of contract law, which tell people what they must do to create a contract that can be enforced by the court; these norms are hypothetical in the sense that they purport to provide reasons that are conditional on other reasons that a subject might or might not have.

Valid legal norms tell subjects what they must do, whether categorically or hypothetically, and thereby define obligations that are treated by officials of the system as binding. Valid legal norms might sometimes seem merely to encourage certain behaviors but even in those cases they define legal obligations. A law giving a tax break to those who purchase automobiles with optional emissions-reduction technologies defines obligations on the part of officials to honor the promised reduction in taxes. While it might be conceptually possible for a legal norm merely to encourage an act, legal systems do not typically trade in norms that encourage some act; they characteristically trade in norms that require acts.

Similarly, the rule of recognition that regulates official behavior is also authoritative in the sense that it tells officials what they *must* do to make, apply, and enforce law and is treated by officials as binding them. It seems to be a conceptual requirement for the existence of a legal system that the rule of recognition includes some norms that are categorical in character; it is not implausible to think that every conceptually possible legal system must include a norm that requires judges to apply valid legal norms in deciding disputes among citizens. In contrast, it is not obviously a conceptual requirement for the existence of a legal system that the rule of recognition contains some norms that are hypothetical. It might be, if the Incorporation Thesis is true, that there could be a legal system with a rule of recognition that validates all and only mandatory moral norms; these norms would be valid in virtue of content—without formal promulgation or recognition.

But if the Incorporation Thesis is false, it would appear to be a conceptual requirement for the existence of a legal system that the rule of recognition contains some hypothetical norms governing how valid legal norms can be promulgated; if the only criteria of validity are source-based, then all valid legal norms would have to have an authoritative source in official promulgation. Since the relevant recognition norms would have to be hypothetical because norms that merely define the permissible procedures for making valid law cannot provide any reasons for officials to make law, they are capable only of providing conditional reasons that apply to officials with an antecedent desire to make law. Even so, these norms also tell officials what they *must* do provided that they have certain antecedent reasons to recognize, apply, or enforce law.

While it should be clear that it is a conceptual truth that legal systems have something that counts, according to ordinary usage, as practical authority over subjects, it should also be clear that it is *not* a conceptual truth that legal systems have legitimate practical authority over subjects—at least, not on the descriptive concept of a legal system defined by ordinary usage. It is straightforwardly false to think that, on that purely descriptive usage, every law or legal system is morally justified; given that we commonly speak of wicked laws and legal systems, it is clear that ordinary linguistic practices do not require that something be morally justified to count as either a law or a legal system.

The issue of whether a legal system necessarily instantiates power or *de facto* authority is somewhat more complicated. Depending on one's views concerning whether sanctions are a conceptually necessary feature of a legal system, it might or might not be true that legal systems necessarily have power. If, on the one hand, sanctions are not a conceptually necessary feature of a legal system, there could be a legal system that does not have power because, in the absence of available sanctions, it lacks a reliable means to coerce compliance. If, on the other, sanctions are a conceptually necessary feature of a legal system, then it is at least *prima facie* plausible to think that it is a conceptual truth that legal systems have power.

Even so, the claim that a legal system authorizes sanctions as a response to non-compliance does not imply that it has power because it does not imply that those mechanisms are sufficient to reliably coerce compliance. It might be that (1) such mechanisms are inadequate to produce compliance in instances in which people are disposed not to comply; and (2) people in the system are inclined to comply in the vast majority of cases without regard to whether there are sanctions authorized for non-compliance. For this reason, it is probably not true that it is a conceptual truth that legal systems have power—even if it is a conceptual truth that legal systems authorize sanctions for violations of mandatory legal norms.

The issue of whether a legal system has *de facto* authority is similarly nuanced. A legal system has *de facto* authority if and only if (1) it is generally successful in imposing its will on subjects; and either (2) claims legitimate authority over subjects or (3) is believed by subjects to have legitimate authority over them. To begin, it is not entirely clear whether it is a conceptual truth that legal systems are generally successful in "imposing their will" on subjects. It is, of course, a conceptually necessary condition for the existence of a legal system that the behavior of citizens generally satisfies the requirements of valid legal norms, but this does not imply that what explains their conforming behavior is that the legal system is generally successful in imposing its will on them. *P* is accurately characterized as imposing her will on *Q* with respect to doing *r* only insofar as *Q*'s doing *r* is motivated in large measure by it being *P*'s will that *Q* do *r*—at least in instances in which *Q* is inclined to do otherwise. If subjects' conforming behavior is not generally motivated by its being the collective will of the officials that they comply with valid legal requirements, then something could be a legal system without being a *de facto* authority.

But regardless of whether a legal system is properly characterized as generally successful in imposing its will on citizens, it is clear that legal systems exercise practical authority under a claim of right conferred by law insofar as they tell citizens what to do and treat valid legal norms as creating *obligations* on the part of citizens. As far as our ordinary linguistic and legal practices are concerned, this seems so clearly true that no plausible theory of the descriptive concepts of law or authority could deny this on the modest approach to conceptual analysis adopted in this volume.

Further, it is not clear that it is a conceptually necessary condition of a legal system that *either* it claims legitimate authority over subjects *or* is believed by subjects to have legitimate authority over them. Certainly, it is not a conceptually necessary condition for the existence of a legal system that citizens accept it as legitimate. I know, for example, that the U.S. has something properly characterized as a legal system on the relevant usage, but I do not know whether citizens generally believe this system is morally legitimate—or even whether most understand the notion of legitimacy well enough to have a coherent belief about the legitimacy of the U.S. legal system. They might, for all I justifiably believe, or they might not. As far as citizens are concerned, all that is conceptually necessary for the existence of a legal system is that their behavior generally satisfies valid legal norms; it might be that citizens are naturally inclined to refrain from the kinds of socially disruptive acts that are prohibited by the valid legal norms of the system. Accordingly, for the disjunction in the topic sentence of this paragraph to be true, it must be the case that law claims legitimate authority in every conceptually possible legal system *in which citizens do not generally believe* the legal system has legitimate authority over them.

One way this disjunction could be conceptually true is, of course, if either of the disjuncts is conceptually true; as a matter of logic, if *p* is conceptually true, then so is *p* or *q*. If it is true that every conceptually possible legal system claims legitimate authority, then it is trivially true that every conceptually possible legal system either claims legitimate authority or is believed by citizens to have legitimate authority. But if it is not a conceptual truth that law claims legitimate authority in every conceptually possible legal system in which citizens do not generally believe the legal system has legitimate authority over them, then the issue of whether any particular legal system has *de facto* authority is a contingent one that requires empirical investigation to resolve.

This suggests that there might be more to the taxonomy of practical authority than is captured by the notions of *de facto* and legitimate authority. It is clearly a conceptual truth, if ordinary usage is the touchstone, that legal systems *have* something properly characterized as practical authority and that this authority is necessarily legal, as opposed to legitimate, in character. Insofar as it is not a conceptual truth that legal systems have either *de facto* authority or legitimate authority, the concepts of *de facto* authority and legitimate authority do not exhaust the relevant notions of practical authority as they apply to legal systems.

Either way, there is nothing in any of this that seems obviously inconsistent with the possibility of moral criteria of validity. Positivists who reject inclusive positivism believe that the possibility of moral criteria of validity is incompatible with a legal system's having the kind of authority that every legal system can, as a conceptual matter, be presumed to have. Insofar as there is some kind of tension between inclusive positivism and the conceptual claim that law is an authority of some kind, it will have to be found in deeper and more specific commitments with respect to the nature and justification of practical authority, such as are expressed below in the service conception of authority.

5. The service conception of authority

Raz articulates his service conception of authority in the form of several claims about the nature and justification of practical authority. It is these more specific commitments that are thought to be inconsistent with the conceptual possibility of moral criteria of legal validity. Insofar as an institutional normative system has moral criteria of validity, it lacks, according to exclusive positivists, some property that is, according to the service conception, a conceptually necessary element of practical authority. Since it is a conceptual truth that legal systems instantiate practical authority and that institutional normative systems with moral criteria of validity do not, it is not conceptually possible for there to be a legal system with moral criteria of validity.

According to the service conception of authority, the conceptual point or function of authority is to resolve disputes among subjects by determining what they should do in a manner that takes into account and weighs all of the applicable reasons that antecedently apply to the subjects. Otherwise put, the point of authority is to *serve* subjects by deciding for them what they should do given the reasons that apply to them in the relevant situations. Authority serves its subjects by mediating between them and the reasons that antecedently apply to them by providing mandatory directives properly grounded in those reasons.

But to minimally perform this mediating function of authority, an authoritative directive must be capable of *replacing* the subject's assessment of the applicable reasons in her practical deliberations. If it cannot replace the subject's own assessment of the reasons, then the subject must assess them to come to a decision about what she should do. In this case, the directive fails to mediate between the subject and the reasons that apply to her because it does not in any way change the way the subject must think about the reasons; there is simply nothing done by the directive that is plausibly characterized as mediating between the subject and those reasons—or, for that matter, as serving its subjects.

The following, then, expresses a conceptual truth about practical authority, on the service conception of authority:

The Preemption Thesis: The conceptual point of practical authority is to tell subjects what they must do by issuing mandatory directives that can replace the subjects' own assessments of the applicable reasons in their deliberations about what to do.

While the service conception of authority does not imply that authoritative directives must *actually* replace the subjects' judgments in their practical reasoning, it does imply that authoritative directives must *be capable of* replacing their judgments in their practical reasoning. Any directive that cannot replace these judgments cannot do anything that is properly characterized as *serving* subjects by mediating between them and the relevant reasons.

The Preemption Thesis implies that authoritative directives must be capable of providing the subject with a *first-order* reason to do what the authority directs her to do. Insofar as the Preemption Thesis asserts that mandatory authoritative directives must be capable of functioning to replace the subject's own assessments of what right reason requires her to do, they must be capable of providing first-order reasons for action that are of the same kind that the subject's own assessments of the balance of applicable first-order reasons would yield.

Further, authoritative directives must also be capable of providing the subject with a *second-order* reason not to act on her own assessment of the applicable first-order reasons. Insofar as authoritative directives must be capable of precluding subjects from acting on their own assessments of the applicable first-order reasons, they must provide some kind of reason for subjects not to act on their assessments of those reasons. Insofar as they provide a reason for subjects not to act on their own assessments of the applicable first-order reasons, they provide a reason for action that is about reasons and that is hence second-order in character.

There is nothing in the Preemption Thesis that implies that a subject of an authoritative directive is precluded from assessing for herself what the balance of reasons objectively requires her to do; it merely implies that the subject of an authoritative directive may not act on her assessment of the balance of reasons. Preemptive reasons, unlike what Hart calls "peremptory" reasons, do not preclude, or even purport to preclude, a subject from considering what her own assessment of the underlying reasons would require.[4] As far as the Preemption Thesis is concerned, there is nothing in the character of an authoritative directive that would bar subjects from deliberating, debating, or arguing about what the balance of first-order reasons requires of them; an authoritative directive purports, at most, to bar subjects from *acting* on their own assessment of the reasons.[5]

[4] On Hart's view, commands are intended to "cut[] off *deliberation*, debate, or argument" and hence provide second-order *peremptory* reasons that bar subjects from even considering what the balance of first-order reasons require them to do. H.L.A. Hart, *Essays on Bentham* (Oxford: Clarendon Press, 1982), 254.

[5] Raz's claim that it is the nature of authority to issue directives that bar subjects from acting on their own assessments of the balance of relevant first-order reasons seems too strong. There is no reason to think in the case where the subject's assessment of the balance of reasons *agrees* with the authority's assessment that the subject is barred from acting on her assessment when it dictates that she should do what the authority has directed her to do. If I refrain from committing murder only because it is morally wrong and not because it is illegal, I have done nothing to either violate the

Both the first-order and second-order reasons that an authoritative directive purports to provide are content-independent. Propositions that are authoritative in virtue of being directed by a practical authority are authoritative in virtue of source rather than content. Since the normativity of such propositions is thus source-based rather than content-based, the first-order reason to act as the authority prescribes and the second-order reason for the subject not to act on her own judgment of what is required by the balance of first-order reasons are both content-independent. An authoritative proposition purports to bind subjects to do what the proposition directs regardless of what their own assessments of the reasons might yield and regardless of what the proposition directs.

The Preemption Thesis is purely descriptive. It states a thesis about the point or function of practical authority and hence makes no normative claims about authority. To say, for example, that the function of an automobile is to reliably transport people from one place to another place states a purely descriptive claim about an automobile. Knowing the point or function of a thing can help us to determine whether it is a good thing of its kind; an automobile that can, because of its design, transport persons only short distances at very slow speeds is not a good example of its kind. But the idea that one can evaluate the quality of an automobile in terms of how well it performs its function does not entail that statements identifying its function are normative or evaluative. Insofar as the Preemption Thesis merely *describes* the point or function of practical authority, it is purely descriptive.

In contrast, the two remaining theses fleshing out Raz's service conception of authority are normative in character. The first is a normative thesis with respect to the character of the reasons on which an authoritative directive should be based. Given that the point of practical authority is to serve subjects by mediating between them and the reasons that antecedently apply to them, an authority's directives should be grounded in, and reflect, the authority's assessment of what those reasons dictate. Raz expresses this thesis as follows:

The Dependence Thesis: All authoritative directives should be based, among other factors, on reasons which apply to the subjects of those directives and which bear on the circumstances covered by the directives.

The Dependence Thesis expresses a normative claim about how practical authorities should go about performing this mediating function. A practical authority performs this mediating function, in part, by determining *for* the subjects what the balance of relevant reasons dictates with respect to how they

legally authoritative directive prohibiting murder or to impugn the (legal) authority of the officials, system, or norm.

should behave. If the function of authority is to issue directives that provide subjects with both first-order reasons for doing what the authority requires and second-order reasons not to act on their own assessments of the reasons that antecedently apply to them, then the directives of an authority should be based on and reflect the authority's assessment of those reasons as they apply to the subjects. There is no meaningful sense in which an authority could realize this function of *serving* its subjects by *mediating* between them and the reasons that antecedently apply to them if the authority's directives do not reflect the authority's assessment of those reasons.

Though normative, the Dependence Thesis does not express a morally normative claim. Properly construed, the Dependence Thesis does not assert that authoritative directives should, as a matter of political morality, be based on and reflect the authority's assessment of the reasons that antecedently apply to the subjects—although that claim might also be true. The Dependence Thesis expresses a claim that is functionally normative: given that the function of authority is to serve subjects by determining for them what the balance of reasons requires them to do, authoritative directives should be based on and reflect the relevant reasons. While it might also be true that authorities should, as a matter of political morality, base their directives on the balance of the relevant reasons, the point is that authorities could not do what they are supposed to do, given their function, without grounding their directives in an assessment of the reasons that antecedently apply to the subjects. The Dependence Thesis, as Raz intends it, expresses a claim that is functionally normative, as opposed to morally normative.

Similar sorts of functionally normative claims apply to automobiles. Once the function of an automobile is known, it is not difficult to extrapolate claims that purport to explicate what an automobile must do in order to be capable of even minimally performing its function. Given that the function of an automobile is to reliably transport people from one place to another, an automobile's engine must, as a functionally normative matter, be capable of being started. The point here is not that an automobile that cannot be started will not perform its function well; it is rather that an automobile *cannot* perform its function unless it can be started. Both this thesis and the Dependence Thesis state normative claims that are purely functional in character.

Thus construed, the Dependence Thesis expresses a thesis about the nature of authority, and not a thesis about the justification of authority. If a directive that does not reflect the underlying reasons is thereby rendered *incapable* of performing the mediating conceptual function of practical authority, then such a directive is no more plausibly characterized as authoritative than a vehicle that lacks any mechanism to start its engine is plausibly characterized as an automobile. It is part of the nature of an automobile, given its conceptual function, that there is some mechanism by which it can be started. An automobile with a broken starter is a broken automobile but it is still an automobile; something that utterly lacks a mechanism to turn its engine on is not an automobile at all—except in, as Fuller might put it, "the Pickwickian sense in which a void contract is a contract."[6]

The service conception includes not only theses that purport to explicate the *nature* of practical authority; it also includes a thesis about the *justification* of practical authority:

> **The Normal Justification Thesis (NJT):** An authority is justified to the extent that its subjects are more likely to comply with what the balance of reasons requires if they follow the authority's directives than if they follow their own assessments of what the balance of reasons requires.

Practical authority, then, is justified over a subject only insofar as the subject "is likely to better comply with reasons which apply to him (other than the alleged authoritative directives) if he accepts the directives of the alleged authority as authoritatively binding, and tries to follow them, than if he tries to follow the reasons which apply to him directly" (*EPD* 214).

There are a number of observations that should be made here about NJT. First, like the Dependence Thesis, NJT expresses a normative thesis about authority; however, unlike the Dependence Thesis, NJT is *morally* normative in character. Raz characterizes NJT as "a moral thesis about the type of argument which could be used to establish the legitimacy of authority"[7] and locates NJT among other theories of moral legitimacy:

> As John Bell pointed out to me, if there is a common theme to liberal political theorizing on authority it is that the legitimacy of authority rests on the duty to support and uphold just institutions, as, following Rawls, the duty is now called. But that duty is of course dependent on a prior understanding of which institutions are just. The account here offered is meant as a beginning of an answer to that question. (*AJ* 28)

The legitimacy of authority, on Raz's view, turns on whether it has certain moral properties: "If [a legal system] lacks the *moral* attributes required to endow it with legitimate authority then it has none" (*EPD* 215; emphasis added). The Dependence Thesis, construed to express a morally normative thesis, might also be true of authority but is intended to express a thesis that is only functionally normative. In contrast, NJT clearly expresses a moral thesis about the conditions an authority must satisfy to be legitimate.

[6] See Lon Fuller, *The Morality of Law*, Rev.ed. (New Haven, CT: Yale University Press, 1969), 39.

[7] Joseph Raz, "Authority and Justification," *Philosophy and Public Affairs*, vol. 14, no. 1 (Winter 1985), 18; emphasis added. Hereinafter *AJ*.

Second, unlike the Dependence Thesis, NJT does not express a functionally normative claim about what is minimally required for authority to be capable of performing its function of mediating between subjects and the reasons that antecedently apply to them. A practical authority that fails to satisfy NJT is not thereby rendered *incapable* of serving subjects in this way; all the authority must do to *succeed* in serving them is to make better decisions about what subjects should do based on the reasons that antecedently apply to them. An authority that fails to satisfy the Dependence Thesis cannot minimally serve its subjects by mediating between them and the reasons that antecedently apply to them because such an authority cannot do what is conceptually required to mediate between subjects and the reasons that apply to them. Whereas the Dependence Thesis is functionally normative and not morally normative, NJT is morally normative and not functionally normative.

Finally, although there is no conceptual link between epistemic and practical authority (apart from their being two different species of the genus authority), NJT is a normative theory of authority that connects the two in the following way. If NJT is true, then whether or not a *de facto* authority, *P*, has morally legitimate practical authority over *Q* depends in the "normal" case on whether *P* is an epistemic authority with respect to *Q* on the matters that fall within the scope of *P*'s practical authority. *P* has epistemic authority over *Q* with respect to a class of issues *only if P* is more likely than *Q* to be correct about those issues. If NJT is true, then *P* has morally justified practical authority over *Q* with respect to a class of acts in the normal case only if *P* has epistemic authority over *Q* with respect to whether acts in that class comport with the balance of first-order reasons that antecedently apply to *Q*.

The Preemption Thesis, NJT, and the Dependence Thesis also apply to advice. Insofar as the point of advice, like that of authority, is to serve the subject by mediating between the subject and the reasons that antecedently apply to her, something like the Dependence Thesis is also true of advice: any piece of advice "should be based, among other factors, on reasons which apply to the subjects of [that advice] and which bear on the circumstances covered by the [advice]" (*EPD* 214).

The relationship between a piece of advice and the underlying reasons appears tighter than it is between an authoritative directive and the underlying reasons. It is true that a piece of "advice" that does not even purport to be grounded in an assessment of the reasons that antecedently apply to the subject is simply not worth considering by the advisee because there is no reason to think that it is likely to be correct. But a suggestion that does not even purport to be grounded in an assessment of the underlying reasons is just not plausibly characterized as advice. If you ask me for my advice on whether you should do *p* and I make my suggestion based on the outcome of a coinflip, I have not given you anything that would count as advice. According to ordinary linguistic conventions, someone who asks me for advice is implicitly asking me to weigh all the relevant reasons and make a recommendation based on the outcome of my assessment of those reasons.

In contrast, it is not obvious that a directive that counts as authoritative cannot, as a conceptual matter, be grounded in a coinflip. If a judge in a case orders me to do something I am otherwise unwilling to do on the strength of a coinflip and the decision survives appeal, then it seems reasonable to characterize the order as authoritative. Notwithstanding that a judge's directive in that case would be illegitimate, such a directive would still arguably be authoritative, according to ordinary usage because (1) it would still be issued by the judge under a claim of legal right; (2) it tells me what I must do; (3) it would still be treated as binding on me; and (4) it would succeed in imposing the will of the judge on me. Given that a piece of advice cannot, as a conceptual matter, be grounded in a coinflip, the above suggests that the mediating role of advice, as a conceptual matter, requires a tighter connection between the prescription and the underlying reasons than is required by the mediating role of authority.

Something like NJT is also true of advice. It makes sense for us to seek out and take advice only from people we have some reason to think are likely to provide advice that is sound in the sense that its content prescribes the act best supported by the applicable reasons. Accordingly, it is plausible to think that a subject is justified in seeking and taking advice from another person only insofar as the subject is "better likely to comply with the reasons which apply to him (other than the alleged [piece of advice]) if he accepts the [advice] … and tries to follow [it] than if he tries to follow the reasons which apply to him directly" (*EPD* 214).

There is, however, this difference between NJT as applied to authority and NJT as applied to advice. NJT is clearly morally normative in the former case in the sense that it defines the conditions of morally legitimate practical authority, but it is not obviously morally normative in the latter. It seems, to my mind, odd to think that someone needs a moral justification in the ordinary case either to seek or take advice. In essence, seeking advice amounts to no more than asking someone's opinion, and taking advice amounts to no more than acting on someone else's opinion; in neither case does there seem to be even a *prima facie* issue of moral justification.

Nor do there seem to be any moral norms governing *giving* advice that do not also govern most ordinary speech acts that would hence tell us anything in particular about the nature of advice. It is true that one has a moral duty to give advice in good faith or to be sincere in offering advice, but that duty seems to apply to most types of communicative acts. It is also true that the duties of sincerity and good faith seem to entail that a piece of advice should be grounded in one's best assessment of the applicable reasons. But once that requirement is satisfied, it seems odd to think that one can justifiably give advice only if one *is*—or has reason to think one is—more likely, as a general matter, to get the relevant issues correct. An authoritative directive, after all, *requires* an act while a piece of advice merely *recommends* it.

As it pertains to advice, NJT is instead more plausibly construed as stating the conditions under which one is prudentially justified in seeking or taking advice from another. People frequently seek out advice for purely prudential reasons. If I am seeking advice on the best way to invest my savings to maximize my gains, I am looking for someone whose advice is most likely to enable me to realize my prudential goals of maximizing my savings. If a person is prudentially justified in doing something insofar as doing that something conduces to the satisfaction of her interests, then NJT seems quite plausibly construed as a principle of prudential justification.

There is thus some dissimilarity with respect to the applicability of NJT to practical authority and its applicability to advice. If the foregoing is correct, then NJT applies differently to advice than it does to practical authority. But this construction of NJT as applied to advice, like the intended construction of NJT as applied to authority, seems to state a plausible principle of *practical* reasoning; principles of prudential justification are no less principles of practical reasoning than are principles of moral justification. If the parallel between advice and authority is a bit weaker here than in the other respects considered above, it remains nonetheless conspicuous.

Something like the Preemption Thesis is also true of advice. If we assume that an advisor is someone who plausibly holds herself out as having expertise with respect to whether certain kinds of actions should be performed, then "[t]he fact that an [advisor suggests] performance of an action is a reason for its performance, which is not to be added to all other relevant reasons when assessing what to do, but should replace some of them" (*EPD* 214). Insofar as the advisor is enlisted to make a suggestion that is based on her evaluation of the reasons that antecedently apply to the subject, the advice should express that evaluation in the form of a prescription that can replace the subject's own assessment of the reasons. Insofar as advice can and should replace the subject's own assessment of the reasons, it should be *possible* for advice to preclude a subject's acting on her own assessment of the reasons; if she accepts and *follows* the advice, then it will have succeeded in precluding the subject from acting on her own assessment of the reasons.

As applied to advice, the Preemption Thesis entails that a piece of advice purports to provide the subject with both a first- and second-order reason to comply with the advice. First, insofar as a piece of advice is intended to replace the subject's own assessment of the applicable reasons in her deliberation, it must, as was true of authoritative directives, provide the same kind of first-order reason for doing something that her own assessment of the reasons would provide. Second, insofar as a piece of advice is intended to replace the subject's assessment of the reasons and to preclude her from acting on her own assessment of the reasons, it purports to provide a second-order reason for the subject not to act on her own assessment of the applicable reasons.

Further, as is true of authoritative directives, the first- and second-order reasons that a piece of advice purports to provide are content-independent. To begin, NJT as it pertains to advice implies that whatever reasons a piece of advice purports to provide are content-independent. Insofar as seeking or taking a piece of advice is justified, whether morally or prudentially, on the strength of the advisor's superior expertise with respect to determining what the applicable reasons require, the piece of advice is justified on the basis of its source, and not its content. This means that whatever reasons a piece of advice provides, they purport to be content-independent. To begin, the relevant first-order reasons are content-independent: if, on the one hand, the advice is to do *p*, it purports to provide a first-order reason to do *p*; if, on the other, it is not to do *p*, it purports to provide a first-order reason not to do *p*. Further, the second-order reasons are also content-independent: regardless of whether the advisor recommends doing *p* or not doing *p*, the advice aims to preclude a subject from acting on her own assessment of the applicable first-order reasons.

Advice and authority have another conceptual feature in common. The Preemption Thesis implies that the content of an authoritative directive must be identifiable by the subject without her having to weigh the applicable reasons for herself; that is, the Preemption Thesis implies the following thesis:

The Identification Thesis: It must always be possible for a subject to identify the existence and content of an authoritative directive without her having to assess for herself what the balance of applicable first-order reasons dictates that she should do.

If the Preemption Thesis is true, then an authoritative directive must be capable of replacing the subject's own assessment of the applicable reasons in her deliberations about what to do. But a directive that *cannot* be identified by the subject without having to assess the applicable reasons is *incapable* of replacing the subject's judgments about the balance of reasons because the subject must assess those reasons in order to ascertain the content of the directive—and hence ends up acting on her own assessment, rather than the putative authority's, of the relevant reasons. For example, if an authority directs the subject simply to do the right thing, the subject must figure out for herself what the right thing to do is in order to determine what the directive requires. If she then acts on that judgment, she is acting on her own assessment of what the right thing to do is rather than on the assessment of the authority.

Insofar as advice cannot be distinguished from authority on the basis of the Preemption Thesis, the Dependence Thesis, and NJT, something like the Identification Thesis would also have to be true of advice—and it is. The conceptual point of advice is for the advisor to make a suggestion grounded in the advisor's assessment of the balance of reasons that can replace in the advisee's deliberations her own assessment of what the applicable reasons dictate that she should do. But a piece of advice that has content that cannot be identified by the advisee without having to assess for herself what the applicable reasons require her to do *cannot* replace the advisee's own assessment of the applicable reasons in her deliberations about what to do.

Consider the suggestion expressed by the sentence "you should do what you think is best." One could, I suppose, argue that someone who offers this thought as a piece of advice has merely given bad advice, but this seems mistaken. If I ask someone what she thinks I should do and she responds with this sentence, I would interpret it as expressing a refusal to give me advice—perhaps for the reason that she did not want to put herself in the position of having given me bad advice on which I acted to my detriment. If this analysis is correct, then the content of a piece of advice, like that of an authoritative directive, must be identifiable by the subject without requiring her to assess the balance of reasons that antecedently apply to her.

What ultimately succeeds in distinguishing a piece of advice from an authoritative directive, of course, is that the latter is a *directive* and is hence mandatory in character. Something that is plausibly characterized as a *directive* purports to bind the subject thereby making the prescribed behavior non-optional in some relevant sense; something that is merely *advice* does not purport to make the suggested behavior non-optional in this or, for that matter, any other ordinary sense of the word.

Law purports to make certain acts mandatory, binding, and non-optional; and this is why it makes sense to think that law is authoritative in some sense that must harmonize with a plausible account of authority. Insofar as the valid norms of law incorporate the minimum content of natural law, they are incorporating not only the content of the relevant norms but also their mandatory character. Insofar as the rule of recognition imposes duties on officials, it makes certain behaviors mandatory in the way that authoritative directives purport to do. Insofar as the legal powers created by valid legal norms and recognition norms define, at the very least, obligations of non-interference on the part of other persons, they purport to make certain behaviors mandatory.

Law seeks to, when necessary, impose its will on subjects—and this is why a conceptual account of law must be consistent with a plausible account of the nature and justification of practical authority.

6. Practical authority and the possibility of moral criteria of validity: The Arguments from Authority

There is nothing in the most general features of practical authority, which are discussed above in the first four sections of this chapter, that is obviously inconsistent with the possibility of moral criteria of validity. At this level of generality, authority merely purports, under a claim of right, to impose its will on subjects by telling them what they must do in a way that, in some sense, binds them. An authoritative directive, then, purports to make certain behaviors non-optional in a manner that provides subjects with a novel content-independent reason contrived to persuade otherwise disinclined subjects to do as the directive requires. There is little reason, on the basis of these general considerations, to think that the directives of an institutional normative system with moral criteria of validity could not perform these general functions of practical authority.

At first blush, it seems easy to think of an institutional normative system with moral criteria of validity that is authoritative with respect to its subjects. Suppose, for example, that the following propositions are true: (1) the God of classical theism exists; (2) God manufactures an objective morality through the social act of issuing directives in the form of the Ten Commandments; and (3) God punishes those who do not conform their behavior, for the most part, to the Ten Commandments with an eternity of torment unmatched in suffering by anything that can otherwise be experienced. Suppose, further, that the vast majority of people believe that (1), (2), and (3) are true and, in consequence, generally conform their behavior to the Ten Commandments—enough to make it possible for people to peacefully live together in a society, as well as for them to cooperate with one another for mutual prudential advantage.

It seems clear, as a matter of ordinary usage, that God satisfies the most general existence conditions for being a practical authority and that God's commands are authoritative with respect to God's subjects. God purports, under a claim of right deriving from God's status as the ultimate sovereign of the universe, to tell people what they must do in a manner that provides reasons for doing what God commands: the threat of an eternity of torment is about as good a reason, if one believes such things are true, as one could possibly have for complying with any directive.[8] Further, these reasons are content-independent in the sense that had God commanded subjects to do otherwise, the prospect of eternal torment would give subjects an equally strong first-order reason to do otherwise and an equally persuasive second-order reason not to act on their own assessment of the reasons. Finally, each of the Ten Commandments purports to make certain acts non-optional and binding on subjects: the threat of an eternity of torment for violating a commandment makes an act about as non-optional and binding as any act could be.

It would appear, at first blush, that the institutional normative system described above satisfies the minimum conditions for a legal system and hence is properly characterized as a system of law. To begin, God (who serves as the only official of the system) seems to be practicing a rule of recognition that requires that God recognize, apply, and enforce as valid norms of the system only those norms that reproduce the content of the moral norms defined by the Ten Commandments; the Ten Commandments thus define moral constraints on the content of valid law and hence define moral criteria of validity. Further, insofar as subjects generally comply with the Ten Commandments, which express the minimum content of natural law, the valid norms of the system are as efficacious as the norms of any legal system need to be.

There is nothing in the conceptual features of practical authority discussed in the first four sections that would preclude characterizing the institutional normative system described above as a legal system—despite the fact that it seems to incorporate moral criteria of validity. If this system is conceptually disqualified from being a legal system on the ground that it has moral criteria of validity inconsistent with law's being authoritative, it would have to be on the strength of the theses that flesh out Raz's service conception of authority. As will be seen below, the idea is that an institutional normative system with moral criteria of validity is incapable of serving its subjects by mediating in the right sort of way between them and the reasons that antecedently apply to them.

[8] As described above, an eternity of torment is not the punishment for any one sin; it is the punishment for living a life that does not "for the most part" conform to the Ten Commandments. Nonetheless, a subject never knows what "for the most part" amounts to in God's judgment, so any violation of a commandment might be sufficient to ensure an eternity of torment for the disobedient subject. Clearly, a system in which (1) the overall quality of one's life is judged by its conformity to the Ten Commandments and (2) one is subject to eternal torment for insufficient conformity to those norms can provide a strong, if not conclusive, reason for complying in every instance with the Ten Commandments. Every sin, on this conception, matters with respect to what one's ultimate fate will feel like.

6.1 Law's claim of legitimate authority: The general strategy of the Arguments from Authority

Raz argues that the conceptual possibility of moral criteria of validity is inconsistent with the nature and justification of practical authority. On this general line of argument, any institutional normative system with moral criteria of validity lacks the kind of authority that any institutional normative system must have, as a conceptual matter, to count conceptually as a legal system.

This does not show that it is conceptually impossible for there to be an institutional normative system with moral criteria of validity; what it shows is that any such system lacks a conceptually necessary feature of a *legal system* and thus does not count as a system of *law*. But this line of reasoning is compatible with the conceptual possibility of institutional normative systems of other kinds that have moral criteria of institutional validity. For example, as far as this line of argument goes, a chess association could have a normative system with moral criteria of validity; that system just would not have practical authority. The claim here is merely that any type of institutional normative system that is authoritative cannot have moral criteria of validity because a system with moral criteria of validity cannot be authoritative. Since legal systems are authoritative or claim to be such, they cannot have moral criteria of validity.

If such reasoning is sound, then it would imply that the institutional normative system that validates all and only norms reproducing the content of the mandatory moral norms defined by the Ten Commandments is not properly characterized as a legal system. Since it incorporates moral criteria of validity, it cannot be authoritative because it lacks a conceptually necessary feature of practical authority. At best, on such reasoning, this institutional normative system would be properly characterized as *pre-legal* despite defining a structure of norms that is perfectly isomorphic to that of anything properly characterized as a legal system.

Raz gives, in essence, three different arguments intended to show the conceptual impossibility of a legal system with moral criteria of validity, but each depends on the following thesis:

The Authority Thesis: Every conceptually possible legal system claims legitimate authority.

According to the Authority Thesis, then, an institutional normative system that does not claim legitimate authority is lacking a conceptually necessary feature of a legal system and hence cannot be a system of law.

The Authority Thesis implies that, as a conceptual matter, law must be *capable* of mediating between law's subjects and the right reasons that apply to them. To begin, on Raz's view, if it is a conceptual truth that law claims legitimate authority, then it must be conceptually possible for a system of law to actually have legitimate authority: "If the claim to authority is part of the nature of law, then whatever else the law is it must be capable of possessing authority" (*EPD* 215). But, further, to be capable of possessing authority, on Raz's view, the law must be capable of serving its subjects by "mediat[ing] between [them] and the right reasons that apply to them" (*EPD* 214).

Raz's service conception of practical authority grounds three main lines of argument against inclusive positivism but all rely on the idea that an institutional normative system with moral criteria of validity is incapable of instantiating legitimate authority and hence lacks a conceptually necessary feature of a legal system. The directives of a legitimate authority, on Raz's view, (1) must, under the Preemption Thesis, be able to replace the judgments of subjects of what the balance of reasons requires them to do; (2) must, under NJT, be such that subjects are more likely to comply with the requirements of right reason by following the authority's judgment of what right reason requires than by following their own judgments; and (3) must express the authority's view about what specifically subjects ought to do.

The basic strategy of these arguments against the Incorporation Thesis is to show that the directives of an institutional normative system with moral criteria of validity cannot be law because they cannot satisfy any of the three necessary conditions for legitimate authority above. The first argument attempts to show that the directives of an institutional normative system with moral criteria of validity cannot satisfy (1) because a subject cannot identify the content of those directives without reading her own assessments of the balance of reasons into it. The second attempts to show that the directives of an institutional normative system with moral criteria of validity cannot satisfy (2) because subjects must follow their own judgments, rather than those of the authority, with respect to what they should do. The third attempts to show that the directives of an institutional normative system with moral criteria of validity cannot satisfy (3) because subjects can identify the content of those directives only by reading into them their own views about what they should do according to right reason. Since, on each of these lines of argument, an institutional normative system with moral criteria of validity is incapable of instantiating legitimate authority, it lacks a conceptually necessary feature of a legal system and cannot be a system of *law*.

6.2 The Authority Thesis, the Preemption Thesis, and inclusive positivism

Raz argues that the Preemption Thesis and Authority Thesis are inconsistent with inclusive positivism. The argument is straightforward. Since the conceptual point of authority is to provide directives that can replace the subject's own assessment of the balance of reasons in her deliberations about what she should do, it must always be possible for a subject to determine what an authoritative directive requires of her without having to assess those reasons for herself; that is, the Preemption Thesis implies the Identification Thesis. Any directive the content of which *cannot* be identified by the subject without assessing the balance of reasons that antecedently apply to her is conceptually disqualified, under the Identification Thesis, as being authoritative.

The problem this poses for inclusive positivism is as follows. The Identification Thesis implies that the content of the law must be identifiable by the subject without having to assess the balance of reasons with respect to what she should do. But a subject cannot identify the content of a norm valid in virtue of moral merit without assessing the underlying reasons with respect to what she should do. To determine what the law requires of a subject under a recognition rule that validates only enacted norms consistent with some mandatory moral norms, the subject must be able to identify the content of the relevant mandatory moral norms that ultimately determines or constrains what the law requires of her. But a subject cannot determine the validity of, say, an enacted norm prohibiting the killing of "innocent persons" without assessing the balance of reasons with respect to what she ought to do, as a matter of morality; in particular, a subject must assess the balance of applicable reasons to ascertain who counts as an innocent person under the law. This implies, on Raz's view, that a rule of recognition that incorporates moral criteria of validity cannot be legitimately authoritative and hence cannot give rise to law because the law *qua* authority is supposed to settle for subjects which persons would count as "innocent" under the relevant moral norm.

6.3 The Authority Thesis, NJT, and inclusive positivism

The second line of argument against inclusive positivism is grounded in the Authority Thesis and NJT. NJT asserts that authority is morally legitimate only if the subject is more likely to do what right reason requires if she follows the authority's judgment about what right reason requires than if she follows her own judgment about what right reason requires. But an institutional normative system with moral criteria of validity is not capable of being legitimate under NJT because a subject cannot identify the content of valid norms without assessing for herself what right reason requires of her. Insofar as the subject must identify the content of a valid norm by assessing for herself what right reason requires, she is, of necessity, *following her own judgment* about what right reason requires, and not the judgment of the authority.

Consider an institutional normative system with a rule of recognition that validates all and only mandatory moral norms, and suppose that a subject must decide whether an institutionally valid norm requires her to do *p*. To determine whether the valid norm requires that she does *p*, she must assess for herself whether the balance of reasons requires that she do *p*. If she is motivated to do what she thinks the valid norm requires with respect to doing *p*, then she will do what she decides the balance of reasons requires with respect to doing *p*: if she decides that the norm requires her to do *p*, then she will do *p*; if she decides that the norm requires her not to do *p*, she will refrain from doing *p*. Since, either way, she cannot avoid following her own judgment of what the balance of reasons requires, it is not possible for her to follow the authority's judgment of what the balance of reasons requires and hence it is not possible for her to better comply with right reason by following the authority's judgment of what the balance of reasons requires than by following her own judgment. For this reason, an institutional normative system with moral criteria of validity cannot instantiate legitimate authority and hence is not properly characterized as a legal system

6.4 The directives of practical authority as expressing its view about what ought to be done

Raz argues that it is a necessary condition for a norm to be legitimately authoritative that "it must be, or be presented as, someone's view on what the subjects ought to do" (*EPD* 221). To be capable of legitimate authority, the directives of a normative system must express the authority's view about which specific act the balance of reasons dictates that subjects must perform. Since a subject can determine what is required by a norm in an inclusive system only by deciding for herself what the balance of reasons requires that she do, she is simply identifying *her own view* about what she ought to do: again, if she decides that the norm requires her to do *p*, then she will do *p*; if she decides that the norm requires her not to do *p*, she will refrain from doing *p*. Since an inclusive rule of recognition requires her to decide for herself, for each act *p*, whether the balance of applicable reasons requires her to do *p* or refrain from doing *p*, it is incapable of expressing the authority's view about what specific act she ought to perform and is hence incapable of being a legitimate authority. Since it is a conceptual truth that law claims legitimate authority and hence is capable of legitimate authority, an institutional normative system grounded in an inclusive rule of recognition is conceptually incapable of being a legal system.

7. Looking ahead: Evaluating the Arguments from Authority

The next three chapters evaluate the Arguments from Authority. Chapters 5 and 6 are concerned with evaluating two theses on which each of the Arguments from Authority depends. Chapter 5 is concerned with challenging the Authority Thesis that it is part of the very nature of law that it claims legitimate authority; I argue that there are no conceptually necessary features of a legal system that are properly interpreted as expressing a claim of legitimate authority. Chapter 6 is concerned with the Identification Thesis; in particular, I argue that there is nothing in the ordinary linguistic or legal practices defining the use of the relevant concept-terms that entails that the nature of *our* concept of authority requires that the content of an authoritative directive be identifiable without recourse to the dependent reasons it is supposed to reflect, balance, and preempt. Insofar as the Identification Thesis is a logical consequence of the Preemption Thesis, the argument of Chapter 6 also purports to refute, albeit indirectly, the Preemption Thesis.

Finally, Chapter 7 attempts to show that the Arguments from Authority incorrectly presuppose that the rule of recognition must be capable of informing subjects of what their non-official obligations are under valid law. The problem is that there is no reason to think that a rule that does not govern non-official behavior must be capable of informing subjects of what other rules that do govern non-official behavior require with respect to such behavior; the rule of recognition defines standards that govern only the law-making, adjudicative, and enforcement acts of officials of the system. Insofar as the Arguments from Authority presuppose that *non-officials* must be able to learn of their obligations from the *rule of recognition*, the arguments fail.

5

Law's Claim of Legitimate Authority

At the foundation of each of the Arguments from Authority is the idea that it is a conceptual truth that law claims legitimate authority (the Authority Thesis) and hence that it is a conceptual truth that law is capable of being legitimate. The problem with inclusive positivism, on these arguments, is that an institutional normative system with moral criteria of validity is incapable of being legitimately authoritative because the subject in such a system cannot determine what the relevant norms require without assessing for herself what she ought to do according to right reason. Since such a system cannot hence vindicate law's claim of legitimate authority, it cannot be a system of law.

There are three related problems that arise in connection with an institutional normative system with moral criteria of validity. First, insofar as the subject of such a system cannot determine what she must do under the norms without assessing the balance of reasons for herself, those norms are incapable of replacing her own judgments in her deliberations about what she ought to do according to right reason. Second, insofar as the subject of such a system cannot determine what she must do under the norms without assessing for herself what right reason requires, it is impossible for her to follow the authority's assessments of what right reason requires and is hence impossible for her to better comply with right reason by following the authority's judgment than by following her own. Third, insofar as the subject of such a system cannot determine what she ought to do under the norms without deciding what she thinks she ought to do according to right reason, the norms cannot express the authority's view about what specifically she ought to do according to right reason. In each case, an institutional normative system with moral criteria of validity is incapable of being legitimately authoritative because it cannot perform some function that something must be able to perform to be authoritative.

Strictly speaking, the claim that causes the problem for inclusive positivism is the claim that it is a conceptually necessary condition for something to count as a system of law that it be capable of legitimate authority—and not the Authority Thesis. The Authority Thesis figures into the argument only insofar as it entails that something must be metaphysically capable of being legitimate to count as a legal system. But since it seems obvious, on any plausible conceptual theory of law, that something must be capable of legitimate authority to count as a legal system, the Authority Thesis, *contra* what is usually thought, plays no essential role in the Arguments from Authority.

Even so, it is important to evaluate the Authority Thesis because it purports to state a fact about the nature of a legal system. One point of this volume is to determine whether the arguments against the Incorporation Thesis succeed, but its overriding point is to facilitate a deeper understanding of the conceptual relationships between law and morality. Insofar as the notion of legitimate authority is a concept with morally normative content, it is important to understand whether it is part of law's nature that it claims legitimate authority. For this reason, this chapter attempts to determine whether the Authority Thesis is true.

1. Understanding the content of a claim of legitimate authority

The Arguments from Authority, as Raz articulates them, rest on the Authority Thesis, according to which it is a conceptual truth that "every legal system claims that it possesses legitimate authority."[1] Insofar as it is conceptual truth that an authority is legitimate if and only if its directives give rise to content-independent moral obligations to obey, the Authority Thesis implies that every conceptually possible legal system claims that its subjects have a content-independent moral obligation to obey legal directives in virtue of having the status of law. It is hence a conceptual truth, according to the Authority Thesis, that law claims that every behavior that is legally obligatory is also morally obligatory *in virtue of being legally obligatory.*

The Authority Thesis asserts a stronger claim than might initially appear. Insofar as it asserts that a claim of legitimate authority is a conceptually necessary feature of a legal system, it implies that Hart's minimum conditions for the existence of a legal system do not exhaust the existence conditions for a legal system. If the Authority Thesis is true, it is also a conceptually necessary condition for an institutional normative system to count as a legal system that some official or institution does something that expresses a claim of legitimacy.

[1] Joseph Raz, "Authority, Law and Morality," *The Monist* (1985), reprinted in Raz (ed.), *Ethics in the Public Domain* (Oxford: Oxford University Press, 1994), 215. Hereinafter *EPD*.

2. Can law make claims? Two possible interpretations

While the Authority Thesis might seem plausible at first glance, it is important to note that it depends crucially on a metaphysical assumption that is far from intuitive—namely, the assumption that legal systems can, like human beings, perform acts that make claims. The problem is that it is not clear that legal systems possess the requisite characteristics that are metaphysically or conceptually necessary to make claims. If they do not possess these characteristics and hence *cannot* make claims, then the Authority Thesis is false.

The worry here arises because of the kind of thing that a legal system is by nature. A legal system has many pieces, which include, most conspicuously, laws; every conceptually possible legal system has a rule of recognition that defines the criteria of validity for that system as well as a set of legal norms that are valid under the rule of recognition. But a legal system also seems to include, as constituents, the various institutions defined by those criteria of validity; these institutions would have to include, as a conceptual matter, judicial institutions but they also would arguably have to include distinct legislative, executive, and enforcement institutions. Each of these institutions is composed, in part, of officials who have duties and powers defined by certain legal norms, which might include those defining validity criteria and first-order norms.

A legal system, as a conceptual matter, appears thus to be an aggregate of these norms, institutions, and officials. If there are no norms, there is no legal system. If the system contains none of the conceptually necessary institutions, there is no legal system. If there are no officials, there is no legal system. Since each of these is a conceptually necessary element of a legal system and a legal system is not identical with any one of them, a legal system must, as an ontological matter, be identical with a set that includes as members all of these objects. Whatever else it might be, then, a legal system is a composite object.

The question is whether and how something that has the defining qualities of a legal system could do something accurately characterized as making claims. Although it is certainly reasonable to question whether whatever claims a legal system makes include a claim of legitimate authority, the initial question is a metaphysical one: is it conceptually possible for a legal system to make claims in a sense that would imply the crucial claim that a legal system must be capable of instantiating legitimate authority?

It is clear, of course, that some of the conceptually necessary pieces of a legal system can make claims. Individual officials can, and sometimes do, make claims about the content of something that is or ought to be law: legislators can, and sometimes do, make claims about the costs or benefits that would result from the enactment of some proposed bill; judges can, and frequently do, make claims about the duties of the parties in legal disputes. Anyone who serves as an official of any kind can make claims partly in virtue of being able to perform various linguistic acts that make statements which bear truth-value.

But some of these conceptually necessary pieces do not seem capable of making claims—at least not on any ordinary understanding of that notion. While it is true that a legal norm can connote the kind of propositional content that might be expressed by a claim, a legal norm is just not the kind of thing capable of *making* a claim in any relevant sense of the phrase.

Notice that the idea that *L* expresses a claim does not imply the idea that *L* thereby *makes* a claim. Sentences express claims but do not make claims; the sentence "capital punishment is unjust" expresses a claim that capital punishment is unjust, but it does not make that claim. Speakers make claims by using sentences that express the content of those claims; I use the sentence "capital punishment is unjust" to make the claim that capital punishment is unjust. I can make claims, in part, because I can perform linguistic acts that express the propositional content I wish to assert as a claim; in contrast, legal norms can express propositional content but cannot perform acts of any kind. Claim-making of the sort asserted by the Authority Thesis, if intended in any sense that conforms to ordinary usage, is an act and as such can be accomplished only by things—such as judges, presidents, and legislators—capable of *doing* something that would count as an act.

But even if it is plausible to think that the propositions expressed by legal norms constitute claims made by those norms, it would still be problematic to think that legal norms make any claims that would warrant attributing a claim of legitimate authority to the legal system. The problem is that legal norms do not appear to express any content properly construed as implying a claim of legitimate authority. For example, the content expressed by the legal norm prohibiting murder is that murder is prohibited by the system of legal norms. Assuming this content expresses a claim, it should be clear that the claim that murder is *legally* prohibited does not imply the claim that murder is *morally* prohibited—much less does it imply the claim that the norm is legitimately authoritative or that murder is morally prohibited in virtue of its being prohibited by a legal norm. There is simply nothing in the norm expressing that murder is legally prohibited that entails any claim, on the ordinary usages that are the topic of this volume, about the moral properties of either the prohibited act, the legal norm, or the legal system to which the norm belongs. The law prohibiting murder lacks the right kind of content even to *express* such a claim.

Nor would it help to aggregate all the legal norms of a system as a means of deriving such a claim. It is simply not plausible to think that all the legal norms of any conceptually possible legal system, taken together, *must* imply a claim of legitimate authority. All that the legal norms of any legal system, taken together, *must* express is that the various acts they govern are either legally required, legally prohibited, or legally permitted: if *A1, A2, A3,* . . . , *An* is a complete list of the acts regulated by the legal norms of the system, then all that the set of a system's legal norms, taken together, must express is that acts *A1, A2, A3,* . . . , *An* are either legally required, legally prohibited, or legally permitted in that system. But the claim that acts *A1, A2, A3,* . . . , *An* are either legally required, legally prohibited, or legally permitted neither asserts nor implies that those acts are either morally required, morally prohibited, or morally permitted—much less that they are morally required/prohibited/permitted in virtue of being legally required/prohibited/permitted, which is what would be needed to express a claim of legitimate authority. If a claim of legitimate authority is properly attributed to every conceptual legal system, it cannot be derived from anything necessarily expressed by the system's legal norms.

But these observations are not germane because the Authority Thesis is a thesis about what is claimed by a *legal system*, and no one of these elements constitutes a legal system. Indeed, to the extent that a legal system is properly conceived to be a unified institution, it must be characterized as a set containing all of these various elements—and a set is a *non*-propositional abstract object, rather than a concrete physical object. But even if we omit the language of sets and abstract objects, it should be clear that the legal system could not be a physical object. While one can see, hear, smell, touch, or taste various elements of a legal system, it should be clear that one cannot see, hear, smell, taste, touch, or taste the legal system itself.

The idea that a non-physical abstract object of this kind can *claim* anything is metaphysically problematic. To begin, it is clear that a *non*-physical *non*-propositional object, unlike physical and propositional objects, cannot even *express* claims. A sentence is a propositional object that can express claims in virtue of being an aggregate of various linguistic entities that bear meaning. But a set that consists of *sets* of norms, *sets* of institutions, and *sets* of persons is not an aggregate of purely linguistic entities; sets of non-physical propositional objects (i.e. norms) are aggregated with sets of non-physical non-propositional objects (i.e. institutions) and sets of physical persons (i.e. officials) to comprise the set constituting a legal system. Even if it were true that every entity contained in one of the sets making up a legal system can express or make claims, there is no way to aggregate those sets to *express* a proposition.

Further, entities that can make claims in any literal sense can do so only in virtue of possessing certain properties. What makes it possible for us to make claims is that we are rational intentional agents who can perform acts using language to communicate content to other similarly abled agents. And each of these properties is necessary for being able to *make* claims in the relevant ordinary sense. The ability to make claims in this sense requires linguistic competence. Rationality is necessary because the ability to use language presupposes the ability to grasp and use concepts. Intentionality is necessary because claims always express content *about* something. The absence of any one of these properties is enough to render a being incapable of making claims. Since legal systems, *qua* abstract object, lack *all* of these capacities, it is not conceptually possible for legal systems to make claims in this sense.

The idea that a legal system can either make or express claims involves a conceptual confusion that rises to the level of a category mistake. As Oxford Online Dictionary defines the notion, a category mistake makes "[t]he error of assigning to something a quality or action which can only properly be assigned to things of another category."[2] The idea that the object denoted by the numeral "2" can make or express claims involves a conceptual confusion that rises to the level of a category mistake; someone who sincerely makes this claim must be confused either about the nature of a number or about the nature of making a claim. But it seems no less conceptually confused to think that a legal system can make claims in some ordinary literal sense than it is to think that the object denoted by the numeral "2" can make claims in the same sense.

The confusion might be somewhat more difficult to see in the former case, but there is nothing in the notion of a category mistake that implies that category mistakes are easy to discern. It is clear that a plant can neither make nor express claims, but it is not clear whether the idea that a plant can make or express a claim involves a conceptual confusion that rises to the level of a category mistake.[3] People frequently attribute certain interests and even mental states to plants that they do not have. One might say on observing a plant's brown leaves that the plant "wants" to be watered. This kind of claim expresses

[2] "Category mistake," *Oxford Online Dictionary*; available at: https://en.oxforddictionaries.com/definition/category_mistake.

[3] Indeed, it is not clear whether it even involves a conceptual confusion. One might be clear on all the relevant notions but think that some plants have the relevant capacities to make claims. That idea might be false, but it is not obviously false in virtue of being conceptually confused; there is nothing in the linguistic conventions for using the term "plant" that entails that plants necessarily lack these capacities. To determine this, one must know more about the world than just the definition of "plant" or the underlying philosophical presuppositions; one would also have to know presumably contingent facts about the empirical properties of everything that counts as a plant.

an error that might rise to the level of a category mistake but whether it does is not clear. Whether it does will depend on conceptual considerations having to do with what counts as having a want, as well as metaphysical considerations having to do with what properties something must have to have wants. If, for this reason, the idea that a plant can make or express claims involves a category mistake, that mistake is not obvious.

One might argue that it is no more obvious that the Authority Thesis involves a category mistake than it is that a plant can make or express claims does. Perhaps the Authority Thesis involves no greater conceptual confusion than the idea that a plant can make or express claims—although a plant is a living physical object while a legal system is a non-propositional abstract object; however, it should be clear that a legal system is simply not the kind of thing that can make or express claims in any ordinary sense of the terms. Whether it involves a category mistake or not, the Authority Thesis is obviously false if construed as asserting that legal systems claim legitimate authority in any literal sense of the term "claim" as ordinary usage defines it.

There are two potential responses here. First, one might think that the objection incorrectly presupposes a literal interpretation of the Authority Thesis. On this line of defense, the Authority Thesis should be interpreted metaphorically to attribute claims to the legal system in the same way that claims are frequently attributed to other types of abstract objects in ordinary and legal practice. The law treats for example, corporations as persons who can sue and be sued because it is useful to do so; to facilitate its aims, the law will attribute claims made by corporate agents to the abstract corporation itself. As long as we respect its intuitive boundaries, there is no decisive reason to reject the use of a device that attributes, in some non-literal metaphorical sense, claims to an abstract object like a legal system.

There are, of course, no obvious objections to using a metaphorical device to describe some element of a legal system and doing so might well yield serviceable insights about the nature of law. One could think of the legal system in metaphorical terms as an author to help us to understand the nature of interpretation as it functions or should function in judicial practices. There is no plausible reason to think that attributing to law an ability to make claims in some metaphorical sense might not disclose something of value about the nature of law.

The problem is that, assuming the Authority Thesis is needed to derive the idea that law must be capable of instantiating authority, it would not imply that idea unless law is capable of making claims in some literal sense. Raz argues that if the law sincerely claims authority, then it must be capable of instantiating authority because the legal practices that construct our concept of authority cannot be conceptually confused about that notion. But this argument is sound only if the relevant sense of claim-making is literal: it is one thing to infer that the law must be capable of being legitimate from the idea that it can and does claim in a literal sense to be legitimate; it is quite another to infer that law must be capable of being legitimate from the idea that law sincerely claims in some purely metaphorical sense to be legitimate.

Either way, a claim of legitimate authority can sensibly be attributed to law only on the strength of the behaviors of its officials. These behaviors might involve deliberately expressive behaviors that make claims in a literal or metaphorical sense, but they need not involve such behaviors. There is no a priori reason to rule out inferences that might be made on the basis of non-expressive behaviors; we are still dealing, after all, with beings capable of making and expressing claims. But whatever behaviors are identified as forming the basis for such claims, they must occur in every conceptually possible legal system since the Authority Thesis attributes such claims to law as a matter of conceptual necessity.

The idea that there are certain behavioral requirements included in the existence conditions for a legal system is not problematic. After all, on a positivist view, the existence conditions for a legal system are at least partly defined by two behavioral requirements. First, it is a necessary condition for the existence of a legal system in *S* that officials in *S* behave in a manner that amounts to their practicing a social rule of recognition that governs the promulgation and adjudication of law in *S*. Second, it is a necessary condition for the existence of a legal system in *S* that people in *S* behave in a manner that generally conforms to the norms validated by the rule of recognition in *S*.

Although each condition states a behavioral requirement, it is plausible to think that the existence conditions for a legal system are exhausted by such requirements because a legal system is a relational object that obtains in some society relative to some population of people whose behavior it regulates. If, on the one hand, there is no one in *S* who practices a rule of recognition governing the promulgation and adjudication of law in *S*, then there is no legal system in *S* because an institutional normative system of the appropriate kind does not exist in *S*. If, on the other hand, there is such a rule of recognition but people in *S* do not obey the norms validated by the rule of recognition, then there is no legal system in *S* because the institutions that the rule purports to bring into existence in *S* do not stand in the appropriate relation to people in *S*.

While there can and *must* be behavioral requirements among the existence conditions for a legal system, the evidence for thinking that the officials must behave in a way that implies a claim of legitimacy must be satisfactory. In particular, there must be a non-question-begging reason for denying the status of law to an institution in which the norms valid under a rule of recognition practiced by officials efficaciously guide non-official behavior but in which officials exhibit none of the requisite behavioral elements that imply a claim of legitimate authority.

I argue below that Raz's argument for the Authority Thesis fails to meet this evidentiary burden. I argue that, on the assumption that a legal system is the kind of thing to which a claim can plausibly be attributed, the behaviors he cites as supporting the Authority Thesis are neither conceptually necessary conditions for the existence of a legal system nor expressive of a claim of legitimate authority. This does not show that the Authority Thesis is false because it does not rule out the possibility that there are other conceptually necessary features of a legal system that imply a claim of legitimate authority. At most, the argument below shows that even if we assume that legal systems are capable of making claims in some relevant sense, we have no reason to believe that they claim legitimate authority.

3. Deriving law's claim of legitimacy from the beliefs and claims of officials

Raz attributes a claim of legitimate authority to the legal system on the strength of certain beliefs and behaviors on the part of officials:

> The claims the law makes for itself are evident from the language it adopts and from the opinions expressed by its spokesmen, i.e. by the institutions of the law. The law's claim to authority is manifested by the fact that legal institutions are officially designated as "authorities," by the fact that they regard themselves as having the right to impose obligations on their subjects, by their claims that their subjects owe them allegiance, and that their subjects ought to obey the law as it requires to be obeyed (i.e. in all cases except those in which some legal doctrine justifies breach of duty). Even a bad law, is the inevitable official doctrine, should be obeyed for as long as it is in force, while lawful action is taken to try and bring about its amendment or repeal (*EPD* 215–16).

There are five practices, then, that imply a claim of legitimate authority that should be attributed to law: (1) the use in the law of such terms as "right" and "duty"; (2) the official designation of legal institutions as "authorities"; (3) the claims of officials that subjects "owe" allegiance to officials; (4) the claims of officials that subjects "ought to obey the law"; and (5) the beliefs of officials that they have a right to impose obligations on their subjects.

Raz does not explicitly attribute these claims and practices to officials of the legal system; rather, he attributes them to unspecified "institutions of law." But if one doubts that a legal system is metaphysically capable of making claims because of its abstract character, one will also doubt that a legal institution is metaphysically capable of making claims because of *its* abstract character. A legal institution is no more a physical object than a legal system is; a legislature or judiciary is made up, in part, of physical objects but it is not a physical object. One can see, hear, smell, touch, and taste judges and legislators, but one cannot see, hear, smell, touch, or taste a legislative or judicial institution.

Even so, we can make sense of the idea that the beliefs, claims, and practices of officials can assert or imply a claim of legitimacy that can metaphorically be attributed to the legal system. Officials are coherently conceived of as representatives of the institutions in which they serve and hence as authorized to speak on behalf the other members of these institutions.[4] Insofar as the beliefs, claims, and practices of those officials who represent the legal system and speak on behalf of other officials of the system imply a claim of legitimacy, it can metaphorically be attributed to the system itself.

4. Do the beliefs and claims of officials imply a claim of legitimacy?

The Authority Thesis asserts that every conceptually possible legal system includes features that make a claim of legitimate authority. Insofar as a legal system's claim of legitimate authority can be derived from (or otherwise explained *only* in terms of) some set of beliefs, claims, or practices instantiated by officials in the system, it follows that officials in any conceptually possible legal system must instantiate some subset of the relevant beliefs, claims, or practices.

This does not mean that the relevant beliefs, claims, or practices that imply the claim to legitimate authority in one conceptually possible legal system must be exactly the same as those that imply that claim in every other conceptually possible legal system. It might be that there are a number of properties, *P1, P2, . . . , Pn* of which instantiation of any one is sufficient to imply such a claim. If so, it is consistent with the Authority Thesis that the claim of legitimate authority is fully constituted in one conceptually possible legal system by the instantiation of *P1* and in another conceptually possible legal system

[4] The idea that one can speak on behalf of an abstract object in a literal sense is no less metaphysically problematic than the idea that an abstract object can make claims. One can speak on behalf of only things that have some capacity to speak; as non-propositional non-physical objects, legal institutions and systems cannot speak for themselves in any literal sense. Strictly speaking, a representative of a group can speak on behalf of only other members of the group.

by the instantiation of *P2*. The Authority Thesis is agnostic with respect to whether the claim of legitimate authority is constituted by the instantiation of exactly the same beliefs, claims, and practices in every conceptually possible legal system.

I argue below that the relevant features identified by Raz as implying a claim of legitimate authority do not warrant accepting the Authority Thesis. First, none of these features implies a claim of legitimate authority because the relevant claims, beliefs, and practices imply nothing at all about the moral properties of the system. Second, there is no reason to think that official acts in every conceptually possible legal system must exhibit one of these features. While it might be true that a claim of legitimate authority can justifiably be attributed to some conceptually possible legal systems, Raz has not given any reason to believe that such a claim must be attributed to all conceptually possible legal systems.

4.1 The use of the language of rights and duties

The first feature of law cited by Raz as implying a claim of legitimate authority is the "language it adopts" (*EPD* 215). Like moral norms, legal norms define protections that we characterize as "rights," as well as requirements that we characterize as "duties." The U.S. Constitution, for example, includes fifteen instances of the term "right," which include its appearance in the First, Second, Fourth, Sixth, Seventh, and Ninth Amendments, and the law of torts prototypically imputes to potential defendants a "duty" of reasonable care.

The use of such language is clearly not coincidental. Legal requirements purport to bind subjects in a manner resembling that in which moral requirements bind moral agents. In law and in morality, the existence of something properly characterized as a "duty" entails that the relevant behavior is required or non-optional. In both cases, the norm states a requirement that is exclusionary in the sense that a violation of a norm cannot be justified by the subject's prudential interests. It is in this sense that a duty of either kind "binds" subjects of the directive creating the duty.

This is a conceptual truth about duties. It is part of the very nature of any kind of duty that it is binding on a subject in the following sense: subjects must do what they have a duty to do regardless of what their preferences might be; failure to satisfy a duty constitutes a wrong for which the subject is properly held accountable. If giving to charity is morally required, then someone who fails to do so has committed a moral wrong for which she can properly be held accountable under the norms of morality. Similarly, if paying taxes is legally required, then someone who fails to do so has committed a legal wrong for which she can properly be held accountable under the law.

This is the hallmark of a duty in the relevant sense: an agent *A* has a duty to do *p* under a class of rules **R** if and only if *A*'s non-performance of *p* is a wrong under **R** for which she can properly be held accountable under the rules of **R**. Given that legal norms purport to make specified acts required in a sense that subjects persons to liability for non-performance, it is quite natural that legal practice would adopt the language of duties in expressing its requirements.

It is equally natural that legal practice would adopt the language of rights in expressing certain requirements of law insofar as the notion of a right is conceptually related to the notion of a duty. Duties correlate, as a conceptual matter, with rights in at least this respect: it is a conceptual truth that *P* has a right against *Q* with respect to act *a* only if *Q* owes a duty to *P* with respect to *a*. It might be that *Q*'s owing a duty to *P* with respect to *a* is not conceptually sufficient for *P*'s having a right against *Q*, but it is conceptually necessary. Either way, it is perfectly natural—and, indeed, predictable—that the law would use the language of rights to describe protections that function the way rights do under moral norms.

No more than these similarities are needed to explain why the law uses the same language to express its requirements that we use to express the requirements of morality. The use in law of such terms as "obligation," "duty," and "right" signifies no more than a collective recognition on the part of lawmakers, judges, and ordinary citizens that the requirements of law define prohibitions that are exclusionary in the same sense that moral prohibitions are exclusionary and that are hence applied and enforced in a way that expresses that exclusionary character.

Law-talk is not unique in co-opting the normative language of morality. We commonly speak of obligations and rights in a host of non-moral contexts that have nothing to do with the law. In addition to legal obligations and rights, we speak of social, institutional, and cultural obligations and rights; the idea that the very use of these terms warrants attributing a belief to speakers that the relevant norms give rise to obligations and rights that are moral in character would imply that members of any club, no matter how trifling its purpose, believe that the club rules defining their obligations and rights also give rise to moral obligations and moral rights. Perhaps that is true in most or even every existing case; however, this is clearly not necessarily true, as a metaphysical, conceptual, or psychological matter.

Further, there is nothing in either ordinary linguistic or legal practices that would warrant the attribution of such a belief to officials on the ground that law-talk uses some of the same language as morality-talk. As discussed in Chapter 2, courts recognize the possibility that a mandatory legal norm might be sufficiently wicked that it gives rise to no moral obligation to obey; thus, there is nothing in the lexical meanings of the terms that would entail that laws must be just and hence that legal obligations and rights give rise to moral obligations and rights. Indeed, there is nothing conceptually confused in the idea that what the law requires might be so wicked that citizens have a moral obligation to disobey it. As far as ordinary usage is concerned, there is nothing in the meaning of the relevant terms that would warrant the attribution of such a belief to people simply in virtue of using the relevant terms.

The idea that one can attribute a belief to officials that legal obligations and legal rights define or give rise to moral obligations and moral rights on just the strength of their use in both contexts of "obligations" and "rights" is problematic not only because there is nothing in the meanings of the two terms that entails any moral content; it is also problematic in virtue of attributing an error theory of law to every speaker of the language. As discussed in Chapter 2, the strong natural law claim that it is a necessary condition for something to count as a valid legal norm that its content be morally just implies an error theory of law.[5] Since the claim that legal obligations and legal rights necessarily give rise to moral obligations and moral rights presupposes this strong natural law claim, it also implies an error theory of law.

In the absence of a sociological survey that shows that most speakers of the language hold this view, it is uncharitable to attribute an error theory of law to speakers of the language simply on the basis of practicing a linguistic convention regarding the use of the terms "obligation" and "right." Without such sociological verification, the use of such language provides no support for the Authority Thesis.

[5] For what it is worth, the idea that some claim *C* implies an error theory and the idea that *C* commits a category mistake are logically independent. To begin, the idea that *C* commits a category mistake does not entail the idea that *C* implies an error theory; the idea that law claims legitimate authority seems to commit a category mistake but does not imply an error theory of anything. Conversely, the claim that *C* implies an error theory does not imply that *C* commits a category mistake. The claim that morality is not objective implies an error theory of morality in the sense that most of our folk moral judgments would be false if that claim is true, but it does not imply that our folk moral judgments involve a category mistake. The problem is not that there is some conceptual confusion with respect to our use of the relevant terms; it is rather that those terms do not pick out some moral property that exists in the universe independently of our own beliefs and practices.

4.2 Officials' belief that they have a right to impose obligations

The idea that a claim of legitimate authority can be attributed to a legal system on the strength of the language used by law enjoys a *prima facie* plausibility because the claim of legal authority and the language used by the law share an important property. A claim of legitimate authority is a *public* claim that could, in principle, be derived from other *public* features of law. Insofar as it is a conceptually necessary condition of law that it is publicly promulgated and hence is a public entity, the language in which it is expressed is also public. It is quite natural to think that a public claim of legitimate authority can be inferred from the public language in which law is framed.

One somewhat surprising property from which Raz attempts to derive a public claim of legitimate authority seems to be a private mental state unconnected with some public act on the part of officials. As Raz puts the point, law's claim of legitimate authority "is manifested [in part] by the fact that ... [officials] *regard themselves* as having the right to impose obligations on their subjects" (*EPD* 215–16; emphasis added).[6]

The property of regarding oneself as having a right of some kind to impose obligations on citizens is an *attitude* constituted by purely internal beliefs and dispositions. To say that officials regard themselves as having such a right expresses no more than that (1) they believe that they have such a right; and (2) they have certain normative dispositions to behave in certain ways. Beliefs and dispositions are purely mental states that might be expressed in acts, but they need not be. I have many beliefs and dispositions that I have never acted on because I have never found myself in circumstances in which both would be activated in a way that would culminate in some act on my part. On this line of reasoning, then, a claim of legitimate authority can reasonably be attributed to the legal system on the strength of beliefs and dispositions that need not be acted on or publicly expressed.

[6] There are a couple of points about the character of the relevant rights and obligations that should be made. First, the right officials believe they have to impose obligations on their subjects must be construed as a *moral* right. A belief on the part of officials that they have a merely *legal* right to impose such obligations would not provide any support for attributing a claim of *moral* legitimacy to law. Second, the character of the obligation they believe they have a right to impose is most plausibly construed as legal; thus construed, the idea is that they believe they have a moral right to impose *legal* obligations on subjects. It is not just that those are the only obligations that are necessarily imposed by a mandatory legal norm; it is also that it is implausible to think that anyone has a moral right to impose *moral* obligations on subjects. When someone comes into my home, she has a moral obligation not to start smashing my property. This is an obligation that I can waive, but it misdescribes the situation to think that I have imposed that obligation on her in the exercise of some general moral right to impose moral obligations.

One might think that, given the nature of what officials are and must do, it is not conceptually possible for someone to be properly characterized as an official without sometimes doing something official that expresses the relevant attitudes. Officials are officials, on this line of argument, in virtue of what they *do* in contexts in which law is recognized, applied, and enforced; a judge is only a judge insofar as she entertains and adjudicates disputes between citizens.

But this is not obviously true. It is arguably possible to conceive of a legal system, like a "society of angels," in which judges never have to decide cases because citizens never have the kinds of conflicts that give rise to legal disputes requiring judicial adjudication. In this world, the citizens and the law would have some properties that they lack in the world of our experience: (1) the law would have to be sufficiently clear that disagreement among citizens about what the law requires never occurs; (2) citizens would have to be sufficiently motivated always to do what the law requires; and (3) it would have to be clear to all citizens that the behavior of every other citizen always complies with the law. In such a system, it would still be necessary to designate certain persons as judges just in case there are disputes. Those persons designated as judges would have to have the relevant beliefs and dispositions but would never have to do anything that expressed those beliefs and dispositions.

If such a state of affairs is conceptually possible, then the idea would have to be that the instantiation by officials of just the relevant mental states (which include the belief and associated dispositions) warrants attributing a claim of legitimate authority to the legal system. On this line of reasoning, then, the fact that officials have the belief that they have a right to impose legal obligations on subjects along with the associated dispositions implies a claim of legitimate authority.

There are two problems with this view. First, there is nothing in the claim that officials *believe* they have a right to impose legal obligations on citizens that would warrant attributing a claim of legitimate authority to the legal system. Unstated beliefs and dispositions are just not the kinds of thing that can express or make claims, either by themselves or together. Public claims can reliably be attributed to people only on the strength of public behaviors that are partly expressive in character.

Second, there is no reason to think that officials typically believe that they have a *moral* right to impose legal obligations on citizens. If the idea is that such a belief can be inferred from the public acts of officials, it is problematic. The most that can reliably be inferred from the adjudicative acts of judges is that they believe they have a *legal* right to impose legal obligations on citizens because their powers and duties as officials are defined by the law itself. Judges, for example, have authority to decide legal disputes because the law affords them that authority. There is nothing in any of this that would entail either that they have a *moral* right to impose legal obligations on citizens or that they *believe* they have such a moral right.

It might be true that many judges believe they have some sort of moral right to impose legal obligations on citizens because they believe the system is morally legitimate, but it cannot be assumed that judges, as a matter of conceptual necessity, have such a belief. The idea that a judge might impose legal obligations on subjects without believing that she is morally justified in doing so is neither conceptually incoherent nor psychologically impossible. Whether all or even most officials in a legal system have this belief is an empirical issue that can be resolved only by sociological investigation.

This is not to suggest that one can never reliably infer a mental state expressing a motive from an act of some kind, but there will always be more than one such mental state that can plausibly be inferred. For example, it might be true that one can usually infer that a person is hungry from the fact that she is eating. But there are other mental states that would explain why a person is eating: a person might be eating when she is not hungry to maintain a healthy weight or to make sure that she is getting proper nutrition. To suggest that there are difficulties in inferring beliefs and dispositions from public acts is not to claim that beliefs and dispositions can never reliably be inferred from public acts; it is merely to claim that such inferences, even in the most favorable of contexts, are subject to some uncertainty.

Inferring an official's beliefs and dispositions from the fact that she is applying or promulgating some norm as law is subject to no less uncertainty than inferring someone's beliefs and dispositions from the fact that she is eating. Assuming the act of applying or promulgating a norm *R* as law entails support for recognizing it as law, a judge or legislator might support recognizing *R* as law because she believes that *R* is morally legitimate, or she might support *R* because she believes that she needs to in order to maintain some desired level of support from her constituency. There are just as many beliefs and sets of related dispositions compatible with an official's applying or promulgating a norm as law as there are beliefs and sets of dispositions compatible with someone's eating something.

Accordingly, there are two problems with the argument here. First, there is no reason to think that it is a conceptual truth that officials in a legal system regard themselves as having a moral right to impose legal obligations on their subjects. Second, even if officials necessarily regard themselves as having such a moral right, a public claim to legitimate authority cannot be inferred from the purely private unexpressed mental states of officials. The claim, then, that officials regard themselves as having a right to impose obligations on subjects provides no support for the Authority Thesis.

4.3 Officials' claim that subjects owe allegiance

A third line of reasoning attempts to derive a claim of legitimate authority from claims on the part of officials that subjects owe a duty of "allegiance." As Raz puts it, "law's claim to authority is manifested by . . . [officials'] claims that their subjects owe them *allegiance*" (*EPD* 215–16; emphasis added).[7] The idea here is that one can derive law's claim of legitimate authority from a claim made by officials that subjects owe a moral obligation of *loyalty*.

At the outset, it is important to note that a moral obligation of loyalty could not be owed to a legal system. It is far more plausible to think that we owe moral obligations to plants than it is to think we owe moral obligations to legal systems because it is far more plausible to think that plants have interests that can be harmed than it is to think that legal systems have interests that can be harmed. On the one hand, it seems reasonable to think that one can harm a plant because plants, as living things, are plausibly thought of as having interests in getting enough sun and water. On the other hand, it is hard to see how one could harm a legal system because non-living, non-sentient non-physical artifacts do not have interests of any kind.

Consider the claim that legal systems have an interest in justice. It is as silly to claim that legal systems have an interest in justice as it is to claim that legal systems want to be just; they are simply the wrong kind of thing to have interests or desires. Plants are non-sentient objects that lack any state that could plausibly be characterized as a desire, but they are living things that are reasonably thought to have interests and this is why it makes sense to think that they can be harmed instead of merely damaged. It might be true that legal systems and legal institutions, as non-living non-sentient non-physical abstract artifacts, can be *damaged* but they can no more be harmed than an automobile can.

The problem with the idea that these objects can be owed moral obligations is not just that it is false; it is rather that it rises to the level of a category mistake if ordinary usage is the touchstone. The lexical meaning of "category mistake," as Oxford Online Dictionary reports it, is particularly telling in this regard:

[7] The relevant obligation would have to be a *moral* obligation. First, there is no law in legal systems like that of the U.S. that requires "allegiance" of subjects and hence no law that would impute a *legal* obligation of allegiance. Second, the claim that subjects owe a *legal* obligation of allegiance would not assert or imply anything that would support attributing a claim of *morally* legitimate authority to the legal system.

Category Mistake: (n) The error of assigning to something a quality or action which can only properly be assigned to things of another category, for example treating abstract concepts as though they had a physical location.[8]

The example in the definition is directly on point: the idea that an abstract object can be owed a moral obligation seems as much and as clearly a category mistake as "treating abstract concepts as though they had a physical location." It is no less conceptually confused to think that such things could be owed a moral obligation or could be harmed as it is to think they have a physical location.

The same is true of the claim that citizens owe a moral duty of loyalty to the legal system, and this poses a problem for the idea that this claim can plausibly be attributed to officials in every conceptually possible legal system. Perhaps one can argue without conspicuous absurdity that officials of every conceptually possible legal system make a claim that is false. But it is implausible to suppose that it is a conceptual truth that officials make a claim that expresses a category mistake because this would imply that an institutional normative system in which officials do not commit this category mistake is *not* properly characterized as a legal system for that reason.

The only remotely plausible interpretation of the view is that officials claim that subjects owe a moral duty of loyalty to the *officials*, and not that they claim that subjects owe a duty of loyalty to the legal system itself. Officials have interests that can be harmed in virtue of being persons who are alive, sentient, and rational—unlike legal systems, which are abstract objects like the object denoted by the numeral "2" and are hence the wrong kind of thing to which interests can be coherently attributed.

It is certainly possible for officials to believe or claim that citizens owe *them* a moral duty of loyalty since that idea is neither an obvious category mistake nor obviously false in all conceptually possible legal systems, but it is problematic to assume that all or some officials in a legal system necessarily believe or claim this. First, it might be plausible to think that citizens owe a moral duty of loyalty to some officials, but it seems clearly implausible to think that citizens owe a moral duty of loyalty to everyone who is properly characterized as an official of the legal system. It is difficult to make sense of what would be required by a moral duty of loyalty to the President; it is considerably more difficult to make sense of what would be required by a moral duty of loyalty to officials at the Internal Revenue Service.

[8] "Category mistake," *Oxford Online Dictionary*; available at: https://en.oxforddictionaries.com/definition/category_mistake.

Second, it is implausible to think that officials in democratic systems like that of the U.S. necessarily believe or claim that citizens owe *them* a moral duty of loyalty. In a democracy, citizens are not conceived of as *subjects* of the officials who recognize, apply, and enforce law; officials are instead conceived of as public servants who owe a duty to their constituents to serve them. While there might be some plausible metaphorical construction of the claim that citizens should be loyal to their country, such a construction would neither assert nor imply that citizens owe a moral duty of loyalty to officials. If the claim that citizens owe a moral duty of loyalty to officials is true in some conceptually possible legal systems, it is not obviously true in democratic legal systems in which officials are conceived of as public servants.

It might be true that some officials in the U.S. are confused about this and believe that citizens owe them a moral duty of loyalty. It might even be true, although even this sufficiently strains credulity to require empirical evidence, that most officials in every existing legal system believe such a claim. But it is simply false that all or some officials in every conceptually possible legal system believe that citizens owe them a moral duty of loyalty; we can easily conceive of a legal system in which officials reject such self-important nonsense.

Similarly, it might be true that some officials in the U.S. do something that asserts or implies that citizens owe them a moral duty of loyalty. It might even be true that most officials in every existing legal system do something that asserts or implies that citizens owe them a moral duty of loyalty. But it is false that some or all officials in every conceptually possible legal system do something that asserts or implies that citizens owe them a moral duty of loyalty; there is simply nothing in what must be included in the job description of a judge or legislator that would require doing anything that asserts or implies such a claim.

There is nothing in ordinary patterns of usage that even suggests that it is a conceptually necessary condition for the existence of a legal system that even *one* official believes that citizens owe officials a duty of loyalty. There is simply nothing in the nature of law, in the nature of being an official, in the content of the typical job descriptions for legislators or judges, or in the psychology of human beings that entails that someone who serves as an official of a legal system must believe—much less claim—that citizens owe them a duty of loyalty. The idea, then, that officials claim that citizens owe them a duty of allegiance provides no support for the Authority Thesis.

4.4 Designation of officials as "authorities"

Raz argues that a claim of legitimate authority can be derived from the fact that "legal institutions are *officially* designated as 'authorities'" (*EPD* 215; emphasis added). The idea seems to be that a claim of legitimacy can be attributed to law on the ground that the law itself characterizes officials as authorities; after all, the only way that legal institutions could be *officially* designated as "authorities" is through some official act that has the status of law. If the law itself specifically designates these institutions as "authorities" and that term connotes that these institutions are morally legitimate, then law must be understood to claim that it is legitimate.

There are two problems with this line of argument. First, and most conspicuously, the claim that "legal institutions are officially designated as 'authorities'" is not true of even all existing legal systems. Nowhere in the U.S. Constitution are executives, legislators, or judges officially designated as "authorities." Likewise, if the Supreme Court ever refers to Congress as a body of legislative "authorities," such references would not amount to an official *designation* of Congress as an authority; what would be involved in designating something as an authority is not clear, but it is clear that only something with a certain kind of authority that the Court lacks could officially designate Congress as an authority. If it is not true of the U.S. legal system, then it is not true of all conceptually possible legal systems.

Second, even if legal institutions have been officially designated as "authorities," that fact is not enough to warrant attributing a claim of legitimate authority to a legal system. The problem is that, as far as ordinary usage is concerned, one can have practical authority over a class of persons without its being morally justified or its being believed to be justified. A police officer, *P*, might have something properly characterized as practical authority over another person, *Q*, that is neither morally justified or is believed by either *P* or *Q* to be morally justified.

There is nothing obviously problematic from the standpoint of our ordinary linguistic conventions with claiming that Nazi courts had authority over those who appeared before them. Although we might also clarify that such authority was not legitimate, there is nothing in these ordinary linguistic conventions that would require that we characterize such authority as merely *de facto*. Most competent native speakers of English would not understand what I meant if I said that the Nazi courts had merely *de facto* authority over citizens. But if they did understand the statement, they would have inferred what I meant from the context of the utterance based on shared assumptions about the wickedness of the Nazi system. The inference would be grounded in certain facts and shared moral judgments about the Nazis—and not in ordinary linguistic conventions for using the term "authority."

Further, there is nothing in our linguistic conventions that allows for the use of the term "authority" to describe an illegitimate institution only if citizens generally believe that the institution is legitimate. As far as ordinary usage is concerned, Nazi courts are properly characterized as having authority over subjects regardless of whether the subjects believed that those courts or judges had morally legitimate authority over them.

The problem to which this gives rise is that one cannot infer a claim of legitimate authority from the claim that legal institutions are officially designated as "authorities." If what people mean when they use the term "authority" to refer to someone does not, on our linguistic conventions, connote that the person's authority is morally legitimate, then a claim of *morally legitimate* authority cannot validly be inferred from just the use of the term "authority." Since our linguistic conventions allow use of the term "authority" to refer to authorities that are neither morally legitimate nor generally believed to be so, there is nothing in the "designation" of legal institutions as *authorities* that would imply a belief or assertion that their authority is morally legitimate.

To summarize: a claim of legitimate authority must be grounded in beliefs or acts that imply that the law is morally justified; and given the ordinary meanings of the term, there is nothing in the use of "authority" that would assert or imply that the authority of legal institutions is morally justified. Since, as far as our linguistic conventions are concerned, there can be authority that is legal in character without being morally justified, any official designation of legal institutions as "authorities" entails no more than that these institutions have *legal* authority under the laws of the system; such a designation would not imply that what legal authority those institutions have is morally justified and hence would not warrant attributing a claim of legitimate authority to the legal system.

4.5 Officials' claim that subjects have an obligation to obey the law

Perhaps the most promising ground for the Authority Thesis is the idea that officials claim that subjects owe an obligation to obey the law:

> The law's claim to authority is manifested by ... [officials'] claims ... that their subjects *ought* to obey the law as it requires to be obeyed (i.e., in all cases except those in which some legal doctrine justifies breach of duty). Even a bad law, is the inevitable official doctrine, *should* be obeyed for as long as it is in force, while lawful action is taken to try to bring about its amendment or repeal (*EPD* 215–16; emphasis added).

The idea is that officials of the legal system express its claim of legitimate authority by insisting that subjects have a content-independent obligation to comply with valid legal norms regardless of what they require until those laws are repealed or are otherwise properly changed.

It is reasonable to think that officials believe that citizens have a content-independent obligation to comply with the law. Judges are charged with recognizing, applying, and enforcing as law anything that has the appropriate source in legislative or judicial acts regardless of content. Legislators enact law with the expectation that it will be enforced by judges in an exclusionary manner regardless of content. Further, official acts of any kind must satisfy the rules of law defining the duties and powers of officials regardless of the content of those rules. It is hard to understand how someone could competently serve as an official without believing that subjects have a content-independent obligation to comply with the law; while someone who lacked such a belief might not be conceptually disqualified from serving as an official, it is hard to see how they could perform their duties in a competent manner without believing something like this.

But there is no reason to think that officials must believe that the relevant obligation is moral in character; it would also be sufficient for them to competently perform their functions that they believe the only relevant obligations are legal. It is true that judges could not apply and enforce whatever norms happen to have the status of law against citizens regardless of their content unless they believe (or act as if they believe) that those norms give rise to content-independent obligation of *some* kind; to apply and enforce a norm in an exclusionary manner is to treat it as if it gives rise to a content-independent obligation on the part of the subject to comply. Since legal norms give rise to legal obligations that are content-independent in character, all that is necessary to explain how judges can competently perform their duties is that they believe (or act as if they believe) that law gives rise to content-independent *legal* obligations.

The problem here is not just that it is unnecessary to impute to judges a belief that the law gives rise to content-independent moral obligations to explain how they can competently perform their duties; it is rather that such a belief would contribute nothing to explaining how judges can competently do what they do. To carry out their legal duties, judges must apply and enforce *legal* norms against subjects in an exclusionary manner that is also defined by *law*. Courts are not charged, legally or otherwise, with deciding disputes under norms of morality; indeed, courts are frequently barred by law from deciding purely moral disputes and from deciding legal disputes by recourse to moral norms that do not have the status of law.[9] The idea

[9] As discussed in Chapter 2, Federal Rule of Civil Procedure 11(b)(2) provides as follows: "By presenting to the court a pleading, written motion, or other paper—whether by signing, filing,

that officials believe that law gives rise to content-independent moral obligations cannot explain a judge's ability to competently perform her function because a judge's job description requires only that she decide disputes that arise under legal norms.

Perhaps the thought is that officials could not, as a psychological matter, do things that have the effect of coercively restricting the freedom of others in a manner that subjects them to the threat of incarceration unless they believed that legal norms give rise to a content-independent moral obligation to comply. The idea here is that, for example, a judge could not, as a psychological matter, issue an order incarcerating a defendant unless she believed she was morally justified in doing so. On this line of reasoning, the only obvious moral justification for incarcerating a defendant who failed to comply with the law is that she violated a content-independent moral obligation to comply.

There is little reason to suppose that officials could not, as a psychological matter, perform such functions unless they believe that citizens have a content-independent moral obligation to comply with the law. Even the most morally virtuous people are psychologically capable of doing things they believe are morally wrong; no one is free of wrongdoing. While one can hope that most officials are motivated by moral considerations, we know from experience that officials are as capable as anyone else of acting on selfish and even wicked motivations. It seems clear that it is not a conceptually or psychologically necessary condition for officials to be capable of performing their official functions that they believe law gives rise to content-independent moral obligations to comply.

Nor is there any reason to think that there is anything in any official's job description that cannot be done unless she publicly *claims* that the law gives rise to content-independent *moral* obligations to comply. It is true that some officials, such as judges, must occasionally in the course of performing their job responsibilities make claims about what citizens are *legally* obligated to do; however, there is no obvious reason to think that there is anything that

submitting, or later advocating it—an attorney or unrepresented party certifies that to the best of the person's knowledge, information, and belief, formed after an inquiry reasonable under the circumstances . . . the claims, defenses, and other legal contentions are warranted by existing law or by a nonfrivolous argument for extending, modifying, or reversing existing law or for establishing new law." In essence, Rule 11(b)(2) prohibits bringing an action simply on the ground that it is necessary to remedy moral injustice in the law. It is true that an action can be properly grounded in a good-faith argument to change the law for moral reasons; but that presupposes that there can be laws that are morally problematic and that the court has legal authority to change the law for that reason. See Note 16, Chapter 2.

any official must do that would imply a claim about what citizens are *morally* obligated to do. Legislators are not typically required to do anything that would imply any claim about what citizens are obligated to do—either legally or morally. Judges must, in the course of deciding such disputes, make claims about the legal obligations of the parties, but they need not make claims about what morality requires. A judge can apply and enforce a valid legal norm against a citizen without doing anything that asserts or entails a claim about what citizens are morally obligated to do.

This argument for the Authority Thesis fails, then, because there is no reason to think that it is a conceptual truth that even some officials must do something that would entail a claim that citizens have a general content-independent *moral* obligation to comply with the law. Since the only claims any officials need make about the obligations of citizens concern only their legal obligations under the valid laws of the system, the idea that officials claim that "subjects *ought* to obey the law as it requires to be obeyed (i.e. in all cases except those in which some legal doctrine justifies breach of duty)" provides no support for the Authority Thesis.

4.6 The claims taken together

One might concede that none of the features discussed above warrants attributing a claim of legitimate authority to law but argue that some combination of them does. For example, one might think that (1) the instantiation of any three of the above five features is sufficient to warrant attributing a claim of legitimate authority to an institutional normative system and that (2) every conceptually possible legal system exhibits at least three of these features. If (1) and (2) are true, then it follows that every conceptually possible legal system claims legitimate authority. Instantiation of each of the relevant features would be conceptually necessary for a legal system to claim legitimate authority, while instantiation of all of them would be conceptually sufficient for a legal system to claim legitimate authority.

The problem is that we can conceive of something lacking all these features that seems to be a paradigmatic instance of a legal system. Suppose there is a society, *S*, that is as much like that of the U.S. except that all citizens in *S* deny that law *could* be morally legitimate and hence deny that law could give rise to a content-independent moral obligation to comply on the part of subjects. Recognizing the need to keep the peace, they all agree to be governed by a normative system that authorizes coercive enforcement mechanisms for violations of the system's obligations and explicitly contract with one another to conform to those obligations. The officials accept a conventional recognition norm that provides recipes for recognizing, applying, and enforcing the norms of the system, while citizens generally obey the valid norms of the system, which incorporate the minimum content of natural law. But being skeptics about the possibility of morally legitimate systems of law, officials refrain from using the potentially misleading terms "authority," "duty," "obligation," and "right," relying instead on terms like "official," "required," "mandatory," "non-optional," and "permitted" in recognizing, applying, and enforcing, and citizens follow this practice. In addition, officials deny that they are owed any duty of allegiance or loyalty. Despite such skepticism about whether any system could be morally legitimate, these institutional norms are just and justly administered.

Regardless of whether this imagined normative system is properly characterized as "law," it seems to be a morally legitimate system of regulation. All citizens promise to comply with the norms of the system in exchange for the promises of all others to do the same. The norms of the system are just, justly administered, and protect citizens from morally culpable assaults on their persons and property. If we further suppose that the system also contains every norm that any legal system must contain to be morally legitimate, then it seems to satisfy all the standards that are required for a legal system to count as morally legitimate—assuming that their views about moral legitimacy are false. Whether or not the system counts as one of law, it is indisputably a morally legitimate system of governance, if any is.

Further, the system in *S* seems to have all the features that are conceptually necessary for something to count as being authoritative. Citizens all take the internal point of view toward the rule of recognition and the valid norms of the system and hence regard the norms of the system as providing content-independent exclusionary reasons for action. The norms tell citizens what they must do; they are applied and enforced in an exclusionary manner that reflects the exclusionary character of the reasons the citizens believe such norms and orders provide. It is true that citizens refrain from using the term "authority" to avoid a suggestion that the system is morally legitimate and do not believe it is legitimate; but it is not a requirement for something to count as an authority on any plausible conception of the term that citizens use that particular word to describe things with authority. It seems clear that the norms and officials do everything that something must do to be properly characterized as an authority according to ordinary usage. If Nazi courts had authority on this ordinary usage, then so does the system in *S*.

The existence conditions for a legal system are satisfied under any plausible conceptual theory of law. From the standpoint of Hart's minimum conditions for the existence of a legal system, the imagined system is a legal system for the following three reasons: (1) the officials of *S* adopt the internal point of view toward the putative rule of recognition; (2) citizens of *S* generally comply with the norms validated by the putative rule of recognition; and (3) *S* incorporates the minimum content of natural law. But since, by hypothesis, all the norms are just and justly administered, the imagined system would also count as one of law under the traditional interpretation of natural law theory. If we suppose, further, that the system also incorporates those moral principles that justify the application of coercive enforcement mechanisms and shows the existing institutional history in its best moral light, it would satisfy Dworkin's third theory of law. Finally, assume that everyone refers to the norms of the system as "law."

What plausible, non-question-begging reason could there be to deny that this system of rules is a legal system? The only salient difference between the legal system of the U.S. and the institutional normative system in *S* is that officials in the U.S. typically believe (assuming they believe this) that the system is legitimate, while officials in *S* lack such a belief—a difference that seems irrelevant to the characterization of the latter as a system of law. All the major institutions are there: the rule of recognition defines institutions that promulgate, apply, and enforce law. All the citizens of *S* accept the determinations of the officials as reasons for action. The rules of *S* are obeyed to precisely the same extent as the rules of law are in the U.S. It is plausible to characterize *S* as having a legal system because it has all the pieces necessary for efficacious state regulation of behavior even though there is nothing that could be construed as entailing an institutional claim to legitimate authority.

Raz anticipates the possibility of constructing a normative system something like this one as a counterexample to the Authority Thesis:

> [T]ry to imagine a situation in which the political authorities of a country do not *claim* that the inhabitants are bound to obey them, but in which the population does acquiesce in their rule. We are to imagine courts imprisoning people without finding them guilty of any offense; damages are ordered, but no one has a duty to pay them. The legislature never claims to impose duties of care or of contribution to common services. It is not merely ordinary people who are not subjected to duties by the legislature: courts, policemen, civil servants, and other public officials are not subjected by it to any duties in the exercise of their official functions.[10]

Raz's response misses the mark. The issue is not whether there could be an authoritative system that arbitrarily imposes penalties and damages without there being a violation of something that counts as a norm stating a requirement that is applied and enforced in an exclusionary fashion; there could not

[10] Joseph Raz, *The Morality of Freedom* (Oxford: Clarendon Press, 1986); emphasis added. Hereinafter *MF*.

be. But that is not what is going on in *S*. People who are punished are being punished for violating a norm, but officials and citizens simply refrain from using "offense" to refer to the violation. People who are being ordered to pay damages are required to pay them under a norm that makes people liable for negligently causing injury.

The issue is, rather, whether it is conceptually possible for there to be a legal system that does not claim legitimate authority in virtue of using certain language and hence whether it is a conceptually possible for there to be a legal system that does not use terms like "offense" and duty" in characterizing the violations and requirements of norms; that is a different issue. It seems clear from the example above that there could be. There is nothing either in our conceptual practices or our moral views that would require the use of "offense" in characterizing violations of the law that are subject to punitive liability or the use of "duty" to describe requirements of the law that will be enforced against violating subjects in an exclusionary manner; it is enough that we can speak in terms of "violations" and "requirements" and that these terms pick out notions that function in practical reason the way the notions picked out by the terms "offense" and "duty" normally do.

On the strength of this foundation, Raz goes on to argue that the imagined system lacks authority and is hence not properly characterized as a legal system:

> Two things stand out when contemplating a political system of this kind. First, it is unlikely that any such society ever existed. Societies we know about are invariably subject to institutions claiming a right to bind their subjects, and when they survive this is in part because at least some of their subjects accept their claim. Secondly, if such a society were to exist we would not regard it as being governed by authority. It is too unlike the political institutions we normally regard as authorities (*MF* 27).

There are two problems here—one less and the other more important. The less important problem is that the claim that "it is unlikely that any such society ever existed" (*MF* 27) is an empirical claim and is hence not relevant; what matters is whether it is conceptually possible for such a legal system to exist, and not whether the existence of such a system is empirically probable. The more important problem is that Raz's argument asserts without evidence that "we would not regard [such a society] as being governed by authority." To refute the idea that the system like the one constructed above is a system of law, one must provide a plausible reason grounded in ordinary usage to believe that it is not properly characterized using the terms "law" or "authority." Raz's argument fails to do so because it begs the question against the relevant line of argument.

That said, there is nothing in the argument of *this* section that would entail the falsity of the Authority Thesis. Assuming it is conceptually possible for a legal system to make claims, it might be that there is some other conceptually necessary feature of a legal system that warrants attributing to it a claim of legitimate authority; if so, the Authority Thesis is true. What it does show, however, is that the considerations typically adduced in support of the Authority Thesis provide insufficient support for it. But if it could be shown, as seems plausible, that these features are the only ones that imply a claim of legitimate authority that can be attributed to the legal system as a whole, the arguments of this section, like the argument of Section 1 if it is sound, would be enough to falsify the Authority Thesis.

6

Authority, Moral Criteria of Validity, and Conceptual Confusion

There are three Arguments from Authority. The first argues that the norms of an institutional normative system *S* with moral criteria of validity cannot replace the judgments of subjects about what right reason requires because subjects cannot determine what its norms require without figuring out for themselves what right reason requires; since *S* cannot hence satisfy the Preemption Thesis, it cannot be legitimate. The second argues that subjects in *S* cannot better comply with what right reason requires by following the authority's judgments about what right reason requires than by following their own judgments because subjects can determine what its norms require only by judging for themselves what right reason requires and hence can follow only their own judgments; since *S* cannot hence satisfy Normal Justification Thesis (NJT), it cannot be legitimate. The third argues that the norms of *S* cannot express the authority's specific view about what the subject should do because the subject can determine what those norms express only by reading her own views about what she should do into the norms; since the rules hence cannot express what directives must express to be authoritative, *S* cannot be legitimate.

Each of these arguments depends on the idea that our conceptual practices with respect to the term "authority" entail that an institutional normative system cannot be legitimate unless it is conceptually possible for a subject to determine what its norms require without having to decide for herself what she ought to do (the Identification Thesis). This thesis, together with the conceptual truism that a legal system must be capable of instantiating legitimate authority (the Instantiation Thesis), entails the Sources Thesis. Since (1) an institutional normative system with moral criteria of validity cannot be legitimate because its directives cannot be identified by the subject without judging for herself what she ought to do and (2) only institutional normative systems that can be legitimate are legal systems, an institutional normative system with moral criteria of validity cannot be a legal system.

This chapter challenges the Identification Thesis. If *our* conceptual practices with respect to using the terms "law" and "authority" are determined by what competent speakers typically believe and say about law and authority, then those ordinary linguistic practices allow for the possibility of a legitimate legal system with moral criteria of validity; our conceptual practices are thus inconsistent with the Identification Thesis. As the Identification Thesis expresses the core of the service conception of authority, the service conception is inconsistent with the concept of authority as it is defined by our conceptual practices.

1. Identifying the content of our conceptual practices

The content of any concept plausibly characterized as ours is determined by the ordinary linguistic practices that construct the corresponding concept-term's lexical meaning. While logical space contains all possible concepts and hence includes concepts with which we are unfamiliar, *our* concepts are picked out by the conventions that *we* converge in practicing to express certain content. The content of our concept of bachelor equates bachelorhood with being an unmarried man because and only because we have converged on practicing a convention that dictates that the term "bachelor" is correctly used to refer only to unmarried men. Had we converged on practicing a convention that dictates that the word "bachelor" refers only to plants, it would not be true that all bachelors are unmarried men.

This is not to suggest that there is any ontological difference between concepts that are ours and concepts that are not ours. If logical space contains every piece of content that *could* be associated with some concept-term, it includes the content of concepts that are not properly characterized as ours. Our linguistic practices do not bring any concepts into existence. Our linguistic practices determine which of these pre-existing concepts are associated with our use of the relevant concept-term; if we had adopted a different convention for using the term "law," that term would pick out a different one of those pre-existing concepts than the one that it currently picks out.

Our convergent linguistic practices define a mapping of the terms of our language to the pieces of content that we use the terms to express; these pieces of content define the only concepts that are properly characterized as *ours*. Insofar as the project of conceptual analysis is concerned to identify the content of our concepts and the content of our concepts is determined by our convergent linguistic practices, the contents of the relevant concepts of law and authority are defined by those practices for using the concept-terms "law" and "authority." Any conceptual claims about law or authority must hence be evaluated on the basis of whether they conform to the linguistic conventions we practice for using the terms "law" and "authority."

Although the Arguments from Authority are conceptual and hence metaphysical in character, each relies on empirical claims about the content of our linguistic conventions with respect to the use of the terms "law" and "authority." As discussed in Chapter 2, modest conceptual analysis is concerned with identifying the deeper philosophical commitments presupposed by our ordinary linguistic practices with respect to using the relevant concept-term. The crucial claim is—and must be if the Arguments from Authority are properly construed as presupposing a modest approach to conceptual analysis—that speakers of the language converge on practicing linguistic conventions that ultimately preclude the application of the terms "law" and "authority" to an institutional normative system with moral criteria of validity.

This is an empirical claim about the content of our linguistic conventions, and it is stronger than might initially appear. Insofar as our ordinary linguistic conventions determine the lexical meanings of the words "law" and "authority," each of the Arguments from Authority ultimately depends on the claim that the lexical meanings of the terms "law" and "authority" preclude their application to an institutional normative system with moral criteria of validity.

Some caution is needed here. The claim that the lexical meaning of a term precludes its application to something does not imply that the lexical meaning is transparent with respect to the relevant application. As we have seen, it is not clear whether the term "bachelor" properly applies to the Pope even though dictionaries universally report its lexical meaning as "an unmarried man." The problem is that many competent speakers would decline to characterize the Pope as a bachelor on the ground that he is not institutionally eligible for marriage; if most speakers practice a convention that entails that only unmarried men institutionally eligible for marriage are bachelors, then the lexical meaning of the term precludes characterizing the Pope as a bachelor.

In this case, what is reported as the meaning of "bachelor" is not fully accurate because the linguistic conventions that determine the lexical meaning of the term "bachelor" do not entail that every unmarried man is a bachelor, but that is of no importance here. What matters is that the issue of whether the Pope is properly characterized as a bachelor according to the lexical meanings is an empirical issue that requires sociological lexical analysis to resolve.

There are three possibilities here: (1) the term "bachelor" might, according to the conventions that determine its lexical meaning, properly apply to the Pope; (2) the term "bachelor" might not, according to these conventions, properly apply to the Pope; or (3) the conventions that determine the lexical meaning of "bachelor" might be indeterminate with respect to whether the term "bachelor" properly applies to the Pope. In the case where the majority of speakers apply "bachelor" to the Pope, the conventions dictate that the Pope is properly characterized as a bachelor; in the case where the majority of speakers reject the application of the term to the Pope, the conventions dictate that the Pope is not properly characterized as a bachelor; and in the case where there is a significant split, the conventions are indeterminate with respect to whether the Pope is properly characterized as a bachelor.

Philosophical analysis is needed only when the lexical conventions are indeterminate. Such an analysis in the case of the term "bachelor" purports to identify common views about the nature of bachelorhood; in particular, it would purport to determine whether the nature of bachelorhood is exhausted by the compound property of being an unmarried man or whether instead the nature of bachelor includes institutional eligibility for marriage. As claims about the nature of a thing are metaphysical in character, an analysis that purports to clarify the nature of bachelorhood is philosophical in character. A philosophically grounded modest conceptual analysis attempts to explicate the deeper philosophical commitments that ground the lexical convention governing the use of "bachelor" in order to determine whether they resolve the indeterminacy

The same is true of whether the lexical meanings of the terms "law" and "authority" preclude the application of these terms to an institutional normative system with moral criteria of validity. If most speakers use these terms in a way that precludes their application to an institutional normative system with moral criteria of validity, then the lexical meanings are determinate with respect to the issue and entail that there cannot be a legal system with moral criteria of validity. If most speakers use the terms in way that allows their application to an institutional normative system with moral criteria of validity, then the lexical meanings are determinate with respect to the issue and entail that there can be a legal system with moral criteria of validity. If there is a significant split on the issue among speakers, then the lexical meanings are indeterminate with respect to the issue—and a philosophical analysis is needed to attempt to resolve the indeterminacy.

A modest conceptual analysis of law and authority begins with the definitions of the terms that are reported in dictionaries. One representative and highly respected dictionary, Oxford Online Dictionary, reports their lexical meanings as follows:

Law: The system of rules which a particular country or community recognizes as regulating the actions of its members and which it may enforce by the imposition of penalties; and

Authority: The power or right to give orders, make decisions, and enforce obedience.

Notice that, assuming these reports are completely accurate, there can be legal systems with moral criteria of validity since there is nothing in the lexical meanings that precludes applying the terms "law" and "authority" to an institutional normative system with moral criteria of validity. Just as there was nothing in the dictionary definition of "bachelor" that precludes its application to the Pope, there is nothing in the dictionary definitions of "law" and "authority" that precludes their application to an institutional normative system with moral criteria of validity. If the reports above accurately and completely state the application-conditions for the terms and the Arguments from Authority are grounded in the ordinary lexical meanings of these terms, then there is nothing in these meanings that would entail the falsity of the Incorporation Thesis.

It might be, of course, that the reports of the lexical meaning of the terms "law" and "authority" are not fully accurate because the relevant polling failed to inquire about the relevant cases. Just as the dictionary definition of "bachelor" would be inaccurate if the Pope is not a bachelor, the dictionary definitions of "law" and "authority" would be inaccurate if they falsely allow for the possibility of a legal system with moral criteria of validity. In exactly the same way that the definition of "bachelor" would be problematic if it incorrectly fails to preclude the Pope's being a bachelor, the definitions of "law" and "authority" would be problematic if they incorrectly fail to preclude the possibility of an authoritative legal system with moral criteria of validity.

2. The Identification Thesis and the Arguments from Authority

The Arguments from Authority, notwithstanding the differences among them, all depend on three principal ideas. The first is the Authority Thesis, according to which it is a conceptual truth that every legal system sincerely claims legitimate authority.[1] Insofar as "the claim to authority is part of the nature of law" (*EPD* 215), the idea of a legal system that does not sincerely claim authority is conceptually incoherent.

[1] Joseph Raz, "Authority, Law, and Morality," in Raz, *Ethics in the Public Domain* (Oxford: Clarendon Press, 1994). Hereinafter *EPD*.

The second is the proposition that "[i]f the claim to authority is part of the nature of law, then whatever else the law is it must be capable of possessing authority" (*EPD* 215). This conditional claim, together with the idea that every conceptually possible legal system sincerely claims to be a legitimate authority, implies:

The Instantiation Thesis: It is a conceptually necessary condition for something to count as a legal system that it is capable of legitimate authority.

For if every conceptually possible legal system sincerely claims authority and only an institutional normative system capable of being legitimate can sincerely claim authority, then any institutional normative system incapable of legitimacy is conceptually disqualified from being a legal system.[2]

The third idea articulates one of the necessary conditions for an institutional normative system of any kind to be legitimate:

The Identification Thesis: It is a conceptually necessary condition for an institutional normative system to be legitimate that subjects can identify the content of its norms without having to assess for themselves what right reason requires of them.

The Arguments from Authority employ a template that can be summarized as follows. If an institutional normative system cannot be legitimate unless the content of its norms can be identified by the subject without having to determine for herself what right reason requires, then an institutional normative system with moral criteria of validity cannot be legitimate because the subject cannot identify the content of its norms without determining for herself what right reason requires. But if an institutional normative system with moral criteria of validity is incapable of being legitimate and any institutional normative system incapable of being legitimate is conceptually disqualified from being a legal system, then an institutional normative system with moral criteria of validity is conceptually disqualified from being a legal system.

All the claims in this argument template are conceptual and hence metaphysical in character. The claim is that it is *conceptually* and hence metaphysically impossible for a subject of an institutional normative system *S* with moral criteria of validity to determine what she ought to do under its norms without assessing what right reason dictates that she should do. It is therefore *conceptually* and hence metaphysically impossible for *S* to be legitimately authoritative. The idea that an institutional normative system with moral criteria of validity can be legitimate is hence grounded in a conceptual confusion

[2] Raz thus derives the Instantiation Thesis from the Authority Thesis. This is unnecessary, as discussed in Chapter 5, because the Instantiation Thesis cannot plausibly be denied.

about the nature of legitimate authority, as is the idea that such a system can be a legal system.

The Identification Thesis, unlike the Instantiation Thesis, is far from self-evident. The Instantiation Thesis expresses a truism about law that can be derived from an obvious conceptual truth about artifacts: only those things capable of instantiating all conceptually necessary features of an *A* can be an *A*. If this latter claim is true and it is a conceptually necessary feature of law that it can be legitimate, then the Instantiation Thesis must also be true. The Identification Thesis, in contrast, is neither a truism about law nor immediately derivable from obvious conceptual truths about artifacts. Whatever else might be true of the Identification Thesis, it expresses a claim that is neither trivial nor self-evident.

The issue is whether we have any reason to believe that the Identification Thesis is true. Insofar as it purports to be a conceptual truth, the Identification Thesis must be grounded in the linguistic practices that determine the content of the relevant concepts. This, again, does not mean that the Identification Thesis must be transparently entailed by the lexical meanings of the terms in the way that the claim that every bachelor is unmarried is transparently entailed by the lexical meanings of "bachelor" and "unmarried." The Identification Thesis might be entailed by deeper philosophical commitments that are presupposed by our ordinary linguistic practices, but it must still be compatible with the lexical meanings that are determined by those practices.

3. Could law's claim of authority be conceptually confused?

The inclusive positivist might argue that officials who claim legitimate authority and accept the Identification Thesis are confused, but Raz rejects this line of defense:

> [W]hile [legal officials and institutions] can be occasionally [confused,] they cannot be systematically confused. For given the centrality of legal institutions in our structures of authority, their claims and conceptions are formed by and contribute to our concept of authority. It is what it is in part as a result of the claims and conceptions of legal institutions (*EPD* 217).[3]

[3] Raz's use of "systematic" suggests that the relevant confusion has both a vertical and a horizontal dimension. The horizontal dimension requires that the conceptual confusion be widespread. One official's conceptual confusion, no matter how extensive or deep, is not enough to constitute systematic confusion. The vertical dimension requires that the confusion pervade a plurality of core practices regarding the concept. Widespread conceptual confusion about purely peripheral issues is not enough to constitute systematic confusion. Conceptual confusion that has both these

It is helpful to note that there are two ways in which a claim of legitimate authority might be false. If, on the one hand, *S* is an institutional normative system or official, the statement that *S* is legitimate can be true or false. If it is true that *S* is legitimate, it is because *S* has the requisite moral properties, which will differ depending on whether *S* is an institutional normative system or *S* is an official. If it is false that *S* is legitimate, it is because *S* lacks the requisite moral properties. Either way, it is a contingent matter whether *S* is legitimate because whether or not *S* has the requisite moral properties depends on properties of *S* that are contingent: if *S* is an institutional normative system, then whether *S* is legitimate depends on the contingent content of its rules; if *S* is an official, then whether *S* is legitimate depends, among other things, on whether *S* was properly selected to serve as an official. Thus, if *S* is either an institutional normative system or an official lacking legitimate authority, the statement that *S* is a legitimate authority is contingently false.

But if, on the other hand, *S* is not an institutional normative system or an official, then the statement that *S* has legitimate authority is necessarily false. If *S* is a building or a novel, it is clearly false that *S* has authority. One need not know anything more about *S* than that *S* is one of those things to know that it does not have authority. We do not need to know what contingent features a building has to know whether it has authority. It does not because it could not; a building is not the kind of thing that, as a conceptual matter, could have authority. We likewise do not need to know what contingent features a novel has to know whether it has authority. It does not because it could not; a novel is not the kind of thing that, as a conceptual matter, could have authority. The claim that a building or novel has legitimate authority is necessarily false because it is conceptually confused.

In the case where *S* cannot have legitimate authority as a conceptual matter—regardless of whether *S* is a building or a novel—the claim that *S* has legitimate authority expresses a category mistake. The problem in each case is that *S* is not the kind of thing to which the category of authority applies. The category of authority applies only to things that are rational free agents or that are either norms or systems of norms. It makes no more sense to characterize a building as having legitimate authority than it does to characterize a number as making claims or as having a physical location.

The Identification Thesis implies that the claim that an institutional normative system with moral criteria of validity can be legitimate expresses a

dimensions is *system-wide* and hence "systematic" in the relevant sense: it afflicts a large percentage of officials and pervades the entire structure of beliefs regarding the concept. Officials can, on Raz's view, be conceptually confused as long as this confusion lacks either the horizontal dimension or the vertical dimension.

category mistake. Insofar as it is true that an institutional normative system with moral criteria of validity is *conceptually* incapable of being legitimate, it is as much the wrong kind of thing to instantiate authority as a building or a novel. It makes sense to ask of two legal systems which is closer to being legitimate; it makes no sense to ask of a novel and a book which is closer to being legitimate. Something that is conceptually incapable of legitimacy is neither close to nor far from being legitimate; it is just not the kind of thing to which legitimacy is sensibly attributed. If institutional normative systems with moral criteria of validity are conceptually incapable of legitimacy, it is as much a category mistake to attribute authority to them as it is to attribute a claim or physical location to a number.

There are circumstances in which a person might knowingly state claims about authority that express category mistakes. A person might say something that expresses a category mistake about authority for comedic effect. Assuming that it is a category mistake to think that a dog can have authority, an excessively doting dog owner might suggest that the animal has authority as a humorous way of expressing that the owner's life revolves around the dog's desires. Or a person might claim the dog has authority to deceive an alien in circumstances where she believes the alien poses a threat that can be neutralized with such a falsehood.

Alternatively, a person might say something expressing a category mistake without knowing that it expresses a category mistake. Assuming that it is a category mistake to think that a dog can have authority, someone could assert that a dog has authority without knowing that it expresses a category mistake; if one does not know that such a claim is, as a conceptual matter, necessarily false, one can sincerely assert it without knowing that it expresses a category mistake.

But there are certain kinds of category mistakes about authority that cannot be made. If a person (1) understands the nature of authority, (2) understands the nature of the thing about which a claim of authority is made, and (3) intends to make a literal claim attributing authority to the thing, then she cannot *sincerely* claim that something conceptually incapable of authority actually has authority. Thus, if officials sincerely claim authority on behalf of the legal system and understand the nature of authority, then a legal system can fail to have authority because it is unjust but not because it is the wrong kind of thing to have authority. If officials sincerely claim that law has authority, then that claim cannot express a category mistake: law must be the right kind of thing to have authority.

This reasoning seems facially incontrovertible. After all, sincerity obviously precludes the deliberate making of false claims. In ordinary circumstances, a person who claims that a building or novel has authority might instantiate any number of mental states that involve insincerity. Such a person might intend to deceive or to make a joke. But she cannot be characterized as being sincere in the absence of extreme confusion about the concept of authority.

The instantiation of sincerity by a person in ordinary circumstances precludes deliberately making conceptually false claims about authority, but it does not preclude unintentionally making such claims. A person might not realize that some entity *S* is conceptually incapable of authority and might sincerely claim that *S* has authority. If so, there is nothing precluding an official's being conceptually confused about authority and sincerely attributing it to something conceptually incapable of having it.

Raz allows that some officials can be confused about the nature of authority but denies that *most* officials could be confused about it because "their claims and conceptions are formed by and contribute to our concept of authority" (*EPD* 217). Since the content of the concept is determined by the convergence of officials in applying the corresponding concept-term, there cannot be widespread conceptual confusion about authority among officials. Accordingly, while some officials can exhibit conceptual confusions about authority that express category mistakes, it is not possible for most officials to exhibit such conceptual confusions.

Even so, it seems premature to dismiss the possibility of widespread conceptual confusion among officials because some conceptual confusions are more difficult to discern than others. It is certainly true that some mistakes are highly unlikely to occur except under the most unusual circumstances. As an empirical matter, it is extremely unlikely that a competent speaker of the language would think that a building or novel has authority because the conceptual confusion is transparent.

But not all such confusion is so transparent. It was widely believed for many years that space-time is defined by certain Euclidean constraints. In particular, it was widely thought necessary that, given a line *L* and a point *p* off of *L*, there is one and only one line passing through *p* parallel to *L*; that is, it was thought that the very concept of space-time was Euclidean in character. Despite the continuing intuitive appeal of this view, the general theory of relativity presupposes a non-Euclidean concept of space-time in which there are an infinite number of lines passing through *p* parallel to *L*. If the confusion about our universe was partly empirical in character, it was also partly conceptual in character.

The possibility of conceptual confusion about whether space-time is Euclidean can arise among competent speakers precisely because there is nothing in our ordinary linguistic practices that would transparently decide the issue of how many lines pass through *p* that are parallel to *L*. Space-time *appears* to be something that could, as a conceptual matter, be Euclidean in character. The claim that space-time is not Euclidean depends, in part, on empirical considerations about the universe that have nothing to do with our ordinary linguistic conventions for using the relevant concept-terms. Insofar as the claim that space-time is Euclidean involves a conceptual confusion, it is not one that is obvious.

But systematic *conceptual* confusion about authority among competent speakers of the language is not possible because the *nature* of authority is defined by the ordinary linguistic conventions that are practiced by such speakers. A competent user of a term cannot be systematically mistaken about its application because its application-conditions are defined by the way such a speaker uses it. Just as a competent user of the terms "bachelor" and "unmarried" cannot be confused about whether bachelors are unmarried, a competent user of the term "authority" cannot be confused about whether a building can have authority.

Law's claim of authority cannot be conceptually confused, then, because it is constituted by the beliefs, claims, and practices of officials that determine the meaning of the term "authority." If the Incorporation Thesis is inconsistent with the concept of authority as it is defined by the beliefs, claims, and practices of officials, it must be rejected; that thesis cannot be rescued by claiming that most officials are conceptually confused about the nature of authority.

4. Do most officials accept the Identification Thesis?

Raz believes that law's claim of authority cannot be conceptually confused, but officials in legal systems like ours can clearly be conceptually confused. Any official who would include moral language in the terms of a constitution believing that such language incorporates a moral constraint on the content of law would be conceptually confused on this view.

Constitutions often include provisions with language that seems to incorporate moral norms into the criteria of validity. The Eighth Amendment states that "cruel and unusual punishments [shall not] be inflicted." The notion of cruelty has some descriptive content, but it also has morally normative content: to say that a punishment is cruel is to say, among other things, that it inflicts suffering that is morally excessive given the gravity of the offense. It is certainly conceivable that an official might include such language in a constitution in the belief that the relevant moral standard is thereby incorporated into the criteria that determine what counts as valid law in the system.

It is likewise conceivable that a judge might apply what she takes to be a legal rule expressing a criterion of validity as though it incorporates a moral principle. A judge might interpret a constitutional provision prohibiting "cruel" punishments as if it incorporates the relevant moral standard into the criteria that determine what counts as valid law. On this reading, the constitution would invalidate official acts that inflict morally excessive punitive detriment on someone who violates the law.

These are not only possible motivations for including putatively moral language in a constitution or applying it in a particular way; they are also the most probable motivations for these acts. It is true that, if Raz is correct, the Eighth Amendment cannot incorporate moral content into the criteria of validity, but there is no reason to suppose that officials would know this. Given that many legal philosophers deny the Sources Thesis, there is no reason to suppose that philosophical laypersons would believe, much less know, that it is conceptually impossible to incorporate moral norms into the criteria of validity.

One can argue that any person who has this belief is conceptually confused, but this is a move that is plausible only up to a point. The more officials and citizens there are who have this belief, the less plausible it is to think that most officials and citizens are practicing a linguistic convention with respect to the term "authority" that entails the Identification Thesis. If the majority of officials and citizens believe that the constitution authoritatively incorporates moral standards that constrain the content of what counts as law and act on this belief, they could not be practicing a linguistic convention regarding "authority" that implies the Identification Thesis.

The problem is not just that it is conceivable that officials believe it is possible to incorporate moral norms into the criteria of legal validity; the problem is that there are judges in existing legal systems who have this belief and act on it. There is a split among judges about how to interpret those clauses of the Bill of Rights that are expressed in moral language. Originalist Justices like Antonin Scalia believe that a moral term appearing in the Constitution should be construed in accordance with the common understanding of its meaning at the time the relevant provision was ratified. Others like William Brennan believe that recourse to moral argument is necessary to identify the moral content of such terms.

These views about constitutional interpretation reflect views about what the meaning of the constitutional language really *is*. Insofar as originalists believe that the putatively moral language of the Constitution should be interpreted in accordance with the original understanding, it is because they believe that the original understanding of that language conforms to what it really *means*. Insofar as judges like Brennan believe that the putatively moral language of the Constitution should be interpreted as incorporating moral content, it is because they believe that the meanings of that language incorporate such content. But to the extent that their views of constitutional interpretation are grounded in the belief that they correctly identify the meanings of the relevant language, it follows that judges who hold a view like Brennan's are conceptually confused.

Even worse, every official, citizen, and legal theorist who holds a theory of constitutional interpretation like Brennan's would be conceptually confused on Raz's view. It is not clear what percentages of judges, citizens, lawyers, and legal theorists hold the respective views because no rigorous sociological surveys have been done. But it certainly seems possible that most officials, citizens, and legal theorists in our world side with Brennan over Scalia.

This poses a problem for the Identification Thesis. If it is possible that most people in *our* world accept Brennan's view, that is because there is no obvious contradiction between that view and *our* linguistic conventions for using the term "authority." It is not possible that most competent speakers of English accept that a married man can be a bachelor because there is an obvious contradiction between that view and the linguistic conventions for using the term "bachelor" that they understand themselves to be practicing.

The idea that these officials, citizens, and theorists can hold such a view only if they are conceptually confused is problematic. For if, given our linguistic practices regarding the term "authority," it is possible for some linguistically competent citizens, officials, and theorists to reject the Identification Thesis, then it is possible for all of them to do so. On this line of reasoning, if a state of affairs in which some linguistically competent judges believe the Constitution incorporates moral norms is consistent, given our linguistic practices, with its defining a legal system, then so is a state of affairs in which they *all* do. There is no reason to think, for example, that there could not be a legal system, compatible with our linguistic practices, in which every linguistically competent person holds Brennan's view on the possibility that the Constitution incorporates moral norms as criteria of legal validity.

But one cannot consistently hold (1) that it is possible, given our linguistic practices, for all such competent speakers to reject the Identification Thesis and (2) that anyone who rejects the Identification Thesis is conceptually confused. Our linguistic practices regarding the term "authority" imply the Identification Thesis only insofar as most competent speakers do not reject that thesis. If it is possible for most competent speakers to reject the Identification Thesis, then they could not be practicing a linguistic convention that implies or presupposes that thesis.

The Arguments from Authority, then, presuppose that most speakers cannot be conceptually confused about the Identification Thesis because they are practicing a linguistic convention that implies this thesis, but Raz offers no more support for this claim than the following remarks about arbitration:

> Suppose that an arbitrator, asked to decide what is fair in a situation, has given a correct decision .... Suppose that the parties to the dispute are told only that about his decision, i.e., that he gave the only correct decision. They will feel that they know little more of what the decision is than they did before. They were given a uniquely identifying description of the decision and yet it is an entirely unhelpful description (*EPD* 219).

If this is intended to justify a claim about what people believe about the concept of authority, the argument is problematic. It is probably true that most people would feel that an arbitrator who gave her decision in such terms had not performed her function, but this tells us more about the nature of arbitration than it does about the nature of either law or authority. An arbitrator who tells the disputants only that they should do the right thing has clearly not done anything properly characterized as arbitrating the dispute, but that is because the point of arbitration is to resolve disputes about what is the right thing to do by *specifically* identifying what the right thing to do is in the circumstances. Given this, it is clear that an arbitrator cannot perform the arbitration's conceptual function of "resolving" a dispute by telling the disputants only that they ought to do what is right. The conceptual function of an arbitrator is both practical and epistemic—namely, to resolve a disagreement by specifying what exactly disputants must do.

It is true that the conceptual function of law, like the conceptual function of arbitration, is both practical and epistemic, but the conceptual function of *law*—as opposed to, say, the conceptual function of *adjudication*—is not to resolve disputes about which of two specific acts must be performed by some particular person. It is rather to promulgate and apply general norms that provide enough guidance to make it possible for people to live together in society. As far as our linguistic practices are concerned, an enacted norm that prohibits killing "*innocent* persons" is no less law or authoritative because it does not indicate with specificity who counts as "innocent" under that norm.

The same is true of a constitutional norm prohibiting "cruel punishment." As far as our linguistic practices are concerned, the Eighth Amendment is no less authoritative or legal in character in virtue of not specifying exactly what would count as cruel. The rule has always been legally binding and authoritative in the U.S. despite the fact that, prior to any court precedent specifying what counts as cruel, the only way that a subject could determine what it prohibits is by assessing the balance of reasons with respect to cruelty. As far as ordinary usage is concerned, the Eighth Amendment is and has been legally binding and authoritative since its ratification.

It is partly because the functions of law and arbitration are different that each institution is needed. As Lon Fuller puts it, the point of law is to "achiev[e] ... [social] order ... through subjecting people's conduct to the guidance of *general* rules."[4] Law could not succeed in keeping the peace if it characteristically provided guidance that is as specific as an arbitrator's decisions; it is not nomologically possible for a human authority to comprehensively regulate the behavior of human beings by specifying every act that the authority seeks to regulate. Law is an institution that is contrived to keep the peace among beings like us, and that can only be done if behavior is largely regulated through the recognition, application, and enforcement of *general* rules.

Raz's arbitration argument fails to establish the Identification Thesis, then, because it incorrectly presupposes that law and arbitration perform the same conceptual function. Law is needed to provide general rules while arbitration is needed to settle disputes that arise under those general rules, and our linguistic practices with respect to the terms "law" and "arbitration" straightforwardly track that difference. Indeed, it is because law must regulate behavior by such means that a *judicial* agency—which arbitrates legal disputes—is needed to resolve disputes about what those authoritative legal norms require. As far as our linguistic practices go, law and arbitration have different but related functions. Both are authoritative, but each has a different epistemic function. Our ordinary linguistic practices distinguish the two because they have different functions; as far as our linguistic conventions are concerned, law and arbitration are not sufficiently analogous to preclude the possibility of an institutional normative system with moral criteria that is both law and authoritative. There is simply nothing in our linguistic practices that entails a commitment to the Identification Thesis.

Further, there is nothing in our linguistic practices that would entail a commitment to the Preemption Thesis, which expresses the core of the service conception of authority, because the Identification Thesis is logically equivalent to the Preemption Thesis. The proof is trivial. If, on the one hand,

[4] Lon L. Fuller, "A Reply to Professors Cohen and Dworkin," vol. 10 *Villanova Law Review* (1965), 655, 657. Emphasis added. Similarly, John Austin writes that "[a] law ... may be defined as a rule laid down for the guidance of an intelligent being by an intelligent being having power over him." John Austin, *Lectures on Jurisprudence or the Philosophy of Positive Law* (St. Clair Shores, MI: Scholarly Press, 1977), 5. See also H.L.A. Hart, "Postscript" in *The Concept of Law* 2nd Ed. (Oxford: Clarendon Press, 1994).

an institutional normative system cannot be legitimate unless its directives can replace the subject's assessment of the balance of reasons in her deliberations, then an institutional normative system cannot be legitimate unless the content of its norms can be identified by the subject without having to assess the balance of reasons; thus, the Preemption Thesis implies the Identification Thesis.[5] If, on the other hand, an institutional normative system cannot be legitimate unless the content of its norms can be identified by the subject without having to assess the balance of reasons, then an institutional normative system cannot be legitimate unless its directives can replace the subject's assessment of the balance of reasons in her deliberations about what to do; thus, the Identification Thesis implies the Preemption Thesis.

The foregoing empirical considerations refute the service conception of authority. Insofar as the Identification Thesis is logically equivalent to the Preemption Thesis, the above reasoning would also refute the Preemption Thesis. If there is nothing in our ordinary linguistic practices that implies the Identification Thesis, then there is nothing in those practices that implies the Preemption Thesis. If the service conception of authority is intended to explicate the concept of authority as it is determined by our ordinary linguistic practices, then it fails insofar as there is nothing in those practices that implies the Preemption Thesis.

These considerations also refute exclusive positivism if conceptual jurisprudence is concerned to explicate the concept of law as it is determined by our ordinary linguistic practices. Insofar as our ordinary linguistic practices allow for the conceptual possibility of a legal system with moral criteria of

[5] It is worth noting that the Identification Thesis can also be derived from NJT, which is a substantive moral claim about the justification of authority and not a conceptual claim about the nature of authority. NJT asserts that an authority is legitimate insofar as the subject is more likely to better comply with right reason if she follows the authority's assessments than if she follows her own. If NJT is true, then an institutional normative system *cannot* be legitimate if it is not *possible* for a subject to better comply with right reason by following the authority's assessments than by following her own. But it is not possible for a subject to better comply with right reason by following the authority's assessments if the authority's directives cannot be identified, as would be true of an institutional normative system with moral criteria of validity, by the subject without having to assess the balance of reasons. Thus, if NJT is true, then an institutional normative system cannot be legitimately authoritative unless the content of its norms can be identified by the subject without having to assess the balance of reasons.

One might think that the above derivation of the Identification Thesis from NJT is problematic because one cannot derive conceptual claims from substantive moral claims, but the above derivation does not rest only on substantive moral claims. The conceptual claim that an institutional normative system cannot be legitimately authoritative unless the content of its norms can be identified by the subject without having to assess the balance of reasons depends in part on NJT. But it also depends on the conceptual claim that it is not possible for a subject to better comply with right reason by following an authority if its directives cannot be identified without the subject's having to assess the balance of reasons.

validity, those practices are inconsistent with the Sources Thesis. Given that the Incorporation Thesis is merely the negation of the Sources Thesis, our ordinary linguistic practices seem to presuppose the Incorporation Thesis. If there are no other compelling reasons to think that it is conceptually impossible for a legal system to incorporate moral criteria of validity, the Incorporation Thesis would seem to be true as far as *our* concept of law is concerned.

7

To Whom the Rules Apply

Norm Guidance and the Incorporation Thesis

A legal system, like any other artifact, is an object manufactured to achieve some characteristic purpose that corresponds to its conceptual function. Given that a legal system is, by nature, comprised of norms that are recognized, applied, and enforced as law against subjects, it seems clear that the conceptual function of law involves regulating behavior through the guidance of norms. Since it is a necessary condition for something to count as an instance of a type of artifact that it is capable of performing that artifact's conceptual function, it is a necessary condition for an institutional normative system to count as a system of law that its norms are capable of guiding the behavior of its subjects.

This chapter is concerned with two arguments for the claim that the norms of an institutional normative system with moral criteria of validity are incapable of guiding behavior (the Guidance Arguments). The problem, on this line of reasoning, is that neither a rule of recognition that validates norms on the basis of moral merit nor a norm that is valid in virtue of moral merit can properly guide the persons they must be able to guide to perform law's conceptual function. To begin, since non-officials cannot identify what their obligations are under valid law by consulting a rule of recognition that validates all *or* only morally meritorious norms without determining for themselves what the morally meritorious thing is to do, the valid norms cannot properly guide non-official behavior.[1] Further, since a judge who follows such a rule of recognition is already motivated to do the morally meritorious thing in deciding a case, the judge cannot also follow the applicable valid norm because she will make the same decision regardless of whether she consults the valid norm. In both cases, an institutional normative system with moral

[1] A rule of recognition that validates all morally meritorious norms makes moral merit a sufficient condition for validity, while a rule of recognition that validates only morally meritorious norms makes moral merit a necessary condition of validity. A rule of recognition that validates all *and* only morally meritorious norms makes moral merit a necessary *and* sufficient condition for validity.

criteria of validity is incapable of performing law's conceptual guidance function and hence cannot be a legal system.

This chapter challenges the Guidance Arguments. It argues that the guidance function of law does not imply that every legal norm must be capable of guiding or informing the behavior of every person; it implies only that every legal norm must be capable of guiding or informing the behavior of every person *whose behavior it governs*. Since the rule of recognition governs only official behavior, there is no reason to think that subjects must be able to determine what their non-official obligations are under valid law by consulting the rule of recognition. Since a valid legal norm that a judge applies in deciding a dispute involving non-official behavior defines no judicial obligations or powers and hence does not govern judicial behavior, it is not possible for the judge to do anything in deciding the dispute that would count as *following* the valid norm. The Guidance Arguments are problematic, then, insofar as they assume that a rule that does not govern someone's behavior must nonetheless be capable of guiding or informing her behavior.

The Arguments from Authority are problematic for a similar reason. It might be true that a rule of recognition defining moral criteria of validity cannot replace the judgment of a subject with respect to what her non-official behavior should be in her practical deliberations about what to do, but a legal norm must be capable of replacing the judgments of *only* those persons whose behavior it governs. Since the rule of recognition, by definition, governs only official behavior, any norm that governs non-official behavior cannot be a *recognition* norm in the same sense that a married woman cannot be a bachelor. Insofar as the Arguments from Authority presuppose that the rule of recognition must be able to replace the judgments of subjects with respect to what their non-official behavior should be, it falsely presupposes that the rule of recognition must be capable of guiding persons whose behavior it does not govern. Like the Guidance Arguments, the Arguments from Authority fail to refute the Incorporation Thesis.

1. The guidance function of law

It is a truism that law has a conceptual function. If law is an artifact, it must have a conceptual function that expresses its purpose as such. Artifacts are objects, as a conceptual matter, that are manufactured, adapted, or adopted by intentional beings to serve some characteristic purpose; an object that is not intended to do something might be *artificial*, but it is not *artifactual*.

What distinguishes an object that is merely artificial from one that is also artifactual is that the latter is a non-natural object in virtue of being manufactured or adapted by intentional beings to do something while the former is simply a non-natural object. If I throw a bunch of fallen tree branches into a heap, the heap is a non-natural, and hence *artificial*, object in virtue of my having modified the various fallen branches from the natural state in which I found them by grouping them into a heap. But it is not an *artifact* unless I have manufactured or adapted it to serve some purpose for which it can generally be used. If I have manufactured the heap in order to present it to an audience to induce an aesthetic experience, the heap is an art object and hence an artifact. Everything that is artifactual is artificial, but not everything artificial is artifactual.

An artificial object must be *capable* of performing the conceptual function of some artifactual kind to be an artifact of that kind. An object that cannot perform the conceptual function of an automobile unless it is transformed into some other kind of object is not properly characterized as an automobile. It might be possible to make an automobile out of a cardboard box with a sufficient number of modifications, but an unmodified box is not capable of doing what something must be able to do to be an automobile; whatever modifications are needed would *transform* the object from something that was just a cardboard box into something that is not a cardboard box. If law is an artifact, then an object incapable of performing law's conceptual function is not properly characterized as "law."

Like any other artifact, something that is properly characterized as law has a conceptual function, but the term "law" is ambiguous as between two purely descriptive usages. The first picks out or describes an individual norm (*a* law) that is recognized, applied, or enforced by officials in some system, while the second picks out or describes the system (*the* law) of which those laws are constituents. *A* law is a part of *the* law.

The functions of the two are related in the same way that the function of some part of any other artifact is related to the function of the artifact itself. Every essential part of an automobile does something that makes it possible for the automobile to transport persons or things to some intended destination. The function of a steering wheel is to enable the driver to direct the automobile by manipulating its position, while the screws holding the various pieces of a steering wheel together facilitate the performance of the steering wheel's function by preserving its structural integrity; if the parts making up the steering wheel come loose, the steering wheel will come apart and be thereby rendered unable to perform its conceptual function.

The conceptual function of a legal system is to regulate behavior through the guidance of legal norms; these norms purport to guide behavior in a way that makes it possible for subjects to reap the social benefits of living and working together. Since it is not possible to reap such benefits unless socially disruptive conflicts are reduced to a point where something properly characterized as a community is possible, the conceptual function of a legal system is to regulate behavior in a manner that keeps the peace enough to permit the existence of a community among its subjects.

There are two classes of legal norms comprising a legal system. Some of these norms govern legislative, adjudicative, and enforcement activities and hence govern official behavior; these norms construct the rule of recognition and thereby define the criteria that distinguish norms that officials must recognize, apply, or enforce as law from those that they may not recognize, apply, or enforce as law. The remainder of these norms govern the non-official behavior of everyone within the jurisdiction of the system, including officials in their non-official capacities. These norms, along with the institutions they construct and the officials who staff those institutions, are all proper parts of a legal system.

As proper parts of a legal system, legal norms are contrived to perform a function that enables the system to regulate the behavior of those within its jurisdiction. But since a complete specification of the conceptual function of law *qua* norm includes that it guides behavior, it is a conceptually necessary condition for something to count as a legal *norm* that it is capable of guiding behavior. A box is not a legal norm because it is incapable of guiding behavior. A purely descriptive preamble to a law is likewise not a legal norm because purely descriptive content is incapable of guiding behavior.

It might be true that it is a necessary condition for something to count as *a* law that it is capable of guiding behavior, but it is not in virtue of being a *legal* norm that something is capable of guiding behavior.[2] Consider the sentence "citizens must pay taxes with six copper disks shaped like a square circle." Despite the otiose occurrence of the deontic operator "must" in the sentence, it fails to express something properly characterized as a norm insofar as it purports to require someone to do something that is *metaphysically* impossible.

[2] If we assume that the conceptual function of law *qua* norm distinguishes it from other kinds of norms, the conceptual function of law must involve something more than just guiding subject behavior; after all, the conceptual function of anything that counts as a norm is to guide behavior. While legal norms and norms of etiquette are specific subclasses of the general category of artifactual norms, the nature of the subcategory also contributes something to defining the conceptual function of the more specific type of norm; the conceptual function of even a legal norm that reproduces the content of a norm of etiquette will be different from the conceptual function of the norm of etiquette the content of which it reproduces. Part of the difference in the conceptual functions of the two subclasses of norms will be explained by the differences in the content of the respective rules, but part of the difference will have to do with the institutional character of law *qua* system and its conceptual function.

The sentence has the logical form necessary to express a norm in virtue of picking out a class of subjects, describing an act, and featuring a deontic operator that purports to require members of the former to do the latter. But the sentence fails to express something that would count, as a conceptual matter, as a norm because it is metaphysically impossible for even an omnipotent being to do what the sentence purports to require. There could not be a *legal norm* that requires citizens to pay taxes with copper disks in the shape of a square circle because there could not be a *norm of any kind* that requires this.[3] Anything properly characterized as a *norm*, whether legal or otherwise, must be capable of guiding behavior in some relevant sense.

Although something must be *metaphysically* capable of guiding behavior to be a norm, it need not be *nomologically* capable of guiding *our* behavior to be a norm. The sentence "all subjects must jump twenty feet off the ground once a day" expresses something that is properly characterized as a norm insofar as the existence of rational beings that can do that is nomologically possible; such beings might be stronger than we could be or might live on a planet where the pull of gravity is weaker. Either way, the norm it expresses cannot govern *our* behavior because, at this point in time, *we* are nomologically incapable of jumping that high; a norm that requires what is nomologically impossible from persons is metaphysically incapable of governing *their* behavior. Only norms nomologically capable of guiding the behavior of a class of beings are metaphysically capable of governing their behavior. Norm governance presupposes norm guidance.

While every legal norm must be metaphysically capable of guiding behavior, not everything capable of guiding behavior counts as a legal norm. Moral norms are capable of guiding behavior, but that does not make them legal norms. Moral norms, like legal norms, can guide behavior in virtue of being norms. But they have some property that conceptually distinguishes them from legal norms insofar as there can be a moral norm that is not also a legal norm. It is hence a necessary, but not a sufficient, condition for something to count as a legal norm that it is capable of guiding behavior.

More difficult is the issue of whether two norms requiring conflicting actions can be properly characterized, according to ordinary usage, as being norms of the same system. There are some normative systems that clearly cannot contain norms with inconsistent requirements. If morality is objective

[3] It is conceptually possible for officials in something that counts as a legal system to "enforce" content requiring subjects to do what is nomologically impossible, but that would not constitute such content as a norm. If norms must be metaphysically capable of guiding behavior and every conceptually possible law is a norm, then content requiring what is nomologically impossible could not be a law. The enforcement of such content by officials is, as a conceptual matter, a form of oppression that has nothing to do with applying or enforcing norms that have the status of law.

in character and there are two norms requiring conflicting actions of the same persons in the same circumstances, then at least one of those norms is not a moral norm. But it is not as clear that there can be no systems containing norms with inconsistent requirements. Suppose Congress enacts a norm requiring subjects in circumstance *C* to do *a* and subsequently enacts another norm requiring subjects in circumstance *C* to abstain from *a* without stating that the newer norm supersedes the older one. Suppose, further, that it is nomologically possible for subjects to do *a* and that it is nomologically possible for subjects to abstain from *a*. Under these assumptions, it is clear that each piece of content is nomologically capable of governing our behavior. But given that it is *metaphysically* impossible for someone to both do *a* and abstain from doing *a* in *C*, the question is whether both norms are properly characterized as laws of the same legal system at time *t*.

There is nothing in ordinary usage that obviously precludes there being two inconsistent laws in the same legal system. Each is properly characterized as a norm insofar as each has the requisite logical form and is metaphysically capable of guiding behavior; similarly, each norm is metaphysically capable of governing *our* behavior in virtue of requiring something that is nomologically possible to do. It is true that they cannot both be satisfied at the same time, but there is nothing in the concept of *a* law, as defined by our linguistic practices, that *clearly* dictates that a requirement of one norm of the system must be consistent with those of every other norm of the system. At the very least, the statement that one law requires doing something that another law prohibits is not obviously self-contradictory in the same sense that the claim that there can be married bachelors is obviously self-contradictory.

This is not to deny that a legal system should not require inconsistent acts. In the absence of exceptional circumstances, it would be morally wrong for a legal system to do so because it is generally unfair to require subjects to do what they cannot do. Moreover, a legal system that frequently required inconsistent acts is less likely to keep the peace among subjects because the application and enforcement of inconsistent requirements will likely lead to the kind of widespread dissatisfaction that expresses itself in socially disruptive ways. But this says nothing about whether it is conceptually possible for a legal system to require inconsistent acts; it goes only to the likelihood that the system will succeed in efficaciously regulating behavior in a manner that keeps the peace and thereby facilitates social cooperation.

It is for these reasons that most legal systems have laws resolving these inconsistencies by giving legal effect to only the most recently enacted law, but the fact that *laws* are needed to resolve these problems entails that it is conceptually possible for there to be two laws with inconsistent requirements. If it were conceptually impossible for norms stating inconsistent requirements to count as laws of the same jurisdiction, it would not be necessary to adopt a legal norm stipulating which of two conflicting "laws" may be applied or enforced in the system.

Further, there is nothing in the conceptual function of a legal system that straightforwardly precludes the possibility of a legal system with inconsistent laws because the existence of two inconsistent laws does not render the system incapable of regulating behavior in a manner that keeps the peace. There have surely been legal systems with norms defining inconsistent requirements that have nonetheless succeeded in keeping the peace; if one of those norms does not count as law, it is not in virtue of any obvious facts about the relevant usages. Although the inclusion of too many inconsistent requirements in an institutional normative system might render the system incapable of realizing its conceptual purpose, there is nothing in the concepts of a legal norm and a legal system that obviously entails that there can be no inconsistent legal requirements in a legal system.

The conceptual function of a legal system involves the regulation of behavior through norms that can guide subject behavior, but that does not imply that everything that counts as a legal norm must be *efficacious* in guiding behavior for a legal system to perform its function. Suppose Congress enacts a sentence that coherently expresses a norm, but people cannot discern, for contingent reasons, from that sentence which norm is expressed by the sentence and what that norm requires of them. Such an enactment would likely create confusion and discontent; however, the legal system would not thereby be rendered incapable of performing its conceptual function of regulating behavior through the guidance of norms—regardless of whether the enactment is properly characterized as creating a law. It is typically enough for a legal system to achieve its function that people can determine, one way or another, enough of what the norms of the system require to enable them to live together in peace. To efficaciously and fairly regulate anyone's behavior in a world *like ours*, a legal system must provide enough information to inform subjects of what law requires of them; a subject cannot *obey* a law if she does not know what it requires.[4]

[4] The notion of obedience is different from the notion of compliance in the following way. To say that a subject *S* obeys a norm *n* is to say that (1) *n* governs some act of *S*; (2) it is nomologically possible for *S*'s behavior to violate *n*; (3) *S*'s behavior conforms to *n*; (4) *S* believes that her behavior conforms to *n*; and (5) *S*'s conforming behavior was motivated by a desire to satisfy *n*'s requirements—either because *n* is a norm or because *n* will be enforced. To say that *S* complies with *n* asserts no more than that (1) *n* governs some act of *S*; (2) it is nomologically possible for *S*'s behavior to violate *n*; and (3) *S*'s behavior conforms to *n*. A subject can comply with a law without knowing what is required, but she cannot obey a law without knowing what it requires.

The notion of obeying a norm is also conceptually distinct from the notion of *following* a norm, as it is used below. To say that *S* follows *n* is to say that (1) *S* obeys *n*; and (2) *S* obeys *n* because *n*

Legal norms are distinct from other norms in virtue of the unique role they play in facilitating the realization of the conceptual function of a legal system. What distinguishes legal norms from other norms is not that they are metaphysically capable of guiding behavior; every norm is metaphysically capable of guiding behavior. What distinguishes *legal* norms from every other norm is that the officials of a system of *law* recognize, apply, or enforce them as legally binding against those persons to whom they are properly applied under some recognition norm of the system. Legal norms, then, are those propositions nomologically, and hence metaphysically, capable of guiding behavior that will be applied and enforced by officials against subjects; those norms are properly said to *govern* the relevant behaviors of subjects insofar as they may, under a recognition norm of the system, be applied or enforced against subjects who are nomologically capable of satisfying and violating them.

2. Motivational and epistemic guidance

There are two types of norm-guidance that a legal system must provide to be capable of regulating the behavior of law-subjects through the governance of legal norms. First, the law must provide norms metaphysically capable of *motivationally guiding* behavior in the following sense: a norm *n* motivationally guides a person *P* if and only if *P*'s conformity to *n* is motivated by the fact that *n* is a valid norm of the system. To be motivationally guided by *n* is to conform to *n because n* is a norm that governs one's conduct. Second, the law must provide norms metaphysically capable of *epistemically guiding* behavior in the following sense: *n* epistemically guides *P* if and only if *P* learns of her obligations under *n* by consulting *n and* satisfies those obligations under *n*.

Both types of norm-guidance require conforming behavior. *P* is motivationally guided by *n* if and only if (1) *P*'s behavior conforms to *n* and (2) *P* conforms her behavior to *n* because it is a norm of the system. *P* is epistemically guided by *n* if and only if (1) *P* learns of her obligations under *n* by consulting it and (2) *P*'s behavior conforms to *n*. If *P*'s behavior does not conform to *n* after learning what it requires, *P*'s behavior is neither motivationally nor epistemically guided by *n*.

Consider a legal norm that establishes a maximum speed limit of seventy miles per hour on Interstate 5. I am motivationally guided by that norm only insofar as I maintain a speed of under seventy miles per hour on Interstate 5

is a norm of the relevant system. Following a norm entails obeying it but obeying a norm does not entail following it; that is, it is not conceptually possible to follow a norm without obeying it, but it is conceptually possible to obey a norm without following it.

because the rule requires it; insofar as I maintain that speed only to avoid the fine authorized for violations, I am not motivationally guided by the norm. I am epistemically guided by the speed limit norm insofar as I learn of the speed limit by consulting the norm and, in consequence, maintain a speed of under seventy miles per hour while driving on Interstate 5. In both cases, I am guided by the norm only insofar as I maintain a speed of under seventy miles per hour on Interstate 5 and thereby conform my behavior to the norm.

These two types of norm-guidance are logically independent. On the one hand, one can be epistemically guided by a norm without being motivationally guided by it; if I consult the norm establishing a speed limit of seventy miles per hour and conform my behavior to the norm to avoid the fine for speeding, I am epistemically guided by the norm without being motivationally guided by it. On the other hand, one can be motivationally guided by a norm without being epistemically guided by it; if I follow the example of the other drivers and drive at the same speed at which they are driving to ensure that I comply with the speed limit norm because it is a norm and not because it authorizes a sanction for violations, then my conforming behavior is motivationally guided by the rule without being epistemically guided by it.[5]

3. The Practical Difference Thesis, the rule of recognition, and valid legal norms

Scott Shapiro argues that the Incorporation Thesis is inconsistent with the idea that law's conceptual function is to guide behavior.[6] On his view, the norms of an institutional normative system with moral criteria of validity are metaphysically incapable of performing law's guidance function. Since something must be metaphysically capable of performing an artifact's function to be properly characterized as that kind of artifact and law is an artifact, the norms of an institutional normative system with moral criteria of validity are not properly characterized as norms of law insofar as they are metaphysically incapable of performing law's conceptual function.

The Guidance Arguments are grounded in the conceptual truism that something must be capable of guiding behavior to be a norm and hence to be a law. Since a norm can provide either epistemic or motivational guidance,

[5] This assumes that my gauging the speed of other drivers to attempt to learn of the speed limit does not constitute *consulting* the rule.

[6] Scott Shapiro, "On Hart's Way Out," *Legal Theory*, vol. 4, no. 4 (1998), 469–507, 490; emphasis added. Hereinafter *HWO*.

the idea that the conceptual function of law is to regulate behavior through the guidance of norms implies the following thesis about the nature of law:

Practical Difference Thesis (PDT): Every conceptually possible legal norm must be metaphysically capable of either epistemically or motivationally guiding subjects.

PDT is an eminently plausible way to flesh out the conceptual truism that every norm must be capable of guiding behavior as it distinctively applies to law. It is conceptually possible for a piece of propositional content, *n*, to perform law's function of guiding subjects only if *n* is metaphysically capable of changing either what the subject believes about what she should do or what the subject does. If *n* is metaphysically incapable of changing either what the subject believes about what she should do or what she does, it is metaphysically incapable of making the kind of practical difference that something must be able to make to be properly characterized as a legal norm that governs the subject's behavior. Thus, if *n* is metaphysically incapable of either motivationally guiding or epistemically guiding a subject's behavior, *n* cannot make the kind of practical difference that a piece of content must be able to make to be a law.

The two classes of legal norms (i.e. those that govern official behavior and those that govern non-official behavior), as Shapiro interprets Hart, guide behavior in different ways. Since Hart's minimum conditions for the existence of a legal system require that subjects generally comply with laws governing non-official behavior but do not require a specific motivation, the valid legal norms of the system must be metaphysically capable of *epistemically guiding* non-official behavior. But since the minimum conditions for the existence of a legal system require that officials take the internal point of view toward the rule of recognition governing official behavior, the rule of recognition must be metaphysically capable of *motivationally guiding* official behavior.

4. Law and the guidance of non-official behavior

Shapiro articulates two Guidance Arguments purporting to show that the norms of an institutional normative system with moral criteria of validity cannot satisfy PDT. The first attempts to show that the norms of an institutional normative system with moral criteria of validity cannot guide non-official behavior in the requisite manner. The second attempts to show that the norms of an institutional normative system with moral criteria of validity cannot guide official behavior in the requisite manner. Either one of these arguments, if sound, is sufficient to refute the Incorporation Thesis.

4.1 The first Guidance Argument

The first of the two Guidance Arguments attempts to show that it is not conceptually possible for the norms of an institutional normative system with moral criteria of validity to epistemically guide non-official behavior:

> It is hard to see, however, how the law can serve this [guidance] function with respect to rules that are valid in virtue of their moral content .... Marks of authority are supposed to eliminate the problems associated with people distinguishing for themselves between legitimate and illegitimate norms. However, a mark that can be identified only by resolving the very question that the mark is supposed to resolve is useless. Therefore, a norm that bears such a trivial mark ... is unable to discharge its epistemic duties. (*HWO* 494–5)[7]

This entails, on Shapiro's view, that the norms of an institutional normative system with moral criteria of validity cannot guide non-official behavior in a way that would satisfy PDT. The norms of an institutional normative system valid in virtue of moral merit cannot epistemically guide non-official behavior because "[t]elling people that they should act on the rules that they should act on is not telling them anything" (*HWO* 494). If it is conceptually impossible for an institutional normative system with moral criteria of validity to satisfy PDT and it is conceptually impossible for there to be a legal system that does not satisfy PDT, then it is conceptually impossible for there to be a legal system with moral criteria of validity.

[7] In Legality, Shapiro makes a similar argument in terms that reflect his view of law as consisting of shared plans: "If law is to guide behavior in the manner of plans, then it follows that its existence and content cannot be determined by facts whose existence the law aims to settle. For if the existence or content of law were determined in such a manner, then the proper way to ascertain its existence or content would be to deliberate about the merits of different courses of action. But the point of having plans is to obviate this very activity. It would be self-defeating, in other words, to have the plans do the thinking for us if the right way to discover their existence or content required us to do the thinking ourselves .... The problem with inclusive positivism is that it ... violates [this principle]. If the point of having law is to settle matters about what morality requires so that members of the community can realize certain goals and values, then legal norms would be useless if the way to discover their existence is to engage in moral reasoning." Scott Shapiro, *Legality* (Cambridge, MA: Harvard University Press, 2011), 275. The criticisms of the Guidance Argument articulated below are equally applicable to the version of the argument expressed in Legality.

It is worth noting that Shapiro's characterization of law's conceptual function seems to conflict with the Separability Thesis. The only conceptually possible way to *settle* a dispute about what morality requires is to recognize, apply, and enforce the mandatory norm that reproduces the content of the applicable mandatory moral norm. But this entails that only norms capable of settling disputes about what morality requires can count as valid law and hence that the criteria of legal validity necessarily include moral norms constraining the content of law, which is inconsistent with the Separability Thesis.

4.2 Can norms valid in virtue of moral merit epistemically guide non-official behavior?

The claim that it is not possible for norms valid in virtue of moral merit to epistemically guide non-official behavior seems vulnerable to a straightforward objection: if it is possible, as is presupposed by our ordinary practices, for mandatory moral norms to epistemically guide non-official behavior, it would also have to be possible for legal norms valid in virtue of moral merit to epistemically guide non-official behavior. It is hard to see how an official act of recognizing, applying, or enforcing a mandatory moral norm that is antecedently capable of epistemically guiding non-official behavior would render that norm incapable of doing so simply because officials treat it as a mandatory *legal* norm.

Consider an institutional normative system that validates all and only mandatory moral norms. The valid norms of the system would presumably include (1) a prohibition on intentionally killing innocent persons; (2) a prohibition on theft; and (3) a prohibition on engaging recklessly in activities highly likely to cause life-threatening injuries to other persons. Each one of these *valid* norms reproduces the content of the corresponding moral norm and expresses *exactly* as much content with respect to what subjects must do as the corresponding moral norm does.

This seems to entail that it is conceptually possible for an institutional norm valid in virtue of moral merit to epistemically guide non-official behavior. If we are morally accountable for our behavior, it must be possible for us both to discern what a mandatory moral norm requires by consulting the norm and to conform our behavior to that norm. If it is therefore possible for a subject to be epistemically guided by mandatory moral norms governing non-official behavior, then it must also be possible for a subject to be epistemically guided by an institutional norm governing non-official behavior that is valid in virtue of its reproducing the content of one of these mandatory moral norms. Simply giving a norm a new name and treating it as a member of a different class of norms cannot change what subjects can learn about its requirements by consulting it.

Thus construed, the first Guidance Argument misfires immediately. Assuming there are mandatory moral norms governing non-official behavior, an institutional norm valid in virtue of moral merit can do everything it must be able to do to be properly characterized as a law governing non-official behavior. To be properly characterized as a *norm*, a piece of content must be metaphysically capable of epistemically guiding the behavior of subjects; to be properly characterized as *a norm that governs* the behavior of some class of subjects, it must be nomologically possible for subjects to *obey* that norm.

An institutional norm valid in virtue of moral merit is therefore metaphysically capable of epistemically guiding non-official behavior if moral norms are metaphysically capable of doing so.

4.3 Can subjects learn of their legal obligations regarding non-official behavior from the rule of recognition?

One might argue that the foregoing criticism of the first Guidance Argument overlooks that a putative legal system with moral criteria of validity cannot properly inform subjects of *which* norms governing non-official behavior are legally valid. On this line of response, it is metaphysically possible for norms governing non-official behavior to epistemically guide non-official behavior *only if* subjects can discern from the rule of recognition *which* norms are valid. But a rule of recognition that validates all and only moral norms tells subjects no more than that they "should act on the rules that they should act on" is not telling them anything that would help them to determine which norms governing non-official behavior are valid.

The underlying idea is plausible. It is hard to understand, as a practical matter, how a subject S could learn of her non-official obligations under a norm n that belongs to a system Δ by consulting n if S has no reliable way to determine that n *is* a member of Δ without having to figure out whether n *should* be a member of Δ. Practically speaking, there is no way for a subject to determine what she must do according to a norm governing non-official behavior that belongs to the system unless she can determine that something *is* a norm of the system without having to deduce that it *is* a norm of the system on the strength of her judgment that it *should be* a norm of the system. Otherwise, she is relying on her own substantive judgment to identify a norm that is supposed to be identifiable by its authoritative "mark."

The claim here is *not* that it must be conceptually possible for an inclusive rule of recognition to epistemically guide non-official behavior. That claim is clearly false. It is not conceptually possible for a rule of recognition of any kind, source-based or otherwise, to epistemically guide *non-official* behavior because the rule of recognition governs only *official* behavior. It might be true that officials must be able to learn of their obligations under the rule of recognition since it governs official behavior. But there is no reason to think that non-officials must be able to learn of *their* obligations under the rule of recognition because they have none; by definition, the rule of recognition governs only official behavior.

Consider the First Amendment to the U.S. Constitution, which provides that "Congress shall make no law ... abridging the freedom of speech." Since

I am not Congress and I cannot make law, it is conceptually impossible for anything I do to be motivationally guided or epistemically guided by the First Amendment. Since the First Amendment, by its own terms, defines no obligations that bind me as a non-official, my behavior can neither violate nor comply with it and hence can neither be motivationally nor epistemically guided by it. It is simply not conceptually possible for a norm to motivationally or epistemically guide behavior it does not govern. Norm guidance presupposes norm governance.

Insofar as the first Guidance Argument presupposes, as it must, this conceptual truism, the operative claim is that it must be conceptually possible for subjects of a legal system to identify what valid law requires with respect to non-official behavior by consulting the rule of recognition. In order for subjects to determine what valid law requires of them, they must be able to determine which norms are valid, and this can be done only insofar as they can accurately distinguish norms that are valid from norms that are not by consulting the rule of recognition. Since it is not possible for the subject to determine which norms are valid by consulting an inclusive rule of recognition, it follows, on this line of reasoning, that there cannot be a legal system with moral criteria of validity.

The claim that it must be conceptually possible for subjects of valid norms to determine which norms are valid by consulting the rule of recognition does nothing to rescue the first Guidance Argument. If we are morally accountable for our behavior, then it must be true not only that we can be epistemically guided by mandatory moral norms, but also that we can determine which norms are mandatory moral norms. We could not be morally accountable for our behavior were we not capable of determining which norms correctly express moral requirements—i.e. which norms are members of the set of mandatory moral norms. To "know the difference between right and wrong," we must be able to determine (1) which norms belong to the set of mandatory moral norms that govern our behavior and (2) what those norms require of us.

But if a person can determine which mandatory norms are moral norms and hence what her *moral* obligations are under a system of mandatory moral norms, then she can also learn which norms are valid and what her legal obligations are under valid law from a rule of recognition that validates all and only mandatory moral norms. A rule of recognition that validates all and only mandatory moral norms tells competent subjects that mandatory moral norms, which those subjects can and should know govern their behavior, will be recognized by judges as *valid law* and will hence be applied and enforced against them *as such* with respect to their non-official behavior. If the claim is that it must be possible for subjects of a legal system to learn which norms are valid and what their legal obligations are with respect to non-official behaviors from the rule of recognition, there is no reason to think that a rule of recognition that defines moral criteria of validity cannot inform subjects of their non-official obligations to the degree necessary for law to perform its guidance function.

Consider, again, a rule of recognition in an institutional normative system that validates all and only mandatory moral norms; and suppose that the valid norms of the system are backed with coercive enforcement mechanisms. Suppose further that everyone within the relevant jurisdiction is contingently, but not necessarily, infallible with respect to what morality requires of her.[8] If the epistemic issue faced by subjects in this conceptually possible world is to determine which acts are required or prohibited by valid institutional norms, then knowing that all and only mandatory moral norms are valid can tell them exactly what they must do to comply *with the valid norms of the system.*

Notice that someone can be infallible with respect to what morality requires only if she can infallibly determine not only what every mandatory moral norm requires but also *which* norms belong to the system of mandatory moral norms. Subjects in this conceptually possible world can determine from the rule of recognition that every norm they antecedently know belongs to the system of mandatory moral norms is also legally valid: such a rule of recognition tells subjects that their legal obligations governing non-official behavior require them to do what they already know mandatory moral norms require them to do.

The claim that people cannot learn of their obligations with respect to non-official behavior from an inclusive rule of recognition, then, mistakenly assumes that they can learn no more from an inclusive rule of recognition than that "they should act on the rules they should act on." An institutional normative system that tells citizens no more about their non-official obligations than that would be no more informative than a judge's decision that tells litigants that they should do what they should do. But a rule of recognition that validates norms in virtue of moral merit conveys something far more useful than that: it informs citizens that moral requirements will be applied against them as *law* and possibly enforced against them with the police power of the state. Again, if mandatory moral norms are *capable* of informing subjects what they must do to satisfy their moral obligations, then a rule of recognition that validates legal norms in virtue of their moral merits is likewise *capable* of informing subjects what they must do to satisfy their *legal* obligations under valid law with respect to their non-official behavior.

[8] See Chapter 8, Section 3.2, for a straightforward proof that such a world is not only conceptually possible but is also nomologically possible.

It is unlikely, of course, that the system described above could be efficacious in a world *like ours* because we are not contingently infallible about moral issues. But the claim being defended here is not that a system like this could be successful enough in regulating *our* behavior to ensure that we can live and cooperate in peace. The claim is, rather, that there is a conceptually possible world in which such a system can make a practical difference with respect to the non-official behavior of its subjects. Although it is highly unlikely that such a state of affairs would be realized among beings with our abilities and disabilities, it is conceptually possible—and that is all that is needed, strictly speaking, to respond to this line of argument. This construction of the first Guidance Argument fails.

4.4 Must subjects be able to learn of their legal obligations regarding non-official behavior from the rule of recognition?

Notice that this construction of the first Guidance Argument depends on the claim that the conceptual function of the rule of recognition is, in part, to inform subjects of their non-official obligations under valid legal norms. Insofar as the rule of recognition must therefore be capable of informing subjects of their non-official obligations under valid laws, a norm that is incapable of informing subjects of their non-official obligations under the valid norms of the system is not properly characterized as part of a rule of recognition. Since, on this line of reasoning, a putative recognition norm incorporating moral criteria of validity is metaphysically incapable of performing this function, it cannot be part of any conceptually possible rule of recognition that succeeds in giving rise to a legal system.

But it is implausible to suppose that subjects *must*, as a conceptual matter, be able to learn of their legal obligations with respect to non-official behavior by consulting the rule of recognition. The conceptual function of a rule of recognition is to govern the behavior of officials in their legislative, adjudicative, and enforcement activities. It might be true that subjects must be able to learn what their *official* obligations are from the rule of recognition because it defines those obligations, but there is nothing in any plausible conceptual theory of law that would entail that subjects must be able to learn what their *non-official* obligations are from the rule of recognition because it cannot, by definition, govern non-official behavior. There is simply no reason to think that subjects must, as a conceptual matter, be able to learn from a norm that *cannot* govern their behavior what their obligations are under *other norms that do govern their behavior*.

It is, of course, a conceptually necessary condition for the existence of a legal system that the behavior of subjects generally conforms to the valid norms of the system, but it is clearly possible for a legal system to efficaciously guide behavior without subjects being able to learn *from the rule of recognition* what their obligations are under valid law. On the one hand, it is unlikely, given the depressingly low rate of constitutional literacy in the U.S., that many law subjects know much about what the Constitution says or understand how its requirements figure into determining what counts as valid law.[9] On the other hand, the institutional normative system that the Constitution brings into existence is clearly efficacious enough in guiding non-official behavior that it is beyond dispute that this system is a system of *law*. Regardless of whether subjects can identify their non-official obligations by consulting the rule of recognition, it is clear that the U.S. not only has a legal system but one that sufficiently exemplifies the nature of law that it constitutes a paradigm instance of law.

Surprisingly, it is not obviously a conceptually necessary condition for the existence of a legal system that most subjects have even a clue about what *valid law* requires with respect to non-official behavior. If their behavior always happens to conform to the valid institutional norms that would be applied or enforced against them if they behaved differently, the fact that they do not know what those norms require does not clearly preclude characterizing either the valid norms or the system itself as "law"; most of us, after all, are sufficiently disinclined to commit murder, fraud, theft, and a host of other anti-social acts that we would abstain from committing those acts even if they were not prohibited by law and even if we were not aware that these acts are prohibited by law.

One could not plausibly deny that, in conceptually possible worlds like *ours* in which intellectually limited self-interested beings like *us* live in conditions of material scarcity, an institutional normative system in which subjects are better informed about the content of their legal obligations is more likely to keep the peace than one in which subjects are less informed about the content of their legal obligations. But this is relevant only with respect to whether it is *probable* that some given institutional normative system will succeed in keeping the peace in *our* world. This tells us nothing about whether it is

[9] Hart puts this obvious point as follows: "[I]n a modern state it would be absurd to think of the mass of the population, however law-abiding, as having any clear realization of the rules specifying the qualification of a continually changing body of persons entitled to legislate .... We would only require such an understanding of the officials or experts of the system; the courts, which are charged with the responsibility of determining what the law is; and the lawyers whom the ordinary citizen consults when he wants to know what the law is." H.L.A. Hart, *The Concept of Law*, 3rd Ed. (Oxford: Clarendon Press, 2012), 60. Hereinafter *CL*.

conceptually *possible* for an institutional normative system in which subjects know little about the content of their legal obligations can succeed in keeping the peace enough to count as a system of law.

The state of affairs in which an institutional normative system succeeds in keeping the peace in our world without informing subjects of what the norms require is, admittedly, a *fringe* state of affairs; however, to say that a state of affairs is fringe is to say only that it is a highly *improbable* state of affairs in *our* world. Again, the issue with respect to whether the Incorporation Thesis is true is whether it is *possible* for an institutional normative system with moral criteria of validity to do everything it must do to be properly characterized as a system of law—and not whether it is probable that there is a legal system with moral criteria of validity in our world. It is compatible with the Incorporation Thesis that there never has been and never will be a legal system in our world with moral criteria of validity.

It is not even true, as a purely *practical* matter, that a legal system in *our* world could not be efficacious unless subjects are able to ascertain by consulting the rule of recognition which norms are legally valid or what these norms require by way of non-official behavior. Most subjects in existing legal systems have enough of an idea of what valid law requires to steer clear of problems with the law. I knew long before I ever studied criminal law, contract law, and tort law that I am legally obligated not to kill or otherwise assault people, to comply with the terms of my contracts, to refrain from fraud and tax evasion, and to be reasonably careful not to cause injury to other persons. In retrospect, I cannot recall how I knew; maybe I learned from television that the law tends to frown on gratuitous violence, breach of contract, fraud, tax evasion, and negligence. But I know that I, and every sensible person over the age of sixteen I have ever known, knew as much about the law as I did prior to studying it—without having a clue what the rule of recognition is. There are clearly other ways for subjects to learn of what valid law requires with respect to non-official behavior than by consulting the rule of recognition.

4.5 A methodological objection: The argument is illicitly grounded in contestable claims about morality

One might argue that the foregoing analysis is methodologically problematic insofar as it grounds a claim about the nature of law in a contestable claim about morality—namely that we are morally accountable for our behavior. This is problematic because, as Hart puts it, "legal theory should avoid commitment to controversial philosophical theories of the general status of moral judgments" (*CL* 253–4). To avoid committing his theory to such theories, Hart made his commitment to the Incorporation Thesis explicitly conditional on the assumption that moral norms are objective and "left open … the general question of whether they have what Dworkin calls 'objective standing'" (*CL* 253). Insofar as the argument above is grounded in the contestable claim that we are morally accountable for our behavior, it fails to avoid a commitment to controversial philosophical theories of morality and is problematic for this reason.

As it turns out, however, there is nothing methodologically problematic with assuming that we are morally accountable for our behavior. As discussed in Chapter 2, a modest approach to conceptual analysis purports to give us insight into what the world is like *as we structure it* through the conceptual framework we impose on the world through our linguistic and other social practices; that is, conceptual analysis purports to explicate what the world is like as we view it through the social practices we adopt to describe, structure, and make sense of our experience of the world. Given that we converge on a set of conceptual practices that presuppose that we are morally accountable for our behavior, it is perfectly legitimate for a modest conceptual theory of law to take that into account.

This is why it is true, as a general methodological matter, that an explication of the descriptive concept of law defined by *our* conceptual practices "should avoid commitment to *controversial* philosophical theories of the general status of moral judgments." A claim is controversial in virtue of being disputed by a large enough segment of the population that it cannot be plausibly characterized as capturing *our* conceptual practices, which are *ours* in virtue of being widely practiced by *us*.

These conceptual practices would be false if it turns out that there is nothing in the world—as it "really" is independent of the conceptual framework we impose on it—that constitutes a system of morality that governs our behavior, but that is not relevant on a modest approach; what is relevant is whether our conceptual practices presuppose that there is such a system. It would be methodologically illegitimate for a conceptual theory of law to presuppose that morality is objective in character because that claim is not presupposed by our conceptual practices; after all, many people in the relevant community of speakers believe that morality is conventional or "relative to culture." But it is no more problematic for a conceptual theory of law to presuppose that we are morally accountable for our behavior than it is to presuppose that we are not being deceived by a Cartesian evil demon; our conceptual practices clearly presuppose that the material world exists and resembles what our senses tell us about it and that our behavior is governed by a system of moral norms, regardless of whether they are objective in character.

As it turns out, the first Guidance Argument and the Arguments from Authority also depend on the assumption that we are morally accountable for our behavior. The first Guidance Argument is grounded in the claim that "[m]arks of authority are supposed to eliminate the problems associated with people distinguishing for themselves between legitimate and illegitimate norms" and hence presupposes that there are norms that *legitimately* govern our behavior; however, a norm can legitimately govern our behavior only if we are legitimately held accountable under it. The Arguments from Authority are likewise grounded in the claim that the conceptual function of authority is to mediate between subjects and "right reason," which is "right" in virtue of conforming to a correct assessment of what objective norms require, which include norms of morality under which we are properly held accountable.

These arguments, then, all rise or fall with the counterarguments given above. If it were methodologically problematic for a conceptual theory of law to presuppose that there exists a system of mandatory moral norms governing our behavior, then the counterarguments to the first Guidance Argument given above would fail to refute it. But if that assumption is methodologically problematic, the counterarguments above would fail, but so would the first Guidance Argument and the Arguments from Authority for the very same reason.

5. Law and the guidance of official behavior

5.1 The second Guidance Argument

Successfully rebutting the first Guidance Argument is not enough to vindicate inclusive positivism because there is another that purports to identify a second inconsistency between the Incorporation Thesis and PDT. The problem, on this line of reasoning, is that the possibility of moral criteria of validity is inconsistent with the claim that all the relevant norms in a legal dispute are capable of making a practical difference in the deliberations of the *judge*. As Shapiro explains:

> Consider, therefore, the following inclusive rule of recognition: "In hard cases, act according to the principles of morality." In *Riggs*, judges guided by this inclusive rule of recognition would conform with the principles of morality when deciding whether to invalidate the will. Let us further assume that the only relevant principle of morality is that people should not profit from their own wrongs and that the majority in that case believed this to be so .... [T]he principle that no man should profit from his wrongs cannot itself make a practical difference as a legal norm. For if the judge were guided by the inclusive rule of recognition, but did not appeal to the moral principle,

he or she would still end up invalidating the will .... The moral principle, therefore, can make no practical difference once the rule of recognition makes a practical difference, because the judge will act in exactly the same way whether he or she personally consults the moral principle or not. Guidance by the inclusive rule of recognition by itself is always sufficient to give the judge the right legal answer. (*HWO* 496)

The problem, on this line of reasoning, is that a rule of recognition that validates all and only mandatory moral norms requires the judge to do exactly the same thing that is required of her by the applicable norm valid in virtue of reproducing the content of the relevant mandatory moral norm. A rule of recognition directing the judge to apply mandatory moral norms in hard cases dictates that the judge not allow a murderer to take under the will of her victim. But this is exactly the same result dictated by the *Riggs* principle, which is valid in virtue of being a mandatory moral norm, that no person should profit from her own wrong. Once a judge is motivated to conform her behavior to the rule of recognition because it is the rule of recognition, she cannot also be motivated to conform her behavior to the *Riggs* principle because it is a valid norm; thus, it is not possible for both norms to make a practical difference in the deliberations of the judge. Since PDT implies that every legal norm must be capable of making a practical difference, the norms of an institutional normative system valid in virtue of moral merit fail to satisfy PDT and hence, according to the second Guidance Argument, are not properly characterized as law.[10]

The second Guidance Argument seems to refute the Incorporation Thesis. Insofar as an institutional normative system with moral criteria of validity lacks any source-based criteria of validity, every valid norm of the system would be valid in virtue of moral merit. This means, however, that none of the norms valid under its rule of recognition would be capable of motivationally guiding the official behavior of a judge who is motivationally guided

[10] Strictly speaking, what this implies is that norms valid only in virtue of moral merit, like the *Riggs* principle, are not norms of *law*; it does not imply that the system itself is not a system of *law*. If there are a sufficient number of norms in the system valid partly in virtue of having an official source, then it might be that there remain enough norms in the system to warrant characterizing it as a legal system. In that case, the system would, despite any appearances to the contrary, be a legal system that has only source-based criteria of validity. If, for example, a legislature decided to codify the minimum content of natural law, which would also be valid in virtue of moral merit, the norms that express that content might still be properly characterized as norms of *law*. While norms valid only in virtue of moral merit would not be properly characterized as legal norms, there would still be enough content valid in virtue of source to satisfy all the conceptually necessary conditions for the existence of a legal system. But if there are not a sufficient number of norms in the system that have an appropriate source, there would not be enough valid content in the system to satisfy all the conceptually necessary conditions for the existence of a legal system; in that case, the relevant social practices would not give rise to something properly characterized as a legal system.

by the rule of recognition to apply those norms. Since no valid norm of the system is capable of making a practical difference in the deliberations of a judge motivationally guided by the rule of recognition, none would be properly characterized as a legal norm. The system would thereby have a putative rule of recognition without having *any* valid legal norms and would hence clearly not be properly characterized as a legal system. There can be no law without laws.

But insofar as an institutional normative system with moral criteria of validity also incorporates source-based criteria of validity as a necessary condition for a norm to be valid in the system, only the norms of the system that are valid partly in virtue of source can make a practical difference in the deliberations of a judge motivationally guided by the rule of recognition. This means, however, that every norm putatively valid wholly in virtue of moral merit would not be a legal norm under PDT. Since, in this case, there are no norms valid in virtue of moral merit that count as *law*, the system would have, despite appearances to the contrary, only source-based criteria of validity.

Either way, the system is not properly characterized as a legal system *with* moral criteria of validity. If, on the one hand, all the norms expressing, say, the minimum content of natural law have not been officially promulgated and are putatively valid only in virtue of moral merit, then they are not legal norms and the system fails, for that reason, to be a legal system. If, on the other, all the norms expressing the minimum content of natural law have been officially promulgated and are hence valid in virtue of source, then the system is a legal system; those norms would be valid in virtue of having a proper source. But since every norm of the institutional system that is putatively valid wholly in virtue of moral merit would not be a legal norm, the legal system to which that institutional system gives rise would lack moral criteria of *legal* validity.

5.2 Can a valid legal norm governing non-official behavior motivationally guide a judge deciding a case under that norm?

To evaluate the second Guidance Argument, it is crucial to note that there is an ambiguity with respect to the *Riggs* principle. It can be construed as stating either a recognition norm that governs the official behavior of judges or as stating a valid legal norm that governs non-official behavior. On the first construction, the *Riggs* principle defines an obligation on the part of judges not to allow someone to profit from her own wrong; on the second, it prohibits a subject from doing something that amounts to profiting from her own wrong.

The second construction is problematic because the *Riggs* principle is not plausibly treated as a norm governing non-official behavior. To begin, if the opinion of the *Riggs* court is any indication, the *Riggs* principle is a recognition norm governing the official behavior of judges—and not a valid norm governing non-official behavior. As the court explains it, the *Riggs* principle is being treated by the court as governing its authority to enforce wills:

> Besides, all laws as well as all contracts *may be controlled in their operation and effect* by general, fundamental maxims of the common law. No one *shall be permitted* to profit by his own fraud, or to take advantage of his own wrong, or to found any claim upon his own iniquity, or to acquire property by his own crime .... These maxims, without any statute giving them force or operation, frequently control the effect and nullify the language of wills. A will procured by fraud and deception, like any other instrument, *may be decreed void and set aside*, and so a particular portion of a will may be *excluded from probate* or *held inoperative* if induced by the fraud or undue influence of the person in whose favor it is .... So a will may contain provisions which are immoral, irreligious or against public policy, and *they will be held void.* [11]

Insofar as the court takes the *Riggs* principle to govern how it may decide the case, the court is clearly treating the *Riggs* principle as a norm governing *its* official behavior, and not as a norm governing non-official behavior. Thus construed, the *Riggs* principle that "no one *shall be permitted* to profit by ... his own wrong" is not a valid legal norm that governs non-official behavior; it is a norm that governs *judicial* behavior and is hence part of the rule of recognition in virtue of being practiced by the officials of the system.

Further, the *Riggs* principle is just not plausibly interpreted as a norm governing non-official behavior. Construed as such, the *Riggs* principle defines a legal obligation on the part of a subject not to profit from her own wrongful non-official behavior. Thus construed, a subject would violate the *Riggs* principle *not* by engaging in a wrongful non-official behavior from which she profits, but rather by attempting to profit from the wrongful non-official behavior.

This construction might seem intuitively plausible at first blush, as burglary, theft, and robbery would all violate the *Riggs* principle, but it is crucial to note that what this interpretation would prohibit in the case of wills is not murdering a testator to prevent her from changing her will. Rather, this construction of the *Riggs* principle would prohibit a person from attempting to *claim* under the will of someone she murdered. Moreover, on

[11] *Riggs v. Palmer*, 115 NY 506 (1889), at 512. Emphasis added.

this construction, its application would not punish or fine the attempt of the murderer to take under the will of her victim; it would simply require a judge to nullify the will with respect to the murderer's gift under the will. It is, of course, conceptually possible for something like the *Riggs* principle to govern non-official behavior, but this construction is so conspicuously odd and alien to our experience with law that the court never considers it.

But if the *Riggs* principle is construed as governing official behavior, the second Guidance Argument immediately misfires because the *Riggs* principle would simply be a logical implication of a rule of recognition validating all and only mandatory moral norms. Either the *Riggs* principle is properly characterized as a legal norm or it is not. If it is properly characterized as a legal norm despite being incapable of motivationally guiding a judge who is motivationally guided by the rule of recognition, then PDT, as it functions in this argument, is false; it is not a conceptually necessary condition for a norm to count as a valid legal norm that it is capable of making a practical difference in the deliberations of a judge. If, however, it is not properly characterized as a legal norm, it is because our conceptual practices dictate that only first principles of law can count as *norms*. In this case, the *Riggs* principle, construed as governing official behavior, would be a logical corollary of the first principle that the judge should "act according to the principles of morality" (*HWO* 496). But the reason that the *Riggs* principle is not properly characterized as a legal norm would then be that our more general conceptual practices dictate that the more general term "norm" be applied only to first principles—and not because our practices regarding the concepts of law or legal system are inconsistent with the conceptual possibility of moral criteria of *legal* validity. If the second Guidance Argument construes the *Riggs* principle as a recognition norm, which is what it seems clearly to be, it is a non-starter.

The second Guidance Argument fares no better if the *Riggs* principle is construed as a valid norm governing non-official behavior. Construed as a valid norm governing non-official behavior, the *Riggs* principle merely prohibits profiting from a murder. On this construction, the *Riggs* principle was clearly metaphysically capable of motivationally and epistemically guiding Elmer, the defendant in *Riggs*, who murdered his grandfather to prevent him from changing his will. Insofar as the *Riggs* principle, on this construction, defines a legal obligation on his part not to profit from the murder of his grandfather, Elmer could have both (1) determined by consulting it that he should refrain from attempting to claim under his grandfather's will *and* (2) refrained from doing so *because* it was required by the *Riggs* principle.

But the problem with this painfully contorted construction is that a valid norm governing non-official behavior is metaphysically incapable of motivationally or epistemically guiding the judge's behavior because a norm that does not govern a person's behavior is metaphysically incapable of guiding it. Even if the *Riggs* principle is valid in virtue of having a proper source, the judge cannot learn what she is obligated to do as a judge by consulting that principle because it governs nothing the judge *can* do to decide the case. Nor can the judge conform her *official* behavior to the *Riggs* principle because it does not govern that behavior.

It is true that the judge is *applying* the *Riggs* principle *to evaluate Elmer's behavior*, but that changes nothing. The judge does not thereby conform her official behavior to the *Riggs* principle by evaluating Elmer's behavior because one can conform to the *Riggs* principle, construed as governing non-official behavior, only by refraining from claiming under the will of one's murder victim.

That, of course, is something the judge can do at any time, including while she is deciding the case, but there is nothing that the judge can do in deciding the case that would violate that norm because that norm does not govern the judge's *official* behavior. If the judge, while conducting a hearing in the *Riggs* case, were to claim under the will of someone she murdered, the judge would be violating the *Riggs* principle on this interpretation of it; however, the act of claiming under the will of someone the judge murdered would no more be properly characterized as an official act because done during the hearing than a sneeze would be if the judge sneezed during the hearing. While the judge can be both motivationally and epistemically guided by the *Riggs* principle, she can be guided by it only with respect to behavior that is not properly characterized as official behavior.

It might be helpful to consider an example that does not involve a legal norm that is ambiguous as to whether it governs official or non-official behavior. Consider an institutional normative system that validates all and only mandatory moral norms, and suppose that a dispute arises under a norm, valid in virtue of moral merit, that holds automobile manufacturers strictly liable for injuries proximately caused by manufacturing defects. Notice that the strict liability norm does not say anything about what the judge must do to adjudicate disputes under the norm and hence defines no judicial duties; it is the rule of recognition, which defines the powers and duties of officials and validates all and only mandatory moral norms, that requires the judge to apply the strict liability norm when relevant.

The reason is that, since judges are not automobile manufacturers, the rule does not apply to *anything* a judge could do in deciding a case. It is the rule of recognition that requires that the judge apply the valid norm to resolve a dispute *between an automobile manufacturer and someone who claims that an injury was proximately caused by a manufacturing defect*; the rule of recognition thereby defines what the judge must do to decide the case—and not the strict liability norm. The only duty that the relevant valid legal norm defines, by its own terms, is that of the defendant. In deciding the dispute, then, the judge can follow the rule of recognition by applying the relevant valid legal norm, but the judge cannot follow the relevant valid legal norm by applying it to decide the case.

There is a conceptual difference between following a norm and applying a norm. A person *P* follows a norm *n* by doing *α*, in the relevant sense, if and only if (1) *n* requires that *P* do *α*; (2) *P* does *α*; and (3) *P* does *α* because *P* believes that *n* requires that *P* do *α*. In contrast, *P* applies a norm *n* that requires someone to do *α*, in the relevant sense, if and only if *P* evaluates the behavior of someone whose behavior *n* governs (which might include *P*) to determine whether the subject has satisfied *n* by doing *α*.

These two notions are logically independent. One can apply a norm without following it. An arbitrator *P* might, for example, authoritatively decide a contract dispute between *Q* and *R* by deciding whether *R* has performed her duties under the terms of the contract without being, or thereby becoming, a party to the contract. To do that, *P* must apply the relevant valid norms of contract law to *R*'s behavior to determine whether it conforms to the terms of the contract as required by contract law. But, in so doing, *P* does not thereby follow either the terms of the contract or the valid legal norm that requires parties to a contract to perform their contractual obligations. The claim that *P* applies *n* does not logically imply that *P* follows *n*.

Conversely, one can follow a norm without applying it. I might follow a norm that prohibits killing an innocent person simply by refraining always from killing *anyone* because I sensibly believe that it is better not to kill someone the norm allows me to kill than to kill someone the norm does not allow me to kill. But my refraining from killing some particular person does not involve applying the norm to my own behavior because I am not evaluating whether my behavior *has* satisfied the norm. If I beat someone nearly to death and subsequently attempt to evaluate my behavior under the norm prohibiting killing innocent persons, I am applying the norm. But my following the norm prohibiting killing in some particular instance involves an altogether different act from my evaluating whether my behavior satisfies that norm in that instance. The claim, then, that *P* follows *n* neither implies the claim that *P* applies *n* nor is implied by that claim. Knowing that a person has followed a norm tells us absolutely nothing about whether she has applied it, and conversely.

The reason is that the behaviors that constitute one act, as a conceptual matter, do not constitute the other. There is no conceptually possible norm that one can simultaneously apply and follow by doing exactly the same thing. The acts that constitute *P*'s following a norm, *n1*, that requires *P* to apply some other norm, *n2*, to *Q*'s behavior do not constitute applying *n1*. On the one hand, to follow *n1, P* must evaluate *Q*'s behavior by applying *n2*; on the other, to apply *n1, P* must determine whether someone else whose behavior is governed by *n1* has properly applied *n2* to *Q*'s behavior. It might be possible for someone to simultaneously follow and apply a norm, but they will be doing two distinct things at the same time—one of which constitutes following the norm and the other of which constitutes applying the norm.

It is, thus, conceptually impossible for the judge to follow a norm simply in virtue of applying it to evaluate someone else's behavior—regardless of whether that norm governs her behavior. If the norm does not govern the judge's behavior, the act of applying the norm to evaluate someone else's behavior cannot satisfy the requirements of the norm as they pertain to the judge; since the norm does not govern the judge's behavior, it requires nothing of her. But if the norm does govern the judge's behavior, then the judge does not conform her behavior to that norm in virtue of applying it because the acts that constitute applying a norm are different from the acts that constitute following it. Following and applying a norm are different notions that have nothing more salient in common than that the corresponding concept-terms involve doing something with norms.

The problem with this second Guidance Argument is, in essence, the same as the problem with the first—namely that it presupposes that someone's acts must be guided, in some intuitive sense, by a norm that does not govern the relevant acts. There is nothing in any plausible conceptual theory of law that entails that it must be possible for the rule of recognition to epistemically guide or inform non-official behavior because the rule of recognition does not govern that behavior. Similarly, there is nothing in any plausible conceptual theory of law that entails that the valid legal norms that a judge applies to a case involving non-official behavior must be capable of motivationally guiding the judge's official behavior because those norms do not govern the judge's official behavior. Since neither strand of the Guidance Argument shows that the norms of an institutional normative system with moral criteria of validity cannot properly guide someone whose behavior it must be capable of guiding, the Guidance Arguments fail to refute the Incorporation Thesis.

6. Revisiting the Arguments from Authority: To whom the rules apply

The Arguments from Authority are vulnerable to a similar objection. The Arguments from Authority are grounded in the idea that the conceptual function of authority is to provide directives that (1) express the authority's specific view about what the subject should do according to right reason; (2) are capable of replacing the subject's judgment in her deliberations about what she should do according to right reason; and (3) enable the subject to better comply with what right reason requires by following the authority's view than by following her own view.

The Arguments from Authority purport to show that the norms of an institutional normative system with moral criteria of validity can do *none* of these things. Since a subject cannot identify what the relevant norms require except by discerning what she believes right reason requires, those norms are incapable both of replacing her judgment about what she should do in her deliberations about what to do and of expressing the authority's view about what she should do. Likewise, since a subject cannot determine what she should do under the relevant norms without discerning what she believes she should do according to right reason, it is conceptually impossible for her to better comply with right reason by following the authority's judgment than by following her own; since the relevant norms cannot express the authority's view, it is conceptually impossible for her to follow the authority's view.

The similarities between the Guidance Arguments and the Arguments from Authority are conspicuous. An institutional normative system that validates all and only mandatory moral norms cannot make the practical difference in the deliberations of subjects that something must be able to make to be properly characterized as a legal system. As Shapiro describes the problem, "a mark that can be identified only by resolving the very question that the mark is supposed to resolve is useless" (*HWO* 495). As Raz describes the problem, "[a] decision is serviceable only if it can be identified by means other than the considerations the weight and outcome of which it was meant to settle".[12]

The reason for these similarities is that both strategies of argument conceive the notion of practical authority partly in terms of its being capable of playing an epistemic role in "mediating" between subjects and norms. The point of authority, as Shapiro conceives it, is to mediate between "competing standards" by informing subjects which of competing standards they must satisfy. The point of authority, as Raz conceives it, is to mediate between subjects and the reasons that antecedently apply to them by providing directives that can replace their judgments about what they ought to do in their practical deliberations. In both cases, the authoritative character of law requires that law be metaphysically capable of playing these mediating roles in the practical deliberations of subjects.

[12] Joseph Raz, *Ethics in the Public Domain* (Oxford: Oxford University Press, 1994), 219.

This similarity, by itself, is anodyne as far as the Arguments from Authority are concerned, but those arguments share a second feature with the Guidance Arguments that is fatal to each. The Arguments from Authority, like the Guidance Arguments, presuppose that it is a conceptually necessary condition for the existence of law that the rule of recognition is metaphysically capable of informing subjects of their legal obligations with respect to *non-official* behavior. Since a rule of recognition, according to the Arguments from Authority, validating all or only mandatory moral norms is incapable of informing subjects of what their obligations are with respect to non-official behavior, it cannot be authoritative and hence cannot ground an institutional normative system that is properly characterized as a system of *law*.

The problem with both lines of reasoning is, for this reason, exactly the same: there is simply no reason to think, as the Guidance Arguments and Arguments from Authority assume, that one conceptual function of the rule of recognition is to inform subjects of their non-official obligations under the valid norms of the system. If the rule of recognition must, as a conceptual matter, play an epistemic role in informing anyone of what her obligations are or which of competing standards she must follow, it need inform only officials of what they ought to do with respect to recognizing, applying, and enforcing law. Insofar as each of these arguments depends on the claim that the rule of recognition must be able to inform subjects of their non-official obligations, neither gets out of the blocks and neither hence succeeds in refuting the Incorporation Thesis.

8

The Conceptual Possibility of Moral Criteria of Legal Validity

This volume has been concerned with the engagement between the concepts of law and morality as defined by our ordinary linguistic and legal practices. There are only three possibilities with respect to this engagement as it pertains to the criteria of legal validity. The descriptive anti-positivist claims that the criteria of validity *must* include moral constraints on the content of law. The inclusive positivist claims that the criteria of validity *can* include moral constraints on the content of valid law. The exclusive positivist claims that the criteria of validity *cannot* include moral constraints on the content of valid law. These three positions exhaust the logical space of conceptual claims regarding whether the criteria of validity include moral norms: the criteria of validity either must, can, or cannot contain moral constraints on the content of law.

This chapter completes the defense of the Incorporation Thesis undertaken in the last two chapters with a positive argument for the claim that the criteria of validity can incorporate moral constraints on the content of law. The argument constructs a model of an institutional normative system that validates all and only mandatory moral norms in a possible world that resembles ours in every causal respect and shows that the system satisfies every condition plausibly thought conceptually necessary for the existence of a legal system.

1. General methodological considerations

It is important to note the character of the claim that the Incorporation Thesis makes about moral criteria of validity. To begin, it neither asserts nor implies that there are, have been, or ever will be legal systems with moral criteria of validity in our world. Insofar as the Incorporation Thesis makes a claim only about what is conceptually possible, it entails nothing about whether there are, have been, or will be, legal systems in our world with moral criteria of validity. Just as the claim that it is *possible* that Bigfoot exists tells us nothing about *whether* Bigfoot does exist, the claim that it is possible that there are legal systems with moral criteria of validity tells us nothing about whether there are legal systems with moral criteria of validity.

Further, insofar as the Incorporation Thesis makes a claim only about what is conceptually possible, it entails nothing about whether such a system is nomologically possible—i.e. possible in worlds with the same laws of nature that obtain in our world. It is obviously true that what is nomologically possible is conceptually possible, but it is not true that what is conceptually possible is nomologically possible. A state of affairs might be realized only in conceptually possible worlds with causal properties so different from those of our world that their inhabitants have some characteristic that we *could* not have because we and our world are just not built that way.

Consider the idea that it is conceptually possible for there to be a legal system without sanctions in a world where beings are always conclusively motivated by altruistic love. It is not clear that such a claim tells us anything about whether it is nomologically possible for there to be such a system because it is not clear whether it is nomologically possible for inherently self-interested beings like us who live in conditions of material scarcity always to put aside our own interests in the service of altruistic concern for others. If, on the one hand, (1) it is nomologically possible for us always to do this and (2) there are no other features of this conceptually possible world that are nomologically impossible, then this world is both conceptually and nomologically possible. But if, on the other hand, (i) it is not possible for us always to do this and (ii) the regulatory efficacy of the system depends critically on this feature of the subjects' psychology, then such a legal system is conceptually but *not* nomologically possible.

But even if we know that some state of affairs *S* is nomologically possible, that tells us next to nothing about whether it is likely to be realized in our world. The claim that *S* is nomologically possible entails only that the probability of its being realized in our world is greater than zero. This tells us little about whether *S* is likely to be realized in our world because, for all we can infer from the nomological possibility of *S*, it might be that the probability of realizing *S* in our world is .99, or it might be that the probability of realizing *S* in our world is .0000000000000001.

The probability that *S* occurs in a nomologically possible world will vary from one world to the next. What is highly improbable in our world because of some nomologically *contingent* feature of ours might be highly probable in another nomologically possible world that lacks that feature. If the probability that *S* occurs is exactly the same in every nomologically possible world, it is because the feature of beings that fully determines the probability is a *non-contingent* feature of beings that resemble us in all causally relevant ways and is hence a nomologically *necessary* feature of ours. To get a reliable sense for the extent to which moral criteria of legal validity are probable in our world, we would have to know considerably more about the particular features of nomologically possible worlds with moral criteria of legal validity and the extent to which those features are likely to occur in our world.

The foregoing calls attention to a methodological problem with respect to grounding claims about the conceptual possibility of moral criteria of validity in empirical investigation: we can confirm the Incorporation Thesis on the basis of empirical experience, but we cannot disconfirm it. If, for example, we can correctly identify a legal system with moral criteria of validity in our world, that would establish the truth of the Incorporation Thesis. The claim that there *is* a legal system with moral criteria of validity trivially implies the claim that there *could be* a legal system with moral criteria of validity. But, again, it would not follow from the claim that there are no actual legal systems with moral criteria of validity that the Incorporation Thesis is false because the claim that there *is no* legal system with moral criteria of validity in our world does not imply that there *could not be* a legal system with moral criteria of validity. For this reason, a search of past and present legal systems might be inconclusive with respect to determining whether the Incorporation Thesis is true.

But there is an epistemic difficulty that diminishes our ability even to confirm the Incorporation Thesis on the strength of ostensibly favorable empirical observations. It is always possible for theorists to agree on certain acts that constitute a *legal* practice in the courts but disagree on how to characterize that practice. Something that counts as a *legal* practice must be interpreted to characterize it, and it is always possible to disagree on the relevant interpretive claims even when there is no dispute with respect to what the uninterpreted facts are that constitute the practice. Two theorists can look at the same set of acts and agree that they constitute a *legal* practice but disagree with respect to how to characterize those acts in other respects; an inclusive and exclusive positivist might look at a set of judicial practices and agree that these practices are *legal* but disagree about whether the practices are properly characterized as defining moral criteria of validity.[1]

[1] Wilfrid Waluchow identifies certain judicial practices in Canada that he interprets as incorporating moral criteria of validity. Wilfrid Waluchow, *Inclusive Legal Positivism* (Oxford: Clarendon Press, 1994). Stephen Perry responds by arguing that those practices are as plausibly interpreted as implicating only source-based criteria of validity. See, e.g., Stephen Perry, "Two Varieties of Legal Positivism" (Critical notice of Waluchow's *Inclusive Legal Positivism*), *Canadian Journal of Law and Jurisprudence*, vol. 9 (1996).

2. Prerequisites for a model vindicating the Incorporation Thesis

The above discussion suggests that one must do two things to show the conceptual possibility of a legal system with moral criteria of validity. First, one must produce a model of an institutional normative system *in a world like ours* that can plausibly be interpreted as having moral criteria of validity that clearly satisfies every condition plausibly thought to be necessary for the existence of law. Second, to ensure that the model establishes the Incorporation Thesis, it should be incompatible with an exclusivist interpretation.

2.1 The model must describe a world that is nomologically possible

The subjects in a model defining a conceptually possible legal system with moral criteria of validity should resemble human beings with respect to those psychological and physical features that explain why we need law to do what it does in our world. Law is contrived *by us* to regulate the behavior of beings *like us*, and one can sensibly worry that a model that is proposed as a defense of some conceptual claim about law defines a world that is too far removed from ours to tell us anything about law as our conceptual practices define the notion. A model that purports to describe a conceptually possible legal system that regulates the behavior of all-powerful gods is problematic insofar as it is not clear that, given our conceptual practices, the concept-term "law" properly applies to such an institutional normative system.

Consider the society-of-angels model that purports to refute the claim that every conceptually possible legal system authorizes sanctions for violations of valid laws. In describing the model, Raz takes care to specify assumptions that ensure that the angels' world resembles ours in theoretically salient respects:

> [W]e can imagine ... rational beings who may be subject to law, who have, and who would acknowledge that they have, more than enough reasons to obey the law regardless of sanctions. Perhaps even human beings may be transformed to become such creatures. It is reasonable to suppose that in such a society the legislator would not bother to enact sanctions since they would be unnecessary and superfluous. If such a normative system has all the features of a legal system described above, then it would be recognized as one by all despite its lack of sanctions.[2]

[2] Joseph Raz, *Practical Reason and Norms* (Princeton, NJ: Princeton University Press, 1990), 159–60. Emphasis added. Hereinafter *PRN*.

These assumptions are contrived to ensure that the world of the "angels" is one that is possible for beings like us. The angels are contrived to resemble human beings enough to ensure that "human beings [might] be transformed to become such creatures." Human beings could not be "transformed" into such creatures except through the standard material and sociological processes that explain how we come to develop certain physical and psychological features. Insofar as we are rationally self-interested and vulnerable to certain kinds of injury for which we need the protection of a legal system, so are the angels.

The one salient respect in which the angels are different from us is that they are conclusively motivated always to conform their behavior to the law without any need for the prudential incentives needed in our world. In every other salient respect, the psychological and physical characteristics of the angels are the same as ours. Insofar as we could be transformed into beings like angels, it is nomologically possible, if improbable, for us to evolve and develop the motivational qualities that distinguish the angels from what we are at present.

The society-of-angels argument is problematic in one respect that is particularly salient with respect to the project of vindicating the Incorporation Thesis. The problem is that it is just not clear whether the world of the angels is nomologically possible because it is just not clear that self-interested beings like us who live in a world of material scarcity could ever become like the angels. If our conceptual practices assume that law is a distinctively human institution and such a world is not nomologically possible, the model would not succeed in showing the existence of a legal system without sanctions.

To avoid similar concerns about its relevance, a model that purports to vindicate the Incorporation Thesis should describe a world that is nomologically possible. If such a model fails to vindicate the Incorporation Thesis, it will not be because the institutional normative system it describes is inconsistent with law's distinctively human character. It will be because the system it describes fails to satisfy some conceptually necessary condition of law.

2.2 The modeled system must meet Hart's minimum conditions for the existence of a legal system

The model must satisfy Hart's minimum conditions for the existence of a legal system and hence must satisfy the following conditions: (1) the officials in the modeled world must practice a rule of recognition that governs official behavior with respect to recognizing, applying, and enforcing law; and (2) non-official behavior in the model must generally conform to the norms valid under the rule of recognition. Although these two conditions do not exhaust the necessary conditions for law and hence do not define conditions that are jointly sufficient for the existence of a legal system, nothing that fails to satisfy these two conditions is properly characterized as a legal system.

2.3 The modeled system must incorporate the minimum content of natural law

Hart takes the position that it is a "naturally" necessary condition for the existence of a legal system that it incorporates the minimum content of natural law:

> Reflections on some very obvious generalizations—indeed truisms—concerning human nature and the world in which men live, show that as long as these hold good, there are certain rules of conduct which any social organization must contain if it is to be viable. Such rules do in fact constitute a common element in the law and conventional morality of all societies which have progressed to the point where these are distinguished as different forms of social control .... Such universally recognized principles of conduct which have a basis in elementary truths concerning human beings, their natural environment, and aims, may be considered the minimum content of Natural Law .... We can say, given the setting of natural facts and aims, which make sanctions both possible and necessary in a municipal system, that this is a *natural necessity*.[3]

There are five features "concerning human nature and the world in which men live" that, on Hart's view, necessitate the incorporation of the minimum content of natural law into any humanly possible system of municipal law[4]: (1) we are vulnerable to physical and psychological harm; (2) we are largely equal with respect to the physical and psychological qualities that enable us to dominate others; (3) our capacity to be motivated by altruistic considerations is limited given that we are inherently self-interested and experience our wants and needs with a persuasive urgency; (4) the material resources of the world are subject to conditions of scarcity; and (5) we are limited with respect to our intellectual capacities and our strength of will (*CL* 193–7).

But insofar as these five properties are instantiated in every possible world that can tell us something about the nature of law as our practices construct it, they also express what is distinctive about our world that gives rise to our need for a system of law. If law, as we conceive it, is distinctively human in the

[3] H.L.A. Hart, *The Concept of Law* 3rd Ed. (Oxford: Oxford University Press, 2012), 192–3; underlined emphasis added. Hereinafter *CL*. The term "natural necessity," as Hart uses it, is most plausibly construed as referring to nomological necessity.

[4] This requirement applies only to systems of municipal law because systems of international law purport to regulate only the official behavior of nation-states.

sense that "law" applies only to institutions that regulate behavior in worlds with each of these five features, then it is not just a nomologically necessary condition for the existence of a legal system regulating non-official behavior that it includes the minimum content of natural law; it is also a conceptually necessary condition.

To ensure that the model below satisfies every condition plausibly thought of as conceptually necessary for the existence of law, it will be defined to ensure that the norms governing non-official behavior incorporate the minimum content of natural law. The model will thus be structured to include the minimum content of natural law to ensure that it succeeds in vindicating the Incorporation Thesis—regardless of whether law is properly characterized, as a conceptual matter, as an institutional normative system that regulates only the behavior of beings like us in worlds like ours.

2.4 The model must satisfy the service conception of authority

Insofar as it is a truism that every conceptually possible legal system is metaphysically *capable* of instantiating legitimate authority, the model must be defined so that the institutional normative system is metaphysically capable of instantiating legitimate authority. Since the most widely accepted analysis of the nature and justification of authority among conceptual jurisprudents is the service conception of authority, the model should be specified in such a manner that the system it defines is metaphysically capable of instantiating legitimate authority according to the service conception of authority.

This requires that the norms of the constructed system (1) are capable of expressing the authority's view about what subjects ought to do according to right reason; (2) are capable of replacing the judgment of subjects in their practical deliberations about what they should do according to right reason; and (3) are framed in a manner that can be legitimate under Normal Justification Thesis (NJT). Although earlier chapters have raised concerns with the service conception of authority, the modeled legal system will be constructed so as to satisfy the service conception to avoid begging any questions about authority.

2.5 The norms of the system must be metaphysically capable of motivationally and epistemically guiding the behavior they govern

The modeled legal system should be constructed to ensure that it can perform law's conceptual function of regulating the behavior of subjects through norms metaphysically capable of guiding the acts they govern. As discussed above, there are two classes of legal norms that govern different types of behavior: (1) the rule of recognition, which governs official behavior; and (2) the norms valid under the rule of recognition, which govern non-official behavior.

It is a conceptual requirement for something to count as a norm of any kind that *governs* a subject's behavior that it is metaphysically capable of *both* epistemically and motivationally guiding her behavior. To begin, a piece of propositional content *n* can count as a norm governing the behavior of members of some class, *C*, of subjects only if that content expresses what *n* requires of them in a manner that members are metaphysically capable of discerning by consulting *n*. Any piece of propositional content metaphysically incapable of epistemically guiding a class of subjects because, as a nomological matter, they characteristically lack the ability to discern what the norm requires of them by consulting it cannot, as a conceptual matter, be a norm that governs the behavior of members of that class. Any norm that governs members of some class *C* is thus metaphysically capable of *epistemically* guiding their behavior.

There are two ways to see that any norm that governs members of *C* must be metaphysically capable of *motivationally* guiding their behavior. First, the claim that a norm, *n*, is metaphysically capable of epistemically guiding the behavior of members of *C* implies the claim that *n* is metaphysically capable of motivationally guiding their behavior. If *n* is metaphysically capable of epistemically guiding the behavior of members of *C*, then it is nomologically possible for members of *C* both to learn from *n* what it requires and to satisfy *n* after learning what *n* requires. But if members of *C* can conform to *n* partly in virtue of having learned from *n* what it requires, then they can conform to *n* because *n* is a norm; if learning what *n* requires can play some role in a subject's decision to conform to *n*, then the subject can conform to *n* for any rational subjective reason—including that *n* is a norm of the system. Accordingly, any piece of propositional content metaphysically capable of epistemically guiding behavior is also metaphysically capable of motivationally guiding the same behavior.

Second, a piece of propositional content *n* can be a norm that governs the behavior of *S* only if *n* is nomologically, and hence metaphysically capable, of motivationally guiding the behavior of *S*. A piece of propositional content *n* is properly characterized as a norm governing the behavior of *S* if and only if (1) it is nomologically possible for *S* to satisfy *n*'s requirements *and* (2) it is nomologically possible for *S* to violate *n*'s requirements. Insofar as it is nomologically possible for *S* to satisfy *n* and it is nomologically possible for *S* to violate *n*, it is nomologically possible for *S* to *obey n*. Insofar as it is nomologically possible for *S* to obey *n*, it is nomologically possible for *S* to conform her behavior to *n* because *n* is a norm that governs her behavior and hence to be motivationally guided by *n*; if a subject can obey a norm, she can obey it for any subjective reason that is minimally rational. Since everything that is nomologically possible is also metaphysically possible, it is a conceptual truth that every norm governing *S*'s behavior is metaphysically capable of motivationally guiding *S*.

This has the following implications for the concept of a legal norm. Since (1) it is a conceptual truth that every legal norm is a *norm* and (2) it is a conceptual truth that something cannot be a norm governing the behavior of some class of subjects unless it is metaphysically capable of both motivationally and epistemically guiding members of that class, it follows that it is a conceptual truth that every legal norm governing the behavior of members of a class is metaphysically capable of both motivationally and epistemically guiding them.

2.6 The model must be plausibly interpreted as incorporating moral criteria of validity

To vindicate the Incorporation Thesis, the modeled system must be plausibly interpreted as incorporating moral criteria of validity. This means that the model must be specified so that two conditions are satisfied. First, it must be clear that judges believe they are practicing a rule of recognition that incorporates moral criteria of validity. Second, it must also be clear that judges are correctly applying those moral standards more often than not; otherwise, the most that can be confidently asserted about the judges in the model is that they *believe* they are applying standards of morality when they make decisions about whether a particular promulgated norm is legally valid.

2.7 The model should be incompatible with an exclusivist interpretation

Finally, the model should be incompatible with an exclusivist interpretation. Although the fact that a model can plausibly be interpreted as defining an inclusive legal system suggests that the idea of moral criteria of legal validity is coherent and hence that a legal system with moral criteria of validity is conceptually possible, it would be preferable to produce a model that can be interpreted as a legal system *only* insofar as it is construed as incorporating moral criteria of validity. This leaves the exclusive positivist with the comparatively undesirable option of denying the status of law to an institutional normative system that satisfies every condition plausibly thought to be conceptually necessary for the existence of law.

3. Specification of a model vindicating the Incorporation Thesis

3.1 The modeled world is nomologically possible

To ensure that the modeled world can tell us something about law on the assumption that it is a distinctively human institution, the model defines a world that resembles ours both with respect to our causal laws and with respect to the features that give rise to *our* need for regulation by law. In particular, the subjects in this world are self-interested, rational, and vulnerable to the same kinds of psychological and physical harms to which we are. Further, there are not enough material resources in this world immediately available to satisfy all of their wants and needs. Insofar as the model includes those features of our world that explain our need for law, it defines a nomologically possible world.

3.2 The subjects are accidentally infallible

The subjects of this nomologically possible world have intellectual abilities that are limited in the same ways as ours, but they differ from us with respect to their beliefs about morality in the following respects. First, the subjects always agree on what morality requires. Second, the beliefs of the subjects with respect to what morality requires always happen to be correct—whether morality is properly conceived as objective or conventional in character; while any subject of this world could have been wrong on any and even every moral issue, they just happen, as a contingent matter, never to be wrong. Third, their beliefs with respect to what morality requires always happen to be epistemically justified; the subjects always stumble onto a sound argument that justifies their beliefs and are hence in cognitive possession of an epistemic justification for each of their beliefs.

Although these stipulations describe a state of affairs that is *improbable* for beings like us, such a state of affairs is nonetheless *possible* for beings like us. First, it is obviously nomologically possible for any two agents to agree on some particular moral issue; we frequently disagree in our world with other people on some issues but also agree with them on others. Given that it is nomologically possible for any two agents to agree on one moral issue, it is nomologically possible for any two agents to agree on every moral issue. But if it is nomologically possible for any two agents to agree on every moral issue, it is nomologically possible for all agents to agree on every moral issue; there is no reason to think that beings like us could not agree on what morality requires on every issue.

Second, there is a nomologically possible world in which every person always happens to be correct about what morality requires. Since it nomologically possible for me to be correct about what morality requires on one issue, it is nomologically possible for me to be correct about what morality requires on every issue. But since what is nomologically possible for one agent in this regard is nomologically possible for all agents, it is nomologically possible for all agents to be correct about what morality requires on every issue.

Third, there is a nomologically possible world in which every person *knows* what morality requires on every issue. Since it is nomologically possible for me to be epistemically justified and correct with respect to what I believe morality requires on one issue, it is nomologically possible for me to be epistemically justified and correct with respect to what I believe morality requires on every issue. But since what is nomologically possible for one agent to correctly believe and be justified in believing about morality is nomologically possible for all agents, it is nomologically possible for all agents to believe what is correct about what morality requires on every issue and to be epistemically justified with respect to every such belief.

The beings in the model are thus conceived to be *accidentally infallible* with respect to morality—and not essentially or necessarily infallible—in the sense that they always *know* what morality requires. The difference is as follows. Since they always have true beliefs about what morality requires and are always in cognitive possession of an argument that epistemically justifies their beliefs, they always know what morality requires and are hence *infallible* with respect to what it requires. But this infallibility is contingent or accidental in the following respect: although the subjects in this world happen to be correct on every issue, they could have been incorrect with respect to any issue. It is not, to reiterate, that they are smarter or have more reliable access to the requirements of morality; they are as intellectually limited as we are but just happen to stumble on to the right views and the right arguments. Unlike an essentially omniscient God who cannot, either as a conceptual or nomological matter, ever be mistaken about anything, the subjects of this nomologically possible world, like us, could be mistaken on any—or even every—moral issue concerning what they ought or ought not to do.

The assumption that subjects of this world could be mistaken on any moral issue is necessary to ensure that they resemble us in all relevant respects and hence to ensure that their world is nomologically accessible to ours. If not for the fact that the subjects could be wrong, like us, on any moral issue, the resulting world would be too distant from ours to tell us anything about the distinctively human nature of law as our practices, properties, and vulnerabilities define it. The practices that give rise to what we characterize as law are shaped by both *our* vulnerabilities and *our* disabilities, as well as by the content of the norms *we* adopt to regulate the behavior of beings with those vulnerabilities and disabilities.

The beings in this world resemble us in another salient and unfortunate respect that explains why they need law: they often commit, as we do, socially disruptive acts they believe are morally wrong. Insofar as these persons, like us, are strongly self-interested and are commonly moved to act by strong emotions, they frequently act in ways they believe to be morally wrong—or would if they were to consider the issue in the heat of the moment—to promote what they urgently feel to be in their best interests. Given that the material resources of the world are scarce, there will frequently be violent conflicts in this world that breach the peace.

How often these conflicts occur in that world relative to how often they occur in ours is not clear, but it is reasonable to hypothesize that they occur less frequently. The reason is that, in our world, we commonly wind up doing something morally wrong to achieve our own interests because we mistakenly believe the act to be morally permissible; this kind of confusion about morality does not occur in the world I have described—at least not insofar as the subjects dispassionately consider the moral issue. If violent conflicts in the modeled world do not arise because of moral confusion, there are likely to be fewer violent conflicts in that world than there are in ours.

But it should be clear that these socially disruptive conflicts will nonetheless occur in this world with sufficient frequency that something like law is needed to keep the peace. Beings like us frequently commit "crimes of passion" in the heat of a moment in which we are overcome by importunate desires or needs. Most wrongful assaults, for example, are spontaneous crimes of passion that result from the frustration of desires experienced as urgent.[5] Since subjects in the model are as prone to committing violent acts in the heat of passion as we are and since the scarcity of material resources (including romantic and sexual resources) ensure that there will be occasions for conflicts among subjects, there is clearly a need for something like law in their world.

[5] For example, 37.5% of female murder victims are killed by their spouses, and 91% are killed by people they knew. See "Crime in the U.S.," *Uniform Crime Reporting*; available at: https://ucr.fbi.gov/crime-in-the-u.s/2010/crime-in-the-u.s.-2010/offenses-known-to-law-enforcement/expanded/expandhomicidemain; and "29 Intriguing Crimes of Passion Statistics," *Brandon Gaille* (May 23, 2017); https://brandongaille.com/27-intriguing-crimes-of-passion-statistics/.

3.3 A model of an institutional normative system with moral criteria of validity

Given that subjects in this world will often have conflicts that breach the peace, there is a need for something resembling a system of law to help minimize the frequency of such conflicts. Such a system, properly equipped, will operate to reduce the number of conflicts enough that people will acquiesce to, if not actively solicit, this kind of regulation of their behavior. While people in this world differ from us in that they always have correct beliefs about what morality requires, they are sufficiently like us in emotional makeup that their world looks nothing like the Garden of Eden. Some sort of institutional regulation with authorized sanctions for non-compliance will be welcomed as a necessary evil.

These sanctions have the same character that they do in our world. They will sometimes be expressly punitive, as is true of the sanctions intended to punish criminal wrongdoing in our world, but sometimes the point will simply be, as is true of the sanctions associated with tort law in our world, to compensate individuals for injuries wrongly caused by the acts or omissions of others. Sometimes the agencies assigned to adjudicate these norms will decline to enforce certain instruments, like contracts or wills, that are not properly formed as a means of providing what is reasonably contrived to be a prudential incentive to induce subjects to ensure that their instruments are properly formed.

As to the rule of recognition, the officials in this institutional normative system converge on recognizing, applying, and enforcing as rules of the system all and only mandatory moral norms. Moral norms of goodness that merely encourage behaviors as good and do not require them as obligatory are not recognized as valid "legal" norms. For example, the system would include as law those moral norms that prohibit intentionally killing an innocent person but not those that encourage helping others insofar as the relevant acts are morally good but not required. Thus, the officials of the system converge on treating as "law" only those moral norms that specify acts that one "shall" or "must" do—and not those that specify acts that one "should" do.

Further, the non-official behavior of people in this nomologically possible world conforms as much to what is required by valid law as our non-official behavior does in our world. In most cases, the conforming behavior of people, as is true of us, is not motivated by a desire to conform to the law or by knowledge of what the law requires; they are as emotionally predisposed to refrain from acts of murder and theft as we are. In some cases, their conforming behavior, as might be true of some of us, is motivated by a desire to avoid the sanctions authorized for violations of valid law. But there are always cases, as is true in our world, in which a subject undeterred by the sanctions commits a socially disruptive act that violates the law. Even so, subjects conform to the valid norms enough to permit them to live and work peacefully together in something properly characterized as a community.

Finally, subjects in this world generally believe that the norms governing their behavior are morally justified as a necessary but regrettable means of ensuring that they can live together in comparative peace so as to secure the benefits of social cooperation. This applies to the subjects of every class of legal norm: officials generally regard those norms governing official behavior as morally justified, while all subjects within the jurisdiction of the system regard the valid legal norms governing their behavior as morally justified.

As described, the model defines a nomologically possible world with an efficacious institutional normative system that validates all and only mandatory moral norms. It should be clear that an institutional normative system that validates all and only mandatory moral norms is conceptually possible; such a system might not count as a system of law, but the existence of an efficacious institutional normative system that validates all and only mandatory moral norms is clearly conceptually possible. Insofar as it is *nomologically* possible for the self-interested, intellectually limited, vulnerable subjects of such a world to be accidentally infallible, the existence of an efficacious institutional normative system validating all and only mandatory moral norms is also possible for us.

4. Vindicating the Incorporation Thesis: The modeled system is a legal system

There are two issues with respect to whether the model succeeds in vindicating the Incorporation Thesis. The first issue is whether such a system is properly characterized, according to the ordinary usage with which this volume is concerned, as a system of *law*. To be properly characterized as law, the system must (1) satisfy Hart's minimum conditions for the existence of a legal system; (2) contain norms governing non-official behavior that incorporate the minimum content of natural law; (3) satisfy the service conception of authority; and (4) regulate behavior by the recognition, application, and enforcement of norms metaphysically capable of motivationally and epistemically guiding behavior. The second issue is whether the system, if properly characterized as law, is more plausibly interpreted as having an inclusive rule of recognition than as having an exclusively source-based rule of recognition.

4.1 The system satisfies Hart's minimum conditions for the existence of a legal system

The institutional normative system sketched above clearly satisfies Hart's minimum conditions for the existence of a legal system. First, there is a conventional rule of recognition that requires judges to apply and enforce all and only mandatory moral norms against subjects of the system. Insofar as the officials of the system converge on taking the internal point of view toward the rule of recognition and following it in all relevant circumstances, the norm is a conventional norm, and one that binds the officials in virtue of their shared commitments.[6]

Second, subjects in the system generally conform their behavior to the valid norms of the system. Although Hart describes this condition as requiring obedience,[7] this is too strong. The claim that a subject has obeyed a rule implies that the motivation for acting as the rule requires has something to do with the fact that the rule requires it; it might be that the subject is motivationally guided by the rule or it might be that the subject's conformity is motivated by a desire to avoid the authorized sanctions. But there is no reason to think that, as a conceptual matter, the conforming behavior of a subject must always be explained by reference to the rule or its authorized sanctions; the fact that I have never killed a person has nothing to do with the fact that the law prohibits or punishes it. It is sufficient that subjects are motivated to conform to the norm in enough of those circumstances in which they might be tempted to do otherwise that the system succeeds in keeping the peace enough to ensure that life in the community is predictably stable. That requirement is also clearly satisfied by the system constructed above; it is not necessary to inquire into the motivations of citizens that would explain their conforming behavior. Accordingly, both of Hart's minimum conditions are satisfied by the institutional normative system described here.

[6] This neither presupposes nor endorses the Conventionality Thesis. It assumes only that there is a nomologically possible world in which the rule of recognition is a conventional rule. But if the reader finds this characterization objectionable, the rule can be characterized as whatever kind of rule she believes the rule of recognition is most plausibly thought to be. See Chapter 3 for a discussion of whether the Conventionality Thesis is a core thesis of positivism.

[7] As Hart puts it, "those rules of behavior which are valid according to the system's ultimate criteria of validity must be generally *obeyed*" (*CL* 113). Emphasis added.

4.2 The system contains norms that incorporate the minimum content of natural law

The system contains what Hart calls the minimum content of natural law, which Hart defines as "certain rules of conduct which [given certain salient facts about human nature] any social organization must contain if it is to be viable" (*CL* 193). These rules of conduct include prohibitions on theft, violence, and other acts that would threaten "the minimum purpose of survival which men have in associating with each other" (*CL* 193). As these rules of conduct are all mandatory moral norms, they are included in an institutional normative system that validates all and only mandatory moral norms. If it is a conceptually necessary feature of municipal law in worlds nomologically accessible to ours that it contains the minimum content of natural law, then the model of an institutional normative system in this world satisfies that additional condition.

4.3 The system satisfies the service conception of authority

4.3.1 The system has de facto *authority*

The system has *de facto* authority over subjects with respect to both official and non-official behavior. As will be recalled, a *de facto* authority "either [1] claims to be legitimate or is believed to be so, and [2] is effective in imposing its will on many over whom it claims authority".[8]

The system satisfies both conditions for instantiating *de facto* authority. To begin, subjects in the modeled world all believe the system is morally legitimate in virtue of being a necessary evil to make the social benefits of community living possible. Further, the institutional normative system succeeds in "imposing its will on many" subjects by making certain behaviors non-optional and deterring those behaviors with the threat of authorized sanctions. Insofar as the system is *needed*, by hypothesis, to keep the peace and *succeeds* in keeping the peace, it does so only by deterring violence that would otherwise have occurred but for its efficacious regulation. It thus succeeds in imposing its will on those compliant subjects who would otherwise disobey without a threat of sanctions.

[8] Joseph Raz, *Ethics in the Public Domain* (Oxford: Oxford University Press, 1994), 211. Hereinafter *EPD*.

4.3.2 *The norms are capable of expressing the authority's view about what right reason requires and of replacing the subjects' views about what right reason requires*

All the norms of the system are metaphysically capable of expressing the authority's view of what right reason requires and of replacing the judgments of subjects in their practical deliberations about what right reason requires. The rule of recognition expresses the view, implicit in the convergent practices of officials and hence accepted by officials as authoritative, that officials must recognize, apply, and enforce as law against subjects *only* mandatory moral norms; it thereby also expresses the authority's view that individual officials must refrain from recognizing, applying, and enforcing as law against subjects any other norms they might believe (or might have believed if their views were different) right reason requires them to recognize, apply, or enforce.

This view is capable of providing officials with a first-order reason to recognize, apply, and enforce only mandatory moral norms, as well as a second-order reason to refrain from acting on any views they might have with respect to what right reason requires. Insofar as officials take the internal point of view toward the rule of recognition, it provides both a first-order reason to conform their official behavior to the requirements of the rule of recognition and a second-order reason to refrain from acting on their own assessments of what should be recognized, applied, or enforced as law. Although officials converge in treating all and only mandatory moral norms as law, individual officials might occasionally be tempted to depart from the requirements of the rule of recognition on the strength of self-interested reasons or on the strength of transiently biased assessments of what right reason requires. The rule of recognition is thus metaphysically capable of replacing officials' judgments of what right reason requires with respect to their official behavior.

It is true that a rule of recognition that validates only mandatory moral norms does not tell a judge which mandatory moral norm is the applicable one in a dispute, but there is nothing in either the concept of law or the service conception of authority that entails that an authoritative recognition rule must distinguish which valid norm is *applicable* in some dispute from all other valid norms; a rule of recognition that defines purely source-based criteria of validity, after all, is no better equipped to do that work for a judge. There is nothing in any plausible construction of the service conception of authority that entails a denial of the self-evident fact that judges must use their judgment in attempting to determine what valid legal norms are relevant in a dispute and how the relevant legal norms should be applied in deciding it. Adjudication is demanding work.

The valid legal norms of the system are also metaphysically capable of expressing an authoritative view about what right reason requires. The valid legal norms require, as a matter of *law*, that subjects do what they are morally required to do, and subjects understand that these norms will be applied and enforced against them as law. These valid legal norms thus express the authority's view that the *law* requires subjects to comply, or be subject to legal sanctions, with mandatory moral norms when those norms conflict with their prudential interests.

The valid legal norms of the system are also metaphysically capable of providing subjects with both a first-order reason to do what the norms require and a second-order reason not to act on their own judgments of what right reason requires with respect to non-official behavior. To begin, given that it is backed by authorized sanctions, the authority's view that subjects are legally obligated to comply with all and only mandatory moral norms is clearly capable of providing a first-order reason for subjects to comply instead of doing something else they might antecedently be inclined to do. But if one rejects the idea that the relevant first-order reasons can make reference to prudential reasons having to do with a desire to avoid sanctions, the subjects all accept the authority of officials as legitimate and hence rationally treat their directives as providing novel first-order reasons to comply.

Further, the valid legal norms are metaphysically capable of providing subjects with a second-order reason not to act on their own judgments of what right reason requires with respect to non-official behavior. It is clearly metaphysically possible for subjects to rationally treat the fact that law requires a non-official behavior as a second-order reason not to act on their own judgments; since they regard the directives as morally legitimate, those directives are as capable of providing the relevant second-order reasons as the underlying mandatory moral norms are. Thus, the valid legal norms are capable of replacing subjects' own judgments of what right reason requires with respect to non-official behavior.

4.3.3 Is it metaphysically possible for subjects to better comply with what right reason requires by following the authority's view of what right reason requires than by following their own views of what right reason requires?

At first blush, the model seems to run afoul of NJT. The problem is as follows. According to NJT, authority is morally justified only insofar as subjects are likely to better comply with respect to right reason by following the authority's view of what it requires than by following their own views. If moral norms take into account prudential interests and dictate what subjects should do *all things considered* according to right reason, then it is not metaphysically possible for subjects to *better* comply with right reason by following the authority's view than by following their own views because they will always arrive at *exactly the same result* with respect to what right reason requires since the moral standards reflect the balance of all the applicable reasons, including the prudential reasons.

One possible response, of course, is to reject the model on the ground that it does not satisfy the service conception, but this is problematic. Subjects in this world are morally infallible but not morally impeccable; they are no less prone to acting out in socially disruptive ways in virtue of being self-interested than we are and hence are as motivated as we are to act in ways that would breach the peace. It is precisely for that reason that an authoritative system of norms is needed to provide an additional first-order reason to comply with the requirements of right reason. But insofar as the system sometimes deters such behavior, subjects are more likely to better comply with right reason by complying with the law than by acting on the basis of their own transient impulses, inclinations, and subjectively corrupted assessments of what right reason requires.

But this seems to call NJT into question if construed as stating a necessary condition for the legitimacy of a legal system. As described, the system appears to be morally legitimate: the norms (1) are morally just and justly enforced; (2) succeed in keeping the peace; (3) distribute the resources of the society in the manner required by morality; (4) enjoy the consent of subjects; and (5) are such that subjects will better comply with right reason by following them than by following their inclinations, impulses, and corrupted judgments. Although this system does not satisfy NJT, there could not be a system that is morally preferable in *the modeled world.* If *any* legal system authorizing sanctions for violations of law is legitimate in this nomologically possible world, this system is.

Nevertheless, NJT is not properly construed as articulating a necessary condition for the existence of a legitimate authority:

> The normal justification thesis: The *normal and primary way* to establish that a person should be acknowledged to have authority over another person involves showing that the alleged subject is likely better to comply with reasons which apply to him (other than the alleged authoritative directives) if he accepts the directives of the alleged authority as authoritatively binding, and tries to follow them, than if he tries to follow the reasons which apply to him directly (*EPD* 214; emphasis added).

Raz here scrupulously avoids characterizing NJT as providing either necessary or sufficient conditions for legitimacy; NJT expresses the "primary" and "normal" way to show that authority is justified. Insofar as he refrains from using such language, it is presumably because he is aware of the problems that arise if NJT is construed as defining a necessary or sufficient condition for legitimacy.

The most plausible construction of NJT, for reasons of both theoretical substance and interpretive accuracy, is to construe it as compatible with the legitimacy of the system constructed in the model. Thus construed, although the "normal" condition is not satisfied, the system is nonetheless legitimate in virtue of the distinctive properties of the system and its subjects. Since the most salient features of the system are highly improbable in our world, the existence of a legitimate system that does not satisfy NJT does not impugn its status as the "normal" way to justify authority. Insofar as NJT gives the correct answer in the vast majority of cases likely to be encountered in our world, it would remain, if correct, the "normal" strategy for justifying authority.[9] On this construction, the modeled system does not satisfy NJT, but it does not run afoul of it and is hence compatible with the most plausible construction of the service conception of authority.

4.4 The modeled system is capable of performing law's conceptual function of regulation through norm-governance and norm guidance

To show that the modeled system is metaphysically capable of performing law's regulatory function, it must be shown that (1) the valid norms can motivationally and epistemically guide non-official behavior and (2) the rule of recognition can motivationally and epistemically guide official behavior. If both these claims are shown, it follows that the modeled system can do everything it needs to do to perform law's regulatory function.

4.4.1 The rule of recognition is metaphysically capable of motivationally and epistemically guiding official behavior

A rule of recognition that validates all and only mandatory moral norms is metaphysically capable of *motivationally* guiding official behavior. To begin, a rule of recognition that validates all and only mandatory moral norms defines a legal obligation on the part of a judge to apply the relevant mandatory

[9] Even so, the system defined above suggests that NJT would be more plausible if reconfigured to allow for the possibility of a legitimate authority in a world where the authority is *not less likely* than the subjects to correctly discern the requirements of right reason. One potential problem with justifying democratic systems under NJT is that, if the views of officials are *perfectly* representative of those of the subjects, the officials are no more and no less likely than subjects to correctly discern the requirements of right reason.

moral norms as law in adjudicating legal disputes. It is obviously possible for a judge to violate this obligation by applying some norm that does not have the status of law in virtue of moral merit, but it is as obviously possible for a judge to satisfy this obligation by applying the relevant norm that has the status of law in virtue of moral merit.

But insofar as a judge can knowingly conform her official behavior to a rule of recognition, *R*, that requires her to apply all and only mandatory moral norms, she can knowingly conform her official behavior to *R* for any reason that rationally strikes her as persuasive. She can conform her official behavior to *R* because she thinks she must in order to retain her seat on the bench, or she can conform her official behavior to *R* because *R* is the rule of recognition. It should be clear—without recourse to any of the features that distinguish the modeled world from ours—that *R* is metaphysically capable of motivationally guiding judicial behavior.

R is also capable of epistemically guiding *judicial* behavior. In a world in which subjects are accidentally infallible about their moral obligations, the judge can learn which norms she must apply in deciding a dispute by consulting *R*; the judge who is confused about her *legal* obligations can learn from *R* that it requires her to apply and enforce a subject's *moral* obligations in disputes concerning non-official behavior. Since the judge can always correctly identify the content of the applicable legal norm, she can learn what *R* requires of her and satisfy her legal obligations under *R* by consulting *R*. Insofar as the judge would apply different norms if *R* required it, *R* is capable of making a practical difference in the deliberations of a judge.

It is true that the judge must decide for herself how a legal norm valid in virtue of moral merit should be applied to a dispute regarding someone's non-official behavior, but that is also true of a legal norm valid in virtue of having an authoritative source. The judge will have to do exactly the same thing to decide a case that requires applying a valid norm that prohibits recklessly performing acts highly likely to cause life-threatening injuries to other persons regardless of whether it is valid in virtue of moral merit or valid in virtue of source. It does not matter what kind of criteria of validity a rule of recognition defines; the judge will still have to figure out for herself how any relevant valid norm applies in any given case. It is no part of what something must do to be a rule of recognition that it defines a decision procedure that produces right answers to every dispute under the law.

There is another way to see that *R* is capable of epistemically guiding judicial behavior that does not require recourse to the particulars of the model described above. If we are morally accountable for our behavior, then we can be epistemically guided by mandatory moral norms governing non-official behavior. Insofar as this implies we can determine which norms *are* mandatory moral norms that govern non-official behavior, we can distinguish mandatory moral norms that apply to the relevant behavior from all other norms. But this implies that a judge can determine from a rule of recognition validating all and only mandatory moral norms which norm she is legally obligated to apply in deciding a dispute and hence can conform her judicial behavior to the rule of recognition by applying the relevant valid norm to decide the dispute. Thus, judges *in our world* can be epistemically guided by a rule of recognition validating all and only mandatory moral norms, on the assumption that we are morally accountable for our behavior.

A rule of recognition validating all and only mandatory moral norms is thus metaphysically capable of both motivationally and epistemically guiding judicial behavior and hence of performing its guidance function with respect to official behavior. This vindicates the Incorporation Thesis with respect to the guidance function of the rule of recognition.

4.4.2 The norms valid under the rule of recognition are metaphysically capable of motivationally and epistemically guiding non-official behavior

The norms valid under the modeled rule of recognition are metaphysically capable of doing everything they must do to enable law to perform its regulatory function. Since subjects in this world are accidentally infallible with respect to what mandatory moral norms require of them, they are also accidentally infallible with respect to which norms are mandatory moral norms. If they know that the judges are recognizing, applying, and enforcing all and only mandatory moral norms as law, then they have enough information to determine which norms are legally valid (i.e. those that reproduce the content of a mandatory moral norm); what those valid norms require of them with respect to non-official behavior (i.e. exactly the same thing that the corresponding mandatory moral norm requires of them); and can conform their behavior to that mandatory moral norm. Thus, every legal norm that is valid in virtue of reproducing the content of a mandatory moral norm is metaphysically capable of epistemically guiding the non-official behavior of subjects in this nomologically possible world.

Likewise, every legal norm valid in virtue of reproducing the content of a mandatory moral norm is metaphysically capable of motivationally guiding the non-official behavior of subjects in this world. Insofar as it is metaphysically possible for subjects to knowingly conform their non-official behavior to a mandatory moral norm, it is metaphysically possible for subjects to knowingly conform their non-official behavior to that norm for the reason that it is a valid legal norm of the system. It follows that every norm governing non-official behavior valid in virtue of reproducing the content of a mandatory moral norm is metaphysically capable of motivationally guiding the non-official behavior of the subjects of the model.

As was true in the last subsection, there is another way to see that the valid norms of this system can motivationally and epistemically guide non-official behavior without recourse to the particulars of the model. First, if we are morally accountable for our behavior under mandatory moral norms, then it must be metaphysically possible for us to knowingly satisfy those moral norms. But if it is metaphysically possible for us to knowingly satisfy a mandatory moral norm, then it must also be metaphysically possible for us to satisfy that norm *because* it is a moral norm. Thus, if we are morally accountable for our behavior, mandatory moral norms are metaphysically capable of motivationally guiding our behavior.

But if it is metaphysically possible for a mandatory *moral* norm to motivationally guide behavior, then it is also metaphysically possible for a *legal* norm valid in virtue of reproducing its content to motivationally guide behavior. If it is possible for us to knowingly satisfy a mandatory moral norm *because* it is a mandatory moral norm, then it must also be possible for us to satisfy a legal norm valid in virtue of reproducing the content of that mandatory moral norm *because* it is a legally valid norm; simply giving the norm a new name cannot render us incapable of knowingly satisfying a norm that we can otherwise knowingly satisfy *because* it belongs to this or that normative system. It is, then, every bit as possible for us to be motivationally guided by a legal norm valid in virtue of reproducing the content of a mandatory moral norm as it is to be motivationally guided by the mandatory moral norm itself.

Similarly, it is metaphysically possible for us to be epistemically guided by legal norms valid in virtue of reproducing the content of a mandatory moral norm, assuming that we are morally accountable for our behavior. We are morally accountable for our behavior only insofar as it is nomologically possible for us to determine what our moral obligations are and to knowingly satisfy those obligations. This requires that we be nomologically capable of (1) distinguishing mandatory moral norms from other norms; (2) determining what a particular mandatory moral norm requires with respect to non-official behavior; and (3) knowingly satisfying mandatory moral norms governing non-official behavior. But if we have the capacities described in (1), (2), and (3) and we know that judges are applying and enforcing as law all and only mandatory moral norms, then we are nomologically capable of satisfying a legal norm valid in virtue of reproducing the content of a mandatory moral norm and we are nomologically capable of determining what is required of non-official behavior by a legal norm valid in virtue of reproducing the content of a mandatory moral norm by consulting the valid legal norm.

This suffices to show that every legal norm governing non-official behavior valid in virtue of moral merit is metaphysically capable of both motivationally and epistemically guiding the governed behavior and hence suffices to vindicate the Incorporation Thesis with respect to the guidance function of legally valid norms.

4.5 The system precludes an exclusivist interpretation

The system in this world was constructed to preclude its being plausibly interpreted as an exclusivist legal system. While the rule of recognition validating all and only mandatory moral norms is a legal norm in virtue of its being practiced by officials, none of the system's norms can be considered valid in virtue of some kind of official promulgation.

One might argue that the institutional normative system described in the model is a legal system but none of the norms of the system are valid, despite appearances to the contrary, in virtue of reproducing the content of a mandatory moral norm. On this line of reasoning, judicial acts applying and enforcing these norms necessarily involve acts of source-based promulgation; for this reason, every valid legal norm is valid in virtue of being applied and enforced by judges in the course of deciding some legal dispute.

This line of reasoning is problematic insofar as it assumes that judges necessarily have occasion to apply and enforce these norms because citizens necessarily violate them at least some of the time. It is true that citizens might frequently violate these norms but there is no reason to assume that they must do so: if an institutional normative system in a Razian society of angels is a system of *law*, then it is an example of a conceptually possible legal system in which subjects never violate the law; if, further, it is true that we could evolve to become like angels, then it is an example of a nomologically possible legal system in which subjects never violate the law. As long as subjects are aware that there is a legal system that validates norms capable of providing something that subjects can rationally treat as a reason to comply, that is enough to ensure that the appropriate regulatory relationship exists between the legal system and its putative subjects.

Insofar as the conceptual function of a legal system is to regulate behavior so as to permit people to live and work together in peace, the case in which subjects never violate the law would be a case in which the system most completely realizes its conceptual function. The idea that it is a conceptually necessary condition for the existence of a legal system that subjects sometimes violate the law is simply false; there is no plausible reason to think that an institutional normative system that completely realizes law's conceptual function of keeping the peace is conceptually disqualified from being a legal system.[10]

An exclusive positivist could, I suppose, deny that the institutional normative system in the model constitutes a legal system, but this is implausible. The system (1) satisfies the minimum conditions for the existence of a legal system; (2) incorporates the minimum content of natural law; (3) satisfies the service conception of authority; (4) is capable of performing law's regulatory function by providing norms capable of motivationally and epistemically guiding the behavior they govern; (5) authorizes sanctions as a response to violations; and (6) contains only morally just norms and is morally legitimate. Given that it satisfies every plausible candidate for a conceptually necessary feature of law on *both* positivist and anti-positivist theories, there is no plausible reason to think it is not a legal system.

5. Why all the fuss? The probability of inclusive legal systems in our world

One common motivation for accepting the Incorporation Thesis is the thought that there are many existing legal systems that incorporate moral criteria of validity. This seems to have been Hart's motivation for accepting the Incorporation Thesis:

> [Dworkin] treats my doctrine of the rule of recognition as requiring that the criteria which it provides for the identification of law must consist only of historical facts and so as an example of 'plain-fact positivism'. But though my main examples of the criteria provided by the rule of recognition are matters of what Dworkin has called 'pedigree', concerned only with the manner in which laws are adopted or created by legal institutions and not with their content, I expressly state both in this book and in my earlier article on 'Positivism and the Separation of Law and Morals' that *in some systems of law, as in the United States, the ultimate criteria of legal validity might explicitly incorporate besides pedigree, principles of justice or substantive moral values*, and these may form the content of legal constitutional restraints (*CL* 250; emphasis added).

[10] Nor is there any reason to think that it is *nomologically* impossible for a legal system to produce perfect compliance in worlds like ours regulating the behavior of beings like us. A system of law with sufficiently stringent sanctions and a highly accurate mechanism for detecting and attributing violations of law could, in principle, produce perfect compliance. There is comparatively little crime, for example, in societies like North Korea because of the harsh sanctions and the pervasively intrusive character of the available detection mechanisms. A totalitarian legal system is no less a legal system in virtue of being totalitarian.

Justifiably characterizing an existing legal system as inclusive is more complicated than might initially appear. As discussed above, there are prohibitive epistemic difficulties with attempting to vindicate the Incorporation Thesis on the basis of empirical observations—which, in essence, is what is done by someone who accepts it on the belief that there are existing legal systems with moral criteria of validity. The problem is that any *existing* legal system that can be interpreted as inclusive can be as plausibly interpreted as exclusive. A validity decision grounded in the application of some putatively moral norm need not be characterized as involving the application of some authoritative moral criterion of legal validity; it is as plausibly characterized as the result of the judicial exercise of a quasi-legislative discretion to create new law in hard cases. This is why vindicating the Incorporation Thesis requires constructing a world with properties that are possible but vanishingly improbable in our world.

Further, the highly idealized character of the modeled world, though nomologically possible, might confirm the Incorporation Thesis, but it tells us *nothing* about the character of existing legal systems. There are two features of these highly artificial vindicating models that account for their irrelevance in explaining existing legal practices. The first is that judges in those worlds always agree on which norms are valid in virtue of moral merit. The problem is that it is quite unlikely that judges in any legal system as complex as the modern municipal legal systems that motivate conceptual theorizing about law will converge in agreeing on the moral merits of any putative legal norm.

Judges in legal systems like that of the U.S. frequently disagree on how to interpret putatively moral language in constitutions in making validity decisions. Some judges adopt an originalist approach to making validity decisions under the constitution while others adopt a conflicting approach that allows them to interpret that language in a manner that conforms to some set of conventional or critical moral standards; and this disagreement extends to every provision of those constitutions plausibly interpreted as defining a moral constraint on the content of valid law. If it is a necessary condition for the existence of an inclusive legal system that judges converge with respect to their views about which norms are valid in virtue of moral merits, there are no inclusive legal systems in our world—nor are there likely to be.

The second is that these vindicating models must be constructed so that we are epistemically justified in believing that judges are always correct about what morality requires with respect to non-official behavior. The problem here is not just that we are epistemically limited with respect to identifying the substantive requirements of whatever moral norms legitimately govern our behavior. It is also that we are epistemically limited with respect to determining whether there are any moral norms that legitimately govern our behavior and, if so, whether those norms are objective or intersubjective in character. If there are correct answers to these questions that are utterly independent of our social practices, there is simply no epistemically reliable way to tell what they are.

It might be true that we are epistemically justified in believing that *our practices* presuppose that morality objectively governs our behavior, but it is not clear how we could be epistemically justified in believing that this presupposition is true. We might be justified with respect to our beliefs about how the world appears to us, but it is hard to see, as argued in Chapter 2, how we could be justified with respect to our beliefs about how the world really is independently of how it appears mediated through the conceptual framework we impose on it. All we have to go on in figuring out how to get around in our world, with the possible exception of the laws of logic and some trivial arithmetical claims, is how the world appears to us through the filter of the relevant conceptual practices. Meta-ethical nihilism might, for all we know, be objectively true.[11]

This is why the model (1) assumes that morality legitimately governs our behavior and (2) is constructed so that subjects with our limitations always happen to be correct about what morality requires—regardless of whether it is objective or intersubjective. The former was assumed because whether the Incorporation Thesis is true depends on whether there are moral norms that legitimately govern our behavior; if not, the Incorporation Thesis is trivially false. The latter was assumed because we are not in an epistemic position to ground a model of an inclusive legal system in practices that conform to some specified set of norms that we know correctly report the requirements of morality. Even so, if the model is coherent, it establishes the ontological claim that inclusive legal systems can exist in worlds like ours.

But the ontological claim that there can be inclusive legal systems in worlds like ours implies nothing with respect to whether we are in an epistemic position to accurately determine that some existing system succeeds in incorporating moral criteria of validity. It is clear that we can verify whether a system affords courts with authority to bind the other officials with morally mistaken decisions and hence that we are in an epistemic position to reliably rule out that some existing system is inclusive. What we cannot do, however, is infer that a legal system succeeds in incorporating moral criteria of validity from the fact that the officials always agree on the relevant moral issues. If the relevant moral views are incorrect enough of the time—and what counts as

[11] Meta-ethical nihilism, as I use the term, asserts that there are no moral norms that, as an objective matter, legitimately govern our behavior. As the point is sometimes put, there is no right or wrong.

enough of the time is not at all clear—then the system is not properly characterized as inclusive. Insofar as we are not in an epistemic position to reliably decide these matters, we are not in an epistemic position to reliably characterize some existing legal system as inclusive.

The fact that neither the Incorporation Thesis nor the supporting arguments offered in this volume entails anything that would explain legal practice in any existing legal system might seem to validate the views of those who believe conceptual jurisprudence should not be done. The intuition motivating that view is that it is wrong to devote limited resources to solving problems when the solutions have no practical applications with respect to existing legal practices—especially when those resources can be as productively devoted to solving problems that tell us something about what our legal practices should be.

But there is nothing surprising about any of this. It was conceded in Chapter 1 that conceptual claims about law lack both normative implications with respect to what our legal practices should be and practical applications that would enable us to explain existing legal systems. Conceptual theories of law can be quite pretty, but they are otherwise useless.

The uselessness of such theorizing is what is behind the complaint, discussed in Chapter 1, that conceptual jurisprudence should not be done; on this oddly anti-philosophical view, the only justification for pursuing a line of theoretical inquiry is that it is likely to produce something of instrumental value. I argued in Chapter 1 that a line of theoretical inquiry need not be justified by its instrumental value; it is enough to justify pursuing any line of inquiry that it adds to our store of knowledge.

The fact that an inquiry conduces to knowledge does not make it interesting; there are many eminently uninteresting and forgettable truths about the world. Perhaps the truths of conceptual jurisprudence are among them. Either way, I have no illusions about what I have done here: assuming I have somehow gotten things largely right, I am certain that I have said nothing in this volume that *should*, in some objective sense, elicit an interest in the topic where one was antecedently lacking.

That being conceded, I hope that those who have taken the time to sludge through this volume have found something to reward their efforts. If I did not think that there was something valuable in this endeavor, I would not have devoted so many hours to it—and I certainly would not have spent more time on such issues than was absolutely necessary to reap whatever prudential benefits I thought might make it worthwhile. I developed my taste for this topic from the beauty I saw in the work of other conceptual jurisprudents; I hope that others might see a little something here that approximates that beauty.

Index